READING
REVELATION
IN CONTEXT

READING
REVELATION
IN CONTEXT

JOHN'S APOCALYPSE AND SECOND TEMPLE JUDAISM

BEN C. BLACKWELL, JOHN K. GOODRICH
& JASON MASTON

ZONDERVAN
ACADEMIC

ZONDERVAN ACADEMIC

Reading Revelation in Context
Copyright © 2019 by Ben C. Blackwell, John K. Goodrich, and Jason Maston

ISBN 978-0-310-56623-6 (softcover)

ISBN 978-0-310-56624-3 (ebook)

Requests for information should be addressed to:
Zondervan, *3900 Sparks Dr. SE, Grand Rapids, Michigan 49546*

Cover design: LUCAS Art & Design
Interior design: Denise Froehlich

Printed in the United States of America

HB 10.03.2024

To our parents-in-law and grandparents:

Norm and Alice MacDonald,
Rob and Susan Mills,
Bill and Patt Elam,
and Barb Campbell

Mark and Nancy Rush,
and Dotty Rush

Ken and Paula Reed,
David and Julie Sterzing,
Al Murdock and Mildred Reed,
and June Maston

"I know your deeds, your love and faith,
your service and perseverance . . ."

(REVELATION 2:19)

Contents

Foreword

The present volume offers a welcome series of accessible studies that illustrate both the importance and the possibility of throwing light on what has been and continues to be one of the most influential writings in the New Testament on Christian and even contemporary culture: the book of Revelation.

The book of Revelation has a long history of being celebrated as a key source for knowing the final course of history and of being discredited for its potential to provoke extreme forms of religiosity. Although the book styles itself as an apocalypse, that is, as a disclosure "of Jesus Christ" (Rev 1:1), it is frequently regarded as one of the most baffling and difficult early Christian writings to interpret. And yet, the epistolary forms that frame the work (chs. 1–3 and 22:21) suggest that it was written to be sufficiently transparent to audiences of Christ believers among a series of churches in Asia Minor. Thus, in order to communicate, the book demanded a high level of engagement among its hearers and readers, who were expected to receive it with knowing discernment and to adhere to its exhortations (1:3; chs. 2–3; 13:9; 14:12; 18:4; 22:18–19). A significant factor in understanding the apocalypse would have been knowing something about the symbolic imagery on which it drew and how that imagery functioned in its new literary context. Despite offering some interpretive guidance for some of the images (e.g., 1:20; 13:18; 17:9–14), the symbols remain essentially multivalent in character and resist being reduced into exclusionary single meanings that result from one-to-one decoding. Instead, through "participatory imagination," late first-century AD audiences in Asia Minor were invited to position themselves within or in relation to the book's symbolism.

Many of the symbols and images in Revelation are reminiscent of, if not directly drawn from, sources that John, the named author, regarded as sacred, whether in the Hebrew Bible or literature from the Second Temple period. While not any one of these sources is ever formally quoted through introductory formulae such as "it is written," "as it says," or "thus," almost every verse of the text employs language that alludes to one or more of them. Scholars have, in particular, observed in Revelation the presence of tradition associated with Daniel, Isaiah, Ezekiel, Jeremiah, Exodus, and Zechariah, while significant influence and/or parallels have also been noted, for example, with parts of 1 Enoch (Book of Watchers, Book of Parables, Animal Apocalypse, Epistle of Enoch), 4 Ezra, Joseph and Aseneth, Apocalypse of Zephaniah, and a range of texts among the Dead Sea Scrolls. Finally, words and phrases recall writings found in other parts of the New Testament (the Synoptic Gospels, Gospel of John, and the Pauline Epistles). Some of the connections with sources outside the New Testament and what they mean are amply and beautifully illustrated by the essays in this volume.

Alongside its heavy, though creative, reliance on symbolism found in Second Temple Jewish tradition, Revelation preserves one of the most developed "high" christologies among New Testament compositions: Jesus, whom the text designates as "the Lamb" no less than 28 times, shares the throne of God (5:6, 13; 7:9–10, 17; 22:1, 3). In addition, as the Lamb he is not only the exclusive center for redemption for those who are faithful but is also, in his suffering, the single paradigm after which believers pattern themselves (6:9–11; 14:4–5).

Why, we may ask, is it important at all to think about how Revelation is related to other Second Temple writings? At least two reasons come to mind. First, for all the book's emphasis on the exalted Jesus' close relationship to God, it is in many ways *no less Jewish* in character. Curiously, in two places, the text complains about those who regard themselves as "Jews and are not" (2:9; 3:9), implying in some sense the writer's claim to identify with a truer form of Judaism. More importantly, Revelation is so completely informed by the contemporary world of Jewish thought that it is impossible to imagine its message apart from it. Thus, even toward the time of its composition near the end of the first century AD, the book shows little sign—though written in Asia Minor (well away from Judea) and participating in socioreligious conflict with the Roman Empire—of disconnecting from Jewish tradition. Indeed, it demonstrates how much emerging Christian identity in the diaspora could be and was deeply entrenched within Jewish roots from which it could not be separated without losing something essential.

Second, exploring Revelation's connection to Judaism reveals how much the text positioned itself within the discourse of Jewish apocalyptic thought and related traditions that circulated in the first-century Mediterranean world. Though often adopting language that seeks to disclose what is to happen in an imminent eschatological future (1:1, 19; 2:16; 3:11; 4:1; 22:6–7, 12, 20), the book, like foregoing and contemporary apocalyptic literature, also reflects a keen interest in presenting a revealed past and a revealed present. In Revelation, the recent (2:12) and remote past (cf. 13:8) is unmasked as a time of head-on conflict between the worship of God and allegiance to powers thought to be behind the Roman Empire, while the present is divulged as a time when followers of the Lamb are being called to uncompromising faithfulness in the face of economically attractive, yet false and delusional alternatives (chs. 2–3, 13–14, 18). How individual churches addressed in the messages to them in chapters 2 and 3 responded to the text's combination of praise and criticism attributed to Christ is not known. However, it cannot be doubted that in a world order thought to undermine the integrity of faith, the writer hoped and, indeed, expected that they would be able to translate the risen Jesus' words into sustained and uncompromising expressions of faithfulness. As with Jewish apocalypses, the program of religious loyalty in Revelation combined with resistance to evil compromise, while convinced that the future shall involve a radical transformation that is already at work in the present (cf. 3:8). The intimate connection forged between Christ the Lamb and his followers demonstrates something of how the symbols and motifs the book has adopted from ancient Jewish texts function: they are not merely metaphors or images that point to a reality beyond, but rather are seen *in themselves* as innate to the very world God's people inhabit. Sacred tradition, whatever its source, springs to life in the text.

The various forms of intertextuality and comparisons offered in the present volume do more than paint a landscape that serves as background to a communiqué that is actually and exclusively about Christ. Instead, the landscape is itself intrinsic to the story; it is theater stage that participates in the motion and world of the actors. The conversation is lively and breathes energy into efforts to read Revelation in context. Those who pick up this book shall, I think, not be disappointed.

LOREN T. STUCKENBRUCK

As the third in a series of Reading in Context books, this volume has incurred a number of debts. Thanks are due to Katya Covrett, Chris Beetham, and the rest of the team at Zondervan Academic for their professionalism. We are also grateful to all our essayists for producing superb work; it has been a genuine pleasure to work with them. Mark Mathews, who has uniquely honored us by having contributed essays to each of the series volumes, was especially helpful in getting us caught up to speed on Revelation scholarship early in the book's production. Thank you, Mark, for always being so eager to partner with and assist us. We are grateful to David Kim for compiling the author and scripture indices and to our academic institutions (Houston Baptist University and Moody Bible Institute) for supporting our research. Finally, to our families, both immediate and extended, we are deeply thankful for your encouragement and support of our research. We love you!

The Editors
June 6, 2019
The 75th anniversary of D-Day

Abbreviations

Old Testament, New Testament, Apocrypha

Gen	Genesis		
Exod	Exodus	Hag	Haggai
Lev	Leviticus	Zech	Zechariah
Num	Numbers	Mal	Malachi
Deut	Deuteronomy	Matt	Matthew
Judg	Judges	Rom	Romans
1–2 Sam	1–2 Samuel	1–2 Cor	1–2 Corinthians
1–2 Kgs	1–2 Kings	Gal	Galatians
1–2 Chr	1–2 Chronicles	Eph	Ephesians
Neh	Nehemiah	Col	Colossians
Esth	Esther	1 Thess	1 Thessalonians
Ps/Pss	Psalm/Psalms	1–2 Tim	1–2 Timothy
Prov	Proverbs	Heb	Hebrews
Isa	Isaiah	1–2 Pet	1–2 Peter
Jer	Jeremiah	Rev	Revelation
Ezek	Ezekiel	Tob	Tobit
Dan	Daniel	Bar	Baruch
Hos	Hosea	1–2 Macc	1–2 Maccabees
Mic	Micah	Sir	Sirach/Ecclesiasticus
Nah	Nahum	Wis	Wisdom of Solomon
Hab	Habakkuk	2 Esd	2 Esdras
Zeph	Zephaniah		

Dead Sea Scrolls

1QHᵃ	Hodayotᵃ/Thanksgiving Hymnsᵃ
1QM	Milḥamah/War Scroll
4QpIsaᵃ	Pesher Isaiah (4Q161)
1QS	Serek Hayahad/Rule of the Community (also Community Rule)
1QSb/1Q28b	Rule of the Blessings
4QFlor	Florilegium (4Q174)

4Q285	Sefer Hamilḥamah
4QShirShabb	Songs of the Sabbath Sacrifice (4Q405)
4Q504	Dibre Hame'orot[a]/Words of the Luminaries[a]
11QMelch	Melchizedek (11Q13)
CD	Damascus Document

Rabbinic Literature

b. Ḥag.	Tractate Ḥagigah (Babylonian Talmud)
Gen. Rab.	Genesis Rabbah
Lam. Rab.	Lamentations Rabbah
Num. Rab.	Numbers Rabbah
Prov. Rab.	Proverbs Rabbah
m. 'Abot	Mishnah 'Abot
Tg. Ezek.	Targum Ezekiel
Tg. Neof.	Targum Neofiti
Tg. Pal. Num	Palestinian Targum Numbers

Other Ancient Texts

1 En.	1 Enoch
2 En.	2 Enoch
2 Bar.	2 Baruch
3 Bar.	3 Baruch
Ann.	*Annales* (Tacitus)
Apoc. Abr.	Apocalypse of Abraham
Apoc. Mos.	Apocalypse of Moses
Apoc. Pet.	Apocalypse of Peter
Apoc. Zeph.	Apocalypse of Zephaniah
Ant.	*Jewish Antiquities* (Josephus)
Ascen. Isa.	Ascension of Isaiah
Comm. Joh.	*Commentary on John* (Origen)
Crass.	*Crassus (Plutarch)*
Cal.	*Gaius Caligula* (Suetonius)
Cult. fem.	*The Apparel of Women* (Tertullian)
Idol.	*Idolatry* (Tertullian)
Princ.	*First Principles* (Origen)
Ep. Barn.	*Epistle of Barnabas*
Haer.	*Against Heresies* (Irenaeus)

In Apoc.	*Commentary on the Apocalypse* (Victorinus)
Tract. Ev. Jo.	*Tractates on the Gospel of John* (Augustine)
J.W.	*Jewish War* (Josephus)
Jub.	Jubilees
LAB	Liber antiquitatum biblicarum/Book of Biblical Antiquities (Pseudo-Philo)
LAE	Life of Adam and Eve
Life	*The Life* (Josephus)
Mos.	*De vita Mosis/On the Life of Moses* (Philo)
Pss. Sol.	Psalms of Solomon
Sib. Or.	Sibylline Oracles
T. Abr.	Testament of Abraham
T. Adam	Testament of Adam
T. Dan	Testament of Dan
T. Levi	Testament of Levi
T. Mos.	Testament of Moses
T. Sim	Testament of Simeon
Vesp.	*Vespasianus* (Suetonius)

JOURNALS, PERIODICALS, REFERENCE WORKS, SERIES

AYBC	Anchor Yale Bible Commentary
BBR	*Bulletin of Biblical Research*
BCAW	Blackwell Companions to the Ancient World
BZNW	Beihefte zur Zeitschrift für die neutestamentliche Wissenschaft
CBQMS	Catholic Biblical Quarterly Monograph Series
CEJL	Commentaries on Early Jewish Literature
DSD	*Dead Sea Discoveries*
DJD	Discoveries in the Judaean Desert
ESV	English Standard Version
GAP	Guides to the Apocrypha and Pseudepigrapha
JBL	*Journal of Biblical Literature*
JETS	*Journal of the Evangelical Theological Society*
JSJSup	Supplements to the Journal for the Study of Judaism
JSNT	*Journal for the Study of the New Testament*
JSNTSup	Journal for the Study of the New Testament Supplement Series
JSP	*Journal for the Study of the Pseudepigrapha*
JTS	*Journal of Theological Studies*
LNTS	The Library of New Testament Studies

NETS	*A New English Translation of the Septuagint.* Edited by Albert Pietersma and Benjamin G. Wright. New York: Oxford University Press, 2007
NIGTC	New International Greek Testament Commentary
NIV	New International Version
NovT	*Novum Testamentum*
NRSV	New Revised Standard Version
RevQ	*Revue de Qumran*
SNTSMS	Society for New Testament Studies Monograph Series
STDJ	Studies on the Texts of the Desert of Judah
TSAJ	Texte und Studien zum antiken Judentum
WBC	Word Biblical Commentary
WUNT	Wissenschaftliche Untersuchungen zum Neuen Testament

OTHER ABBREVIATIONS

AD	*anno Domini* (in the year of our Lord)
BC	before Christ
ca.	circa (approximately)
DSS	Dead Sea Scrolls
LXX	Septuagint
MT	Masoretic Text
NT	New Testament
OT	Old Testament

Introduction

~~~~~~~~

BEN C. BLACKWELL, JOHN K. GOODRICH,
JASON MASTON, AND MARK MATHEWS

*The text lives only by coming into contact with another text
(with context). Only at the point of this contact between texts
does a light flash, illuminating both the posterior and anterior,
joining a given text to a dialogue.*

M. M. Bakhtin

The book of Revelation, also known as the Apocalypse of John, is widely
considered the most graphic and gripping of the New Testament
documents. Although occasionally sidelined for its incendiary rhetoric and puzzling plotline, Revelation appeals to the sensibilities of popular
Christianity as much as any book of the Bible—indeed, a sermon series on
this portion of Scripture is basically guaranteed to boost weekly church
attendance in most traditions. Such widespread interest is due in no small
measure to the book's copious symbolism and triumphalist eschatological
outlook. Even professional theologians are easily intrigued by the author's
visionary experiences and preoccupation with political and cosmic conflict.
Commentators continue to dispute when and how the events described have
been or will be fulfilled, yet all agree that Revelation vividly forecasts the
certain demise of God's enemies together with the climactic vindication of
God's holy people. John's Apocalypse, then, is a theologically significant
book with a message ripe for contemporary believers. As Richard Bauckham
explains, "The method and conceptuality of the theology of Revelation are
relatively different from the rest of the New Testament, but once they are
appreciated in their own right, Revelation can be seen to be not only one of
the finest literary works in the New Testament, but also one of the greatest
theological achievements of early Christianity."[1]

Written sometime in the latter half of the first century AD to seven

---

1. Richard Bauckham, *The Theology of the Book of Revelation*, New Testament Theology
(Cambridge: Cambridge University Press, 1993), 22.

churches in western Asia Minor, Revelation begins with a Son of Man figure (the risen Messiah) instructing John of Patmos to record everything about to be revealed to him. After an initial report on the ethical shortcomings of the book's original addressees, John is immediately transported to the heavenly throne room. There he witnesses regally adorned elders and ferocious creatures worshiping the sovereign God and falling prostrate before the slain Lamb (Jesus Christ), who enters majestically to take possession of the sealed scroll in God's right hand.

As the Lamb breaks the scroll's seven seals, John receives successive visions of various cataclysmic events enacted by mysterious men on horseback. The breaking of the seals is followed by the sounding of seven trumpets, each of which triggers additional calamities, including natural disasters, the assembling of armies, the rising of beasts, and the murder of prophets. More visions ensue, culminating in the dispensing of seven bowls of plagues and the destruction of Babylon the Great. Satan is then captured, producing a lengthy peace, during which the Messiah and his followers rule the earth together for a thousand years.

But when Satan is released, one last showdown occurs, climaxing in the final defeat of evil, including Satan, Death, and their accomplices, all of whom are cast into the lake of fire. John is then shown the restoring of creation, as the new Jerusalem descends from above, and heaven and earth are joined eternally. There, in that Edenic city, John envisions God dwelling and reigning together with his faithful people forever, the promise of which provides hope and peace in the present for those who persist in their allegiance to Jesus Christ.

The book of Revelation is like a magnificent theme park. Replete with visual and auditory stimuli and brimming with chaos and catastrophe, reading this work is a disorienting, multisensory experience that terrifies nearly as much as it clarifies. While the book often requires more careful study than many armchair theologians are prepared to invest, Revelation may well be, as Ian Paul promises, "the most remarkable text you will ever read."[2]

Not all readings of Revelation, however, are equally insightful. The Apocalypse, like the rest of the Bible, was written at a time and in a culture quite different from our own. Accordingly, reading Revelation responsibly, as most second-year biblical studies students will know, requires careful consideration of a passage's historical-cultural context.[3] This is particularly

---

2. Ian Paul, *Revelation*, TNTC (Downers Grove, IL: IVP Academic, 2018), 1.

3. See Michael J. Gorman, *Reading Revelation Responsibly: Uncivil Worship and Witness—Following the Lamb into the New Creation* (Eugene, OR: Wipf & Stock, 2011), 12–22, who observes

so for an apocalypse like Revelation, whose rhetorical strategy and communicative artistry require special hermeneutical attention. Although it is true that some contextual awareness is better than none, it is also true that failure to immerse oneself within the literary and religious environment of the New Testament world will likely result in not only unconscious imposition of alien meaning onto the biblical text but also a poorer understanding of the otherworldly creatures and apocalyptic symbolism revealed in John's visions.

The history of interpretation demonstrates just this problem. Representatives from several of the major interpretive approaches to Revelation—especially from the so-called futurist and historicist perspectives—have a track record of too hastily identifying concrete referents of John's images without adequately establishing how the author intends for his visions to communicate. One need only survey the ways Babylon and the Beast have been understood through the centuries to realize how eager some theologians are to construe these figures in the likeness of their own contemporary political and religious opponents—whether the papacy, the Nazis, the Russians, or Muslim extremists.[4] It is as G. K. Chesterton remarked: "Though St. John the Evangelist saw many strange monsters in his vision, he saw no creature so wild as one of his own commentators."[5]

Modern scholarship has exposed many of the deficiencies in these ill-founded proposals. Although Revelation clearly contains predictive prophecy, there is a danger in seeking to decode the book's images without first appreciating what John J. Collins refers to as "the allusive and evocative power of apocalyptic symbolism."[6] In other words, while the zealous reader may long to know when and how John's visions have or will come to fruition, speculative interpretation about ambiguous and artistically arranged

---

the importance of recognizing the literary genre(s) of Revelation, especially its Jewish apocalyptic features, and of interpreting the book in the light of this distinct idiom. We do not mean to imply, however, that a historical reading is the only kind needed for responsible interpretation. With Gorman, it is important to note that reading Revelation responsibly also requires consideration of the book's "spirituality," that is, how it relates to "the lived experiences of the Christian faith" (176). As Marianne Meye Thompson eloquently reminds us, "The often unintended result of reading Revelation with a primary focus on its past is that it remains an artifact of the past." Thus, it is important also to ask "how [Revelation] serves in the Christian formation of its readers" ("Reading What Is Written in the Book of Life: Theological Interpretation of the Book of Revelation Today," in *Revelation and the Politics of Apocalyptic Interpretation*, ed. R. B. Hays and S. Alkier [Waco: Baylor University Press, 2012], 155–71, at 157).

4. For the reception history of Revelation 13, see, e.g., Judith Kovacs and Christopher Rowland, *Revelation: The Apocalypse of Jesus Christ*, Blackwell Bible Commentaries (Oxford: Blackwell, 2004), 147–59.

5. G. K. Chesterton, *Orthodoxy* (London: John Lane, 1908), 13.

6. John J. Collins, *The Apocalyptic Imagination: An Introduction to Jewish Apocalyptic Literature*, 3rd ed. (Grand Rapids: Eerdmans, 2016), 20.

revelatory reports may in fact undermine what the author was intending to accomplish. In fact, according to Collins, a Jewish-Christian apocalypse like Revelation "may on occasion achieve its effect precisely through the element of uncertainty."[7] A deeper understanding of how apocalyptic literature functions is therefore required.

When biblical scholars use the language of *apocalyptic*, they are normally referring to a constellation of ideas often featured in texts composed in the literary form known as *apocalypse*, of which Revelation is an example.[8] "Apocalypse," as Collins famously defined it, "is a genre of revelatory literature with a narrative framework, in which a revelation is mediated by an otherworldly being to a human recipient, disclosing a transcendent reality which is both temporal, insofar as it envisages eschatological salvation, and spatial insofar as it involves another, supernatural world."[9] Within this literary type, there exist two main subtypes: *historical apocalypses* (which review sacred history) and *otherworldly journeys* (which tour the cosmos).[10] Regardless of a work's subtype, what is important to recall is that these written accounts describe a "transcendent reality." In other words, the seer is granted either a behind-the-scenes peek of *this* world or a glimpse into an altogether *different* realm. In either case, what is being reported is either entirely *invisible* to those on the ground or at least *not as things appear* to the naked eye. For this reason, it is the interpreter's primary responsibility not so much to decode the vision by identifying the concrete referent of a revealed image, but to recalibrate one's perceptions of their lived experience in light of the revelation received. As David deSilva explains, "An apocalypse . . . puts an everyday situation into perspective by looking at the larger context (the cosmos of faith) that should interpret that situation. From this an apocalypse derives its power to comfort those who are discouraged or marginalized, admonish those whose responses in their situation are not in line with their religious values, and provide the necessary motivation to take whatever action the seer recommends."[11]

Many such Jewish and Christian apocalypses have been studied for millennia, but it was not until the first half of the nineteenth century that this

---

7. Collins, *Apocalyptic Imagination*, 20.

8. John even begins the book by labeling it an apocalypse: "The revelation [Gk. *apokalypsis*] of Jesus Christ" (1:1).

9. John J. Collins, "Introduction: Towards the Morphology of a Genre," *Semeia* 14 (1979): 1–20, at 9.

10. Collins, *Apocalyptic Imagination*, 7.

11. David A. deSilva, *Seeing Things John's Way: The Rhetoric of the Book of Revelation* (Louisville: Westminster John Knox, 2009), 13.

literature was authoritatively identified as a distinct group of writings.[12] This advancement coincided with the discoveries of several ancient Jewish manuscripts and the publication of their critical editions, especially of 1 Enoch and the Ascension of Isaiah. The bulk of these and other works—including some that do not take the form of an apocalypse yet still can be described as *apocalyptic* because they share constitutive traits of the genre[13]—were studied and made accessible in English around the turn of the twentieth century by British scholar R. H. Charles, who drew heavily on them in his own scholarship on Revelation. Charles maintained that these sources offer such valuable contextual insight for exegesis that "the New Testament Apocalypse cannot be understood apart from Jewish Apocalyptic literature."[14] In fact, Charles credited much of his newfound respect for the theological profundity of Revelation to his contextual studies. "The first ground for such a revolution in my attitude to the Book," Charles explained, "was due to an exhaustive study of Jewish Apocalyptic. The knowledge thereby acquired helped to solve many problems, which could only prove to be hopeless enigmas to scholars unacquainted with this literature."[15] Charles is not alone in his appreciation for this body of texts and its significance for unlocking Revelation.[16] In the decades that have followed, his contention has come to be shared by many others, including Bauckham, who remarks, "The tradition of apocalyptic literature is the living literary tradition to whose forms and content [John of Patmos] is most indebted."[17]

---

12. Credit is normally given to Friedrich Lücke, *Versuch einer vollständigen Einleitung in die Offenbarung des Johannes und in die gesammte apokalyptische Litteratur* (Berlin: Edward Weber, 1832).

13. The early Jewish book of Jubilees is one such example. Although Jubilees is a narrative elaboration of the earliest parts of the Old Testament and thus best fits into the literary genre known as *rewritten Scripture*, woven throughout this work are themes commonly found in the apocalypses, such as angelic-mediated revelations of divine mysteries and discourses on eschatology and otherworldly beings. The book of Revelation also has a mixed genre, containing elements of epistolary, prophetic, and apocalyptic literature. Apocalyptic features also appear throughout the rest of the New Testament. See, e.g., Ben C. Blackwell, John K. Goodrich, and Jason Maston, eds., *Paul and the Apocalyptic Imagination* (Minneapolis: Fortress, 2016); Benjamin E. Reynolds and Loren T. Stuckenbruck, eds., *The Jewish Apocalyptic Tradition and the Shaping of New Testament Thought* (Minneapolis: Fortress, 2017).

14. R. H. Charles, *Studies in the Apocalypse* (Edinburgh: T&T Clark, 1913), 4 (see also p. 2). Also, R. H. Charles, *The Revelation of St. John*, ICC (Edinburgh: T&T Clark, 1920), 1:lxv: "without a knowledge of the Pseudepigrapha it would be impossible to understand our author."

15. Charles, *Revelation of St. John*, 1:x.

16. See also, e.g., Austin Marsden Farrer, *A Rebirth of Images: The Making of St. John's Apocalypse* (Westminster: Dacre, 1949); Pierre Prigent, *Commentary on the Apocalypse of St. John* (Tübingen: Mohr Siebeck, 2004), 22–36.

17. Richard Bauckham, *The Climax of Prophecy: Studies on the Book of Revelation* (Edinburgh: T&T Clark, 1993), xii. Loren Stuckenbruck and Mark Mathews go so far as to suggest that it

Yet even as scholars now routinely acknowledge the value of studying Revelation within the context of apocalyptic literature, sustained attention to the book's Jewish historical and literary context is still too often bypassed as a result of the sometimes greater scholarly fascination with the book's relationship to the non-Jewish world, particularly the sociopolitical milieu of the Roman Empire. In many recent sociopolitical studies of Revelation, for example, John's language and imagery are believed to be due to some kind of crisis, whether real or perceived.[18] Some have suggested that life on the ground for late first-century Christians was one of intense persecution during the tyrannical reign of Emperor Domitian (AD 51–96).[19] For others, John's concerns target the ubiquity of the Roman imperial cult in its various forms, most importantly Christian involvement in them, whether voluntary or under duress.[20] Thus, the Roman Empire in Asia Minor offered Christians the opportunity to assimilate into imperial culture and look to the *pax romana* as their source of peace and prosperity, an assimilation John sees as incompatible with allegiance to Christ.

According to still other studies, the Christian community felt marginalized in the shadow of the Roman Empire's excessive wealth and power, which would have triggered envy and resentment in John and his readers.[21] John's rhetoric, viewed from a sociopolitical perspective, serves as anti-Roman propaganda and seeks to pacify feelings of antipathy.

There is no doubt that these and similar sociopolitical approaches to Revelation offer significant resources for understanding the book's message. The range of results produced by these disparate perspectives, however, accentuates the difficulty modern readers face when seeking to specify what

---

"is likely that the writer of Revelation was either directly acquainted (through literary or oral transmission) with several of the major sections of *1 Enoch* or at least had access to traditions that were influenced by these writings" ("The Apocalypse of John, *1 Enoch*, and the Question of Influence," in Loren T. Stuckenbruck, *The Myth of Rebellious Angels: Studies in Second Temple Judaism and New Testament Texts* [Grand Rapids: Eerdmans, 2017], 281–325, at 324).

18. Paul Hanson, *The Dawn of Apocalyptic* (Philadelphia: Fortress, 1975), has been very influential in the modern understanding that apocalypses arise out of situations of crisis. While the earliest apocalypses may have risen out of a setting of crisis, subsequent uses of the genre may have simply been the product of an inherited mode of expression. Although there has been considerable advancement made in the understanding of apocalyptic literature, this idea is still pervasive in much of NT scholarship.

19. Elisabeth Schüssler Fiorenza, *The Book of Revelation: Justice and Judgment* (Philadelphia: Fortress, 1985), and *Vision of a Just World* (Minneapolis: Fortress, 1991).

20. Nelson J. Kraybill, *Imperial Cult and Commerce*, JSNTSup 132 (Sheffield: Sheffield Academic, 1996); Steven J. Friesen, *Imperial Cults and the Apocalypse of John: Reading Revelation in the Ruins* (Oxford: Oxford University Press, 2001).

21. Adela Yarbro Collins, *Crisis and Catharsis: The Power of the Apocalypse* (Philadelphia: Westminster, 1984), 84–107.

John was actually reacting to within the social world of ancient Rome. While the studies mentioned above offer reasonable possibilities, the degree of influence they afford to the Roman Empire's shaping of John's message too often outweighs consideration of how received traditions also likely impacted the author's word choice, writing style, and worldview. This is especially surprising since, as Collins notes, "No other book in the New Testament has such clear and well-established precedents in Jewish literature."[22] Given, then, the nature of the apocalyptic genre and its development during the Second Temple period, it is critical to read Revelation alongside antecedent Jewish apocalyptic traditions.

Even so, many readers of the Bible today, especially in the evangelical tradition, give little, if any, attention to early Jewish texts. For some, this is simply a matter of *familiarity*. Being generally unaware of the literature produced during the Second Temple period, many assume that the so-called "silent years" between the Testaments witnessed little to no development beyond the inherited traditions of the Hebrew Scriptures. Such readers therefore overlook early Jewish literature because they assume that the New Testament was written in a literary and theological vacuum.

For others, this avoidance is a matter of *canonicity*. Although aware of the existence of extrabiblical Jewish literature, these readers often consider ancient religious books lying outside of Scripture to be theologically irrelevant or even dangerous. Accordingly, they bar these works from hermeneutical consideration, basing such avoidance on their commitment to *sola Scriptura* or related post-Reformation doctrines on the clarity and sufficiency of Scripture.

For still other readers, the neglect of Second Temple literature is simply a matter of *utility*. Despite realizing that the Jewish people authored important religious works between the Testaments, many remain unsure how these noncanonical texts can be studied profitably alongside the Bible. They therefore disregard early Jewish literature, being either regretful they do not have the training to apply extrabiblical insights or anxious they might distort the New Testament message if they tried.

While we understand the above concerns, the rewards for even nonspecialists studying Second Temple texts far outweigh the challenges and supposed risks of doing so. Indeed, there are many advantages to becoming familiar with early Judaism and the relevant literature. Bruce Metzger

---

22. John J. Collins, "The Christian Appropriation of the Apocalyptic Tradition," in *Seers, Sibyls, and Sages in Hellenistic-Roman Judaism* (Leiden: Brill, 1997), 115–30, at 115.

assessed the importance of these works (especially **the Apocrypha**) for biblical studies over a half-century ago:

> Though it would be altogether extravagant to call the Apocrypha the keystone of the two Testaments, it is not too much to regard these intertestamental books as an historical hyphen that serves a useful function in bridging what to most readers of the Bible is a blank of several hundred years. To neglect what the Apocrypha have to tell us about the development of Jewish life and thought during those critical times is as foolish as to imagine that one can understand the civilization and culture of America today by passing from colonial days to the twentieth century without taking into account the industrial and social revolution of the intervening centuries.[23]

Concerns about canonicity are also difficult to justify. We too embrace the evangelical and wider Protestant belief in the authority of inspired Scripture. Refusing to engage early Jewish literature on theological grounds, however, goes well beyond this commitment. Even Martin Luther famously insisted that the books of the Apocrypha "are not held as equal to the sacred Scriptures, and nevertheless are useful and good to read."[24] In fact, the Apocrypha was included in most early Protestant printings of the Bible (e.g., Luther's Bible and the King James Version), even if separated into its own section. It was only in the early nineteenth century when Bibles began to be printed without it. Obviously the mishandling of these texts remains a real concern to those in the church, just as it does to many within critical scholarship; over half a century ago Samuel Sandmel warned the academy of illegitimate uses of background material, calling it "parallelomania."[25] Yet the appropriate solution to the misuse of comparative literature is not its outright dismissal but responsible handling by students of Scripture. As Bauckham maintains, "The detailed study of particular items of apocalyptic tradition as they appear in Revelation and in other Jewish and Christian writings

---

23. Bruce M. Metzger, *An Introduction to the Apocrypha* (Oxford: Oxford University Press, 1957), 151–52.

24. Cited in *The Apocrypha: The Lutheran Edition with Notes* (St Louis: Concordia, 2012), xviii. See also how Matthew Barrett defends the sufficiency of Scripture while also urging Protestants to recognize the value of extrabiblical data for the task of hermeneutics: "Such factors demonstrate the high importance of general revelation, even guarding us against certain biblicist caricatures of *sola Scriptura*" (*God's Word Alone—The Authority of Scripture: What the Reformers Taught . . . and Why It Still Matters* [Grand Rapids: Zondervan, 2016], 338–39).

25. Samuel Sandmel, "Parallelomania," *JBL* 81 (1962): 1–13.

is laborious—no doubt one reason why it has rarely been undertaken. But it is essential to the understanding of the background and composition of apocalyptic literature, and can yield significant exegetical results."[26]

Many readers seem particularly anxious about the illegitimate *imposition* of external meaning onto the biblical text. That is a fair concern. What some fail to realize, however, is that comparative studies are (or should be) just as interested in exposing the theological *differences* between texts as observing their *similarities*. Indeed, it was even Bauckham's contention that comparative studies of this sort "[do] not at all . . . deny the individual distinctiveness of Revelation. On the contrary, precisely this method will show how John often uses common apocalyptic traditions in highly creative ways and develops the conventions of the literary genre for his own purposes and by means of his own literary genius."[27] Thus, while one should avoid utilizing early Jewish literature merely as a foil for the New Testament documents, their differences must be highlighted if their individual meanings are to be appreciated and a dialogue between them is to take place. To interpret Revelation responsibly, then, students must not *ignore* Second Temple Jewish literature, but *engage* it with frequency, precision, and a willingness to acknowledge theological continuity *and* discontinuity.

While scholarly studies that situate Revelation within Judaism are plenty,[28] there exist virtually no nontechnical resources for beginning and

26. Bauckham, *Climax of Prophecy*, 39.

27. Bauckham, *Climax of Prophecy*, xii. Collins agrees: "Revelation does indeed modify the typical apocalyptic genre in certain ways, reflecting the Christian conviction that the messiah has already come and that the eschatological age has begun. These modifications do not entail a rejection of the apocalyptic worldview, but actualize it in a particular way, that is not without analogy in Judaism" (Collins, "The Christian Appropriation of the Apocalyptic Tradition," 120).

28. The prevalence of these studies, however, should not be exaggerated. In the early 1990s Bauckham lamented,

> Since the important work of scholars of a previous generation, such as R. H. Charles and I. T. Beckwith, very little fresh work has been done by way of comparing and contrasting Revelation with the rest of the apocalyptic literature, or of tracing the specific literary conventions and apocalyptic traditions which occur both in Revelation and in other apocalypses. Despite the major advances in our knowledge and understanding of the Jewish and Christian apocalypses during the last two decades, much scholarly writing on Revelation gives the impression that all the relevant parallels were pointed out long ago and that interpreters of Revelation have no need to engage in firsthand study of other apocalypses. . . . Yet floods of fresh light can still be thrown on Revelation in this way. (*Climax of Prophecy*, xii)

More studies have appeared since Bauckham's complaint, but much work remains. See, e.g., Edith M. Humphrey, *The Ladies and the Cities: Transformation and Apocalyptic Identity in Joseph and Aseneth, 4 Ezra, the Apocalypse and The Shepherd of Hermas*, JSPSup 17 (Sheffield: Sheffield Academic, 1995); Loren T. Stuckenbruck, *Angel Veneration and Christology: A Study in Early Judaism and in the Christology of the Apocalypse of John*, WUNT 2/70 (Tübingen: Mohr

intermediate students to assist them in seeing firsthand how Revelation is similar to and yet different from early Jewish apocalypses and related literature. This volume seeks to fill this void. In this book we investigate the relation between John's Apocalypse and Second Temple Judaism by bringing together a series of accessible essays that compare and contrast the perspectives and hermeneutical practices of John the Seer and his various kinsmen. Going beyond an introduction that merely surveys historical events and theological themes, this book examines select passages in Second Temple Jewish literature to illuminate the context of John's visions and the nuances of his message.

Following, then, the progression of the Apocalypse, each chapter in this book (1) pairs a major unit of Revelation with one or more sections of a thematically related Jewish text, (2) introduces and explores the theological nuances of the comparator text, and (3) shows how the ideas in the comparator text illuminate those expressed in Revelation. The end of each chapter also contains a short list of other thematically relevant Second Temple Jewish texts recommended for additional study and a focused bibliography pointing students to critical editions and higher-level discussions in scholarly literature. Finally, at the end of the book is a glossary where readers will find definitions of important terms. Whether one reads the entire book or only a few essays, it is our hope that readers will gain a new appreciation for extrabiblical Jewish texts, begin to see the many benefits of studying the New Testament alongside its contemporary literature, and acquire a better understanding of apocalyptic theology as it is presented in the book of Revelation.

Before proceeding to our comparisons, however, it is necessary briefly to survey the events of the **Second Temple period** and the literature that it produced.

Introducing the Second Temple Period and Early Jewish Literature

From the First Temple Period to the Second

In the exodus, a pivotal event in the history of national Israel, Abraham's family was liberated from Pharaoh after nearly four centuries of forced labor.

Siebeck, 1995); Ronald Herms, *An Apocalypse for the Church and for the World: The Narrative Function of Universal Language in the Book of Revelation*, BZNW 143 (Berlin: de Gruyter, 2006); Mark D. Mathews, *Riches, Poverty, and the Faithful: Perspectives on Wealth in the Second Temple Period and the Apocalypse of John*, SNTSMS 154 (Cambridge: Cambridge University Press, 2013).

The Israelites were led by God into the desert and given the Mosaic law at Sinai to regulate Hebrew life and religion, with the sacrificial system at the center of their community (Exod 19:1–8). Separated from the nations through their distinctive way of life (Lev 20:22–26), the Israelites were to keep the commandments that God had given them lest they profane the holy **covenant** and be exiled from the land of promise (Lev 26:14–39; Deut 28:15–68; 30:15–20).

From the conquest of Canaan to the end of the united monarchy, the nation inhabited the land for almost five hundred years. During that era, King Solomon *built the first temple* in the mid-tenth century BC, fulfilling David's original aspiration for the project (1 Kgs 6:1–8:66). After Solomon's death, the kingdom divided, and, following a series of evil rulers, Israel's northern ten tribes (the kingdom of Israel/Samaria) were captured and exiled by Assyria in 722 BC (2 Kgs 17:1–23; 18:9–12). The southern two tribes (the kingdom of Judah) ultimately fared no better. By the beginning of the sixth century, the Babylonians had waged war on Jerusalem, and in 586 BC King Nebuchadnezzar destroyed the city, including the first temple, and exiled many of its inhabitants (2 Kgs 24:10–25:21; 2 Chr 36:17–21).

The Babylonian captivity marks a low point in Israel's history. The nation had faced the full brunt of the Deuteronomic curses as a result of their covenant disobedience. Consequently, the Israelites were without a homeland, just as Yahweh had promised would happen through Moses and the prophets.

Yet even before their captivity, God had also promised that he would return his scattered people to the land and fully restore the nation (Lev 26:40–45; Deut 30:1–10; 32:34–43; Isa 40:1–66:24; Jer 30:1–31:40; Ezek 36:8–37:28). Israel was to experience the glory of its former days, and as it would turn out, they did not remain under Babylonian rule for long. In 539 BC Cyrus of Persia conquered Babylon and famously decreed that all exiles could return to their ancestral homelands (2 Chr 36:22–23; Ezra 1:1–4). Many Israelites therefore gradually returned to and rebuilt Jerusalem. Zerubbabel was instrumental in the rebuilding of the temple, while Nehemiah oversaw the construction of the city walls (Ezra 3:8–6:15; Neh 2:9–6:15). It is the building of this second temple in 516 BC that marks the beginning of the Second Temple period.

The newly renovated city, however, was not what was promised. When Israel's returnees gazed at the new temple's foundation, some celebrated while others cried over its unimpressive stature (Ezra 3:10–13; Hag 2:3). Israel's promised restoration had not arrived at the hands of Ezra and

Nehemiah. As the centuries to follow would demonstrate, the peace and prosperity God swore to his people had yet to be realized in the period immediately following the Babylonian exile. Instead, generation after generation witnessed subjugation and suffering at the hands of still other foreign powers—namely, Medo-Persia, Greece, and Rome—and these experiences significantly colored the texts these Jews produced.

Israel survived under the rule of the Medo-Persian Empire from 539 to about 332 BC, when the Greek Empire led by Alexander the Great conquered the known world. Alexander's rule would not last long. Following his death in 323 BC, Alexander's territories were partitioned among his military generals, who established their own kingdoms (e.g., the Ptolemaic Kingdom in Egypt, the **Seleucid Kingdom** in Syria) and continued the former ruler's systematic spread of **Hellenism**, or Greek culture (1 Macc 1:1–9; 2 Macc 4:7–17). These kingdoms, which were often embroiled in war with one another, also created challenges for the Jews who were positioned geographically between them. The Seleucid Kingdom in particular, under the rule of **Antiochus IV Epiphanes** in 167 BC, raided Jerusalem (1 Macc 1:20–40), desecrated the temple (1:47, 54, 59), outlawed observance of the covenant (1:41–53), and prohibited possession of the Torah (1:56–57). In his pursuit of **Hellenization**, Antiochus banned the Jews' customs (1:41–44) and violently forced their assimilation (1:50, 57–58, 60–64). But Antiochus's persecution was not passively tolerated. The Jewish resistance that arose in response (the **Maccabean Revolt**, 167–160 BC) resulted in the Jews' repossession of the land, rededication of the temple, and institution of the festival of Hanukkah (1 Macc 4:36–59; Josephus, *Ant.* 12.316–25).

With the renewed national sovereignty of the **Hasmonean Kingdom**, various groups held differing opinions about how to manage the political and temple leadership of Israel. This infighting eventually led to the weakening of the Jewish national leadership, and Pompey, a Roman general contemporaneous with Julius Caesar, seized control of Israel in 63 BC, making it a territory of the Roman Republic. Although Rome largely tolerated Jewish religious practices, pressures leading toward political, cultural, and religious assimilation were ever present. Eventually the **Zealots** (a Jewish resistance group) fomented the hopes of another successful revolt. But the Romans, under the soon-to-be Emperor Titus, defeated the Jews and destroyed the Second Temple in AD 70 (Josephus, *J.W.* 6.220–270), thus bringing an end to the **Second Temple period**.

The Second Temple period (516 BC–AD 70) began with the Jews under the control of the Persians and ended under the control of the Romans.

This was without question a time of crisis for the Jewish people, and devout men and women reflected on their experiences in a variety of ways. With the continuous pressures of consecutive foreign nations pushing the Jews toward assimilation, numerous Second Temple Jewish literary works preserve their thoughts and hopes about God and life in the covenant. These reflections survive in the numerous literary works produced during this period. We turn now to survey these texts.

Overview of Second Temple Jewish Literature

The Second Temple Jewish writings were composed by numerous authors in multiple languages over several hundred years. They derive from geographical provenances extending over much of the **Ancient Near East**. There is no easy way to characterize or categorize these texts. Still, scholarly surveys of ancient Judaism normally assign individual Second Temple Jewish texts to one of three main literary bodies—the Septuagint, the Apocrypha, and the Pseudepigrapha—collections which were unrecognized by the original authors, having been determined by later editors and scholars. Accordingly, these corpuses overlap in different places.

The **Septuagint** (abbreviated **LXX**) is a collection of Jewish texts in Greek that includes the Greek translation of the Old Testament as well as other Jewish writings. It was the most widely used Greek version in antiquity, though other Greek versions also existed. The Old Testament **Apocrypha** (also called the **deuterocanonical** books) are a subset of the texts found in the Septuagint (though not in the Hebrew Bible) that were accepted as authoritative by patristic (and medieval) Christians and included in the Vulgate (a Latin translation that became the authoritative version for the medieval church).[29] Different Christian groups have variations in their **canonical** lists related to the Apocrypha, but the primary collection includes the books of Tobit, Judith, Additions to Esther, the Wisdom of Solomon, Sirach (Ecclesiasticus), Baruch, the Epistle of Jeremiah, Additions to Daniel (the Prayer of Azariah, Song of the Three Young Men, Susanna, and Bel and the Dragon), and 1 and 2 Maccabees. Certain churches also afford special status to works such as 1 and 2 Esdras (= "Ezra" in Greek), the Prayer of Manasseh, and Psalm 151. In addition to the Greek translation of the Hebrew Bible and what later became known as the Apocrypha, the LXX

---

29. The canonical status of these texts for patristic Christians is unclear, but they did treat them as authoritative. These texts were later included in the Old Testament by Roman Catholic and Orthodox Christians because of their reception by the church in the patristic period.

also includes, in certain copies, the books of 3 Maccabees, 4 Maccabees, 1 Esdras, the Psalms of Solomon, and Odes of Solomon (including the Prayer of Manasseh).

The Old Testament **Pseudepigrapha** (meaning "falsely attributed writings") is a diverse body of ancient Jewish works, many of which claim to be authored by famous Old Testament persons although they did not write them. Some Septuagint works mentioned above are also falsely attributed. For example, neither the Wisdom of Solomon nor Psalms of Solomon were authored by Israel's third king, though they bear his name. In distinction to the Septuagint and the Apocrypha as fixed bodies of texts, all early Jewish religious literature not considered to be (deutero)canonical are commonly placed in the open category of pseudepigrapha—aside from **Philo, Josephus**, and the **Dead Sea Scrolls**.[30]

While these classifications (especially Apocrypha) are widely used and indeed useful for classifying texts that may be considered authoritative in certain religious traditions, an alternative and more descriptive way to group these writings is according to genre. We survey the main early Jewish literary genres below.[31]

The first early Jewish literary genre to be familiar with is *history*. Several works fall into this category, including 1–2 Esdras and 1–2 Maccabees. The books of 1–2 Esdras (Vulgate) refer to the books of Ezra and Nehemiah and thus report Israel's immediate postexilic history.[32] The books of 1–2 Maccabees chronicle important events between the biblical testaments, including the **Maccabean Revolt**. Together, the early Jewish histories are essential for understanding the events, influences, challenges, and commitments of the Second Temple Jewish people.

A second early Jewish literary genre is *tales*. According to James Vander-Kam, these are "stories with no serious claim to historicity but [which] aim to inculcate wise teachings through the stories and the speeches they narrate."[33] To this category belong such books as Tobit, Judith, Susanna, 3 Maccabees, and the Letter of Aristeas. These works normally cast important, sometimes

---

30. Loren T. Stuckenbruck, "Apocrypha and Pseudepigrapha," in *Early Judaism: A Comprehensive Overview*, ed. J. J. Collins and D. C. Harlow (Grand Rapids: Eerdmans, 2012), 173–203, at 191–92.

31. Our overview generally follows the categories of James C. VanderKam, *An Introduction to Early Judaism* (Grand Rapids: Eerdmans, 2001), 53–173.

32. The contents of 1–2 Esdras differ in the ancient Greek (LXX) and Latin (Vulgate) corpuses in which they were transmitted. The title 2 Esdras, for instance, can refer to the apocalyptic work also known as 4 Ezra; in other cases it refers to the book of Nehemiah (Vulgate), or to the books of Ezra and Nehemiah combined (LXX).

33. VanderKam, *An Introduction to Early Judaism*, 69.

heroic, men and women at the center of their narratives in order to model Jewish piety and inspire trust in God's promises.

Our third genre is *rewritten Scripture*. Often books belonging to this group also take a narrative form, since these works typically reproduce, paraphrase, and elaborate on the accounts of specific Old Testament events and characters. To this category belong such books as Jubilees (a retelling of the biblical events from creation to Mt. Sinai) and the Genesis Apocryphon (an expansion of select patriarchal narratives). Also considered by some scholars as rewritten Scripture are the Life of Adam and Eve (an account of the advent of death and restoration of life) and the Testaments of the Twelve Patriarchs (an elaboration on Jacob's final words to his twelve sons in Genesis 49), the Testament of Adam (the first human's final words to his son Seth), and Joseph and Aseneth (a romance based on the patriarch's presumed marriage to a gentile in Genesis 41:45, 50; 46:20). Works such as these are important for demonstrating how biblical literature was interpreted during the Second Temple period, when exegetical commentaries were quite rare.[34]

Fourth among the early Jewish literary genres is *apocalypse*, which normally consists of otherworldly visions given to a human recipient (seer) through the mediation of a supernatural, sometimes angelic, being. Most Jewish apocalypses were written in the second and third centuries BC during times of great distress. They therefore seek to bring comfort to suffering Jewish communities by providing a heavenly perspective on past, present, and future events. Often coded in elaborate symbolism, these visions typically anticipate the eventual cessation of evil and political oppression. Early Jewish apocalypses include 4 Ezra, the Sibylline Oracles, the Testament of Moses, the Apocalypse of Zephaniah, and several portions of 1 Enoch: the Book of Watchers (1 En. 1–36); the Similitudes/Parables of Enoch (1 En. 37–71); the Astronomical Book (1 En. 72–82); the Book of Dreams (1 En. 83–90); and the Apocalypse of Weeks (1 En. 91:11–17; 93:1–10).

The fifth and sixth genres, *poetry* and *wisdom literature*, are similar in both content and style to their antecedent biblical literature (Job, Psalms, Proverbs, Ecclesiastes). Hebrew poems are normally songs of praise and lament utilizing meter and structural parallelism. The songs written during this period of Jewish history commonly entreat the Lord for deliverance from pain and oppression. Examples include the Psalms of Solomon, the Prayer of Manasseh, and the Prayer of Azariah and Song of the Three Young Men.

---

34. Cf. Molly M. Zahn, "Rewritten Scripture," in *The Oxford Handbook of the Dead Sea Scrolls*, ed. T. H. Lim and J. J. Collins (Oxford: Oxford University Press, 2010), 323–36.

Wisdom literature appeals to common experience in order to instruct people how to live virtuously. Examples include Sirach (Ecclesiasticus), the Wisdom of Solomon, and perhaps Baruch and the Epistle of Enoch (1 En. 91–108).[35]

Four additional collections deserve special mention, the origins of which we know far more about than the various works previously surveyed. First are the works of Philo (ca. 20 BC–AD 50). A diaspora Jew influenced by Platonism from Alexandria, Egypt, Philo authored numerous philosophical treatises and exegetical studies on the Pentateuch. Second are the books of the historian Josephus (AD 37–ca. 100). Once a Jewish Pharisee and military leader, Josephus was taken captive during the war against Rome and eventually made a Roman citizen and dependent of Emperor Vespasian. Josephus's four extant works include a history of the Jewish people (*Jewish Antiquities*), an account of the Jerusalem War (*Jewish War*), a work in defense of Judaism and the Jewish way of life (*Against Apion*), and an autobiography (*The Life*).

Third are the **Dead Sea Scrolls (DSS)**. Although the majority of the scrolls discovered near **Qumran** are ancient copies of the Old Testament or versions of apocryphal and pseudepigraphal texts (e.g., Tobit, 1 Enoch, Jubilees), many are **sectarian** documents—works that describe how the Dead Sea community originated and was organized and how members of the community should live and worship. These works are labeled by the Qumran cave number in which they were found (1Q, 4Q, etc.) and a cataloging number, though many have other shortened names describing their content (e.g., 1QS = Rule of the Community; 4Q504 = Words of the Luminaries). Citing the Damascus Document is more complex. Although two medieval manuscripts (abbreviated CD) were originally found in Egypt, ten ancient manuscripts were discovered in the Qumran caves (4Q266–73; 5Q12; 6Q15). All together, the textual tradition is abbreviated DD.

The fourth collection is the rabbinic literature. This literature is extensive and consists of the Mishnah, the Jerusalem Talmud, the Babylonian Talmud, the Targumim, and a variety of other writings. The Mishnah and Talmuds come from after the NT period, while some of the Targumim and other writings may stem from the NT period. While one must be careful about imposing later traditions on the earlier period, when used properly the rabbinic writings can shed much light on the practices and beliefs of Judaism in the first century.

Our goal here has been to provide only a concise overview of certain foundational elements for understanding early Jewish history and literature.

---

35. VanderKam, *An Introduction to Early Judaism*, 115–24.

For a full account, the reader should consult the resources listed below. Having oriented ourselves to the first-century Jewish context, we now turn to read Revelation in conversation with some of these Second Temple Jewish texts.

FOR FURTHER READING

For the most comprehensive overview of early Jewish literature, see Craig A. Evans, *Ancient Texts for New Testament Studies: A Guide to the Background Literature* (Peabody, MA: Hendrickson, 2005), which summarizes the literature and provides the bibliographic details for critical texts, research tools, and key scholarly works. The volume's appendixes also show how Jewish literature can illuminate the New Testament. See also David W. Chapman and Andreas J. Köstenberger, "Jewish Intertestamental and Early Rabbinic Literature: An Annotated Bibliographic Resource Updated (Part 1)," *JETS* 55 (2012): 235–72, and David W. Chapman and Andreas J. Köstenberger, "Jewish Intertestamental and Early Rabbinic Literature: An Annotated Bibliographic Resource Updated (Part 2)," *JETS* 55 (2012): 457–88.

Standard Translations of Early Jewish Literature

Bauckham, Richard, James R. Davila, and Alexander Panayotov, eds. *Old Testament Pseudepigrapha: More Noncanonical Scriptures*. Grand Rapids: Eerdmans, 2013.

Charlesworth, James H., ed. *The Old Testament Pseudepigrapha*. 2 vols. New York: Doubleday, 1983–1985.

Coogan, Michael D., Marc Z. Brettler, Carol Ann Newsom, and Pheme Perkins, eds. *The New Oxford Annotated Apocrypha: New Revised Standard Version*. Rev. 4th ed. Oxford: Oxford University Press, 2010.

García Martínez, Florentino, and Eibert J. C. Tigchelaar, eds. *The Dead Sea Scrolls Study Edition*. 2 vols. Leiden: Brill, 1997–1998.

Pietersma, Albert, and Benjamin G. Wright, eds. *A New English Translation of the Septuagint*. Oxford: Oxford University Press, 2007.

Introductions to Early Jewish Literature

Chapman, Honora Howell, and Zuleika Rodgers, eds. *A Companion to Josephus*. BCAW. Chichester: Wiley-Blackwell, 2016.

Collins, John J. *The Apocalyptic Imagination: An Introduction to Jewish Apocalyptic Literature*. 3rd ed. Grand Rapids: Eerdmans, 2016.

Collins, John J., and Daniel C. Harlow, eds. *Early Judaism: A Comprehensive Overview*. Grand Rapids: Eerdmans, 2012.

deSilva, David A. *Introducing the Apocrypha: Message, Context, and Significance.* Grand Rapids: Baker, 2002.

Helyer, Larry R. *Exploring Jewish Literature of the Second Temple Period: A Guide for New Testament Students.* Downers Grove: InterVarsity Press, 2002.

Kamesar, Adam, ed. *The Cambridge Companion to Philo.* Cambridge: Cambridge University Press, 2009.

Mason, Steve. *Josephus and the New Testament.* 2nd ed. Peabody, MA: Hendrickson, 2002.

Murphy, Frederick J. *Apocalypticism in the Bible and Its World: A Comprehensive Introduction.* Grand Rapids: Baker, 2012.

Nickelsburg, George W. E. *Jewish Literature between the Bible and the Mishnah: A Historical and Literary Introduction.* 2nd ed. Minneapolis: Fortress, 2011.

Strack, H. L., and G. Stemberger. *Introduction to the Talmud and Midrash.* Edinburgh: T&T Clark, 1991.

VanderKam, James C. *An Introduction to Early Judaism.* Grand Rapids: Eerdmans, 2001.

VanderKam, James C., and Peter Flint. *The Meaning of the Dead Sea Scrolls: Their Significance for Understanding the Bible, Judaism, Jesus, and Christianity.* San Francisco: HarperCollins, 2002.

CHAPTER 1

The Parables of Enoch and Revelation 1:1–20: Daniel's Son of Man

BENJAMIN E. REYNOLDS

John's Apocalypse includes numerous fascinating visions and revealed mysteries, the first of which is presented in Revelation 1. After introducing the revelation he received from God (1:1–3), John addresses it to seven churches in Asia: Ephesus, Smyrna, Pergamum, Thyatira, Sardis, Philadelphia, and Laodicea (1:4–6, 11). He writes in a manner typical of New Testament letters: "John, to the seven churches in the province of Asia: Grace and peace to you from him who is, and who was, and who is to come, and from the seven spirits before his throne, and from Jesus Christ, who is the faithful witness, the firstborn from the dead, and the ruler of the kings of the earth" (1:4–5a). This greeting from Father, Spirit, and Jesus Christ climaxes with its description of Jesus as Messiah, witness, resurrected one, and king, before it leads immediately into a doxology to Jesus (1:5b–6).

Revelation 1:7–8 links the opening of Revelation with the first of John's visions (1:9–20). In 1:7, John quotes from the Old Testament to indicate that Jesus Christ (1:5–6) is both the cloud-riding "one like a son of man" envisioned by Daniel (7:13) *and* the "pierced" messenger of God prophesied by Zechariah (12:10).

Revelation 1:9 then begins the narrative section of the book and introduces John's first vision. While he was on the island of Patmos, John had a vision, but as happens on a number of occasions in Revelation, John first *hears* and then *sees* (e.g., Rev. 5:5, 6; 7:4, 9). First, John *hears* a voice behind him that sounds like a trumpet, and the voice tells him to write what he sees and to send it to the seven churches (1:10b-11). Then, when John turns around, he *sees* a figure that looks like a human being standing among seven golden lampstands. John's various descriptions of this human-like figure (Rev 1:13–15) draw on portrayals of the visionary figures in Daniel (7:9–14; 10:2–9, 15–17) and Ezekiel 1.

Figure 1.1: John's Old Testament Quotations

Revelation 1:7	Daniel 7:13a	Zechariah 12:10b
"Look, he is coming with the clouds,"	and there before me was one like a son of man, coming with the clouds of heaven.	
and "every eye will see him, even those who pierced him";		They will look on me, the one they have pierced,
and all peoples on earth "will mourn because of him." So shall it be! Amen.		and they will mourn for him as one mourns for an only child, and grieve bitterly for him as one grieves for a firstborn son.

While Revelation presents Jesus as Daniel's son of man using imagery from Daniel 7, 10, and Ezekiel 1, it is not alone in using Daniel 7 to describe the Messiah. Three early Jewish apocalypses also describe visionary experiences of a messiah figure using imagery from Daniel 7's "one like a son of man"—the Parables of Enoch, 4 Ezra, and 2 Baruch. For our purposes, we will focus on the Parables of Enoch. When we read Parables alongside Revelation 1, John's vision of Jesus as Daniel's son of man and Messiah comes to life.

The Parables of Enoch

"AND I ASKED THE ANGEL OF PEACE . . .
ABOUT THAT SON OF MAN"

The early Jewish work known as 1 Enoch consists of seven separate texts, including the Book of the Watchers (chs. 1–36), the Parables of Enoch (chs. 37–71), the Book of the Luminaries (chs. 72–82), the Dream Visions (chs. 83–90), the Epistle of Enoch (chs. 91–105), the Birth of Noah (chs. 106–7), and another Enoch text (ch. 108). Each text was written separately and later collected to form the composite work known as 1 Enoch. These texts concern the experiences of Enoch, the seventh from Adam, who "walked faithfully with God; then he was no more, because God took him away" (Gen 5:24). The Enoch traditions attempt to explain this mysterious phrase but were not written by the biblical Enoch. The date of the Parables has been questioned because it was not found among the Dead Sea Scrolls, and the earliest extant versions are thirteenth and fourteenth-century Ge'ez (Ethiopic) manuscripts. However, the majority of scholars now agree that the Parables of Enoch is a Jewish text written in the late first century BC or early first century AD.

Evoking Old Testament Figures. The Parables of Enoch contains the "vision of wisdom that Enoch saw" (37:1) and includes three "parables" (37:5) that he received (38:1–44:1; 45:1–57:3; 58:1–69:29).[1] Our main interest with the Parables, however, is the figure of the son of man. The following quotes highlight some features of this figure.

> [1] There I saw one who had a head of days,
>   and his head was like white wool.
> And with him was another, whose face was like the
>   appearance of a man;
>   and his face was full of graciousness like one of the holy angels.
> [2] And I asked the angel of peace, who went with me and
>   showed me all the hidden things, about that son of man
>   —who he was and whence he was (and) why he went
>   with the Head of Days.
> [3] And he answered me and said to me,
> "This is the son of man who has righteousness,
>   and righteousness dwells with him.
>   And all the treasuries of what is hidden he will reveal;
> For the Lord of Spirits has chosen him,
>   and his lot has prevailed through truth
>   in the presence of the Lord of Spirits forever." (1 En. 46:1–3)

> [2] And in that hour that son of man was named in the presence of the
>   Lord of Spirits,

---

1. All translations are from George W. E. Nickelsburg and James K. VanderKam, *1 Enoch: The Hermeneia Translation* (Minneapolis: Fortress, 2012).

and his name, before the Head of Days.
³ Even before the sun and the constellations were created,
    before the stars of heaven were made,
his name was named before the Lord of Spirits. (48:2–3)

¹ And thus the Lord commanded the kings and the mighty and the
    exalted and those who possess the land, and he said,
"Open your eyes and lift up your horns,
    if you are able to recognize the Chosen One."
² And the Lord of Spirits [seated him] upon the throne of his glory,
    and the spirit of righteousness was poured upon him.
And the word of his mouth will slay all the sinners,
    and all the unrighteous will perish from his presence. (62:1–2)

The son of man figure in the Parables of Enoch is clearly a reinterpretation of Daniel's "one like a son of man." The Enochic figure appears with "one who had a head of days, and [whose] head was like white wool" and is described as having a "face like the appearance of a man" (1 En. 46:1–2; Dan 7:9–10, 13–14). Although called "Son of Man," Enoch's figure is most often referred to as "Chosen One," which reflects the Lord's chosen servant in Isaiah (42:1; 43:10). The figure is also called "Righteous One" (1 En. 38:2; 53:6) and "Anointed One," signifying that he is the Messiah (1 En. 48:10; 52:4). In the Parables, then, the designations Righteous One, Anointed One, Chosen One, and Son of Man all refer to the same figure.

Preexistence and Eschatological Judgment. Beyond attributing these designations to him, the Parables also depicts the Son of Man as possessing notable attributes and participating in specific activities. This figure will judge the kings of the earth after being seated on the Lord of Spirits' throne (1 En. 45:3; 61:8; 62:2–6; 69:27–29). His judgment takes place through speech, echoing the messianic prophecy in Isaiah 11:4 (1 En. 62:2; see also Isa. 49:6). That the Son of Man sits on the Lord of Spirits' throne of glory implies a close relationship with God. The Parables of Enoch also depicts the Son of Man as a preexistent figure, since he was named before creation and was hidden in God's presence "before the world was created" (48:2, 6; 62:7). Following the judgment of the wicked, the Son of Man of the Parables will dwell with the righteous forever (62:13–14). He thus shares in the identity of several scriptural figures, and also identifies closely with God and his people.

Revelation 1:1–20

"I SAW . . . IN THE MIDST OF THE LAMPSTANDS ONE LIKE A SON OF MAN"

Evoking Old Testament Figures. Turning to John the seer's vision of "one like a son of man," we find many striking similarities with the Parables of Enoch. The figure that John sees in Revelation 1:12–20, like the Son of Man in the Parables of Enoch, is depicted with language from Daniel 7:13. This connection is made obvious in the similar phrase "one like a son of man" (Rev 1:13) and the citation of Daniel 7:13 in Revelation 1:7: "he is coming with the clouds." In addition, the sharp double-edged sword coming from the mouth of the Son of Man (Rev 1:16; also 2:12, 16; 19:15, 21) draws on Isaiah 11:4 and 49:2 and is similar to the act of judging that the Enochic Son of Man does through his speech (1 En. 62:2). Revelation also links the "one like a son of man" from Daniel 7 with Davidic messianic expectation, just as the Enochic figure is called "Anointed One." In Revelation, Jesus is called Christ ("Messiah"), the Lion of Judah, and the Root of David (Rev 1:5; 5:5; cf. Gen 49:9; Isa 11:1).

Preexistence and Eschatological Judgment. Like the Son of Man in the Parables, the figure that John sees takes part in judgment (1 En. 69:27; Rev 14:14–16) and sits on God's throne (1 En. 45:3; 61:8; 62:2; Rev 3:21). Both figures are preexistent: Jesus says that he is "the First and the Last" (Rev 1:17; 2:8; 22:13; cf. Isa 41:4; 44:6; 48:12). Additionally, there is a close relationship between the Son of Man in Revelation and the people of God. Similar to how the righteous in the Parables of Enoch dwell with the Son of Man (1 En. 62:14), John sees Jesus present among the seven golden lampstands, which signifies his presence with the seven churches (Rev 1:12, 20).

Angelic Appearance and Divine Identity. The Parables and Revelation both describe the physical appearance of their respective figures in ways evocative of angelic beings. The Parables merely states that the Son of Man looks like a human being and that "his face was full of graciousness like one of the holy angels" (1 En. 46:1), whereas John provides more physical details, describing Jesus in terms similar to the *angel* in Daniel 10:5–6 (see Figure 1.2).

While Jesus in John's vision looks like the angel in Daniel 10, his white hair reflects that of the Ancient of Days in Daniel 7:9, indicating Jesus's similarity with God. This similarity is also noticeable in two declarations that Jesus and God make of themselves. Both state that they are "the first and . . . the last" (Isa 44:6; 48:12; Rev 1:17) and "the Alpha and the Omega" (Rev 1:8; 22:13). The relationship between God and Jesus in Revelation, one that verges on a shared identity, is therefore much stronger than the relationship between the Parables of Enoch's Lord of Spirits and Son of Man.

Figure 1.2: Jesus and Daniel 10's Angel

Daniel 10:5–6	Revelation 1:12–15
"I looked up and there before me was	"And when I turned I saw . . .
a man	someone like a son of man,
dressed in linen,	dressed in a robe reaching down to his feet
with a belt of fine gold from Uphaz around his waist.	and with a golden sash around his chest.
His body was like topaz,	
his face like lightning,	
	The hair on his head was white like wool, as white as snow,
his eyes like flaming torches,	his eyes were like blazing fire.
his arms and legs like the gleam of burnished bronze,	His feet were like bronze glowing in a furnace,
and his voice like the sound of a multitude."	and his voice was like the sound of rushing waters."

Son of Man, Dead and Raised to Life. Another difference centers on the significance Revelation gives to Jesus's death and resurrection. After John falls down, Jesus declares: "Do not be afraid. . . . I am the Living One; I was dead, and now look, I am alive for ever and ever! And I hold the keys of death and Hades" (1:18). The Enochic Son of Man makes no such claim, even though he is seated on the Lord of Spirits' throne of glory and judges the wicked. In fact, if 1 Enoch 70–71 are original, Enoch is taken up into heaven (Gen 5:24; 1 En. 39:3; 70:1–2) and declared to be the Son of Man (71:14).[2] Before this declaration, however, Enoch falls on his face before God, experiences a transformation, and blesses God (1 En. 71:11). Jesus, on the other hand, comes as Daniel's son of man and does not fall on his face before God

---

2. Chapters 70 and 71 are sometimes considered to be later additions to the Parables of Enoch.

like Enoch (Rev 1:7, 13). Jesus, the Lion of Judah and the Lamb, boldly takes the scroll from God's right hand, being worthy to open it because he was slain (Rev 5:5–7). Jesus died and was raised to life, but rather than blessing God, he receives blessing and praise from the four living creatures and the twenty-four elders who fall down before *him* (Rev 5:8–14). Revelation's Son of Man, therefore, may be understood as a more exalted figure than that of the Parables, perhaps even sharing in the divine identity.

Reading the Parables of Enoch alongside Revelation 1 highlights similar expectations concerning Daniel's son of man, while also drawing attention to the ways the same Old Testament texts could be understood differently. John the seer presents Jesus as Daniel's "one like a son of man," Isaiah's servant, the Davidic Messiah, and one who shares characteristics with God. Many of these themes are repeated in the messages to the seven churches (Rev 2–3), in the throne room scene (Rev 5), and in the vision of the rider on the white horse (Rev 19). John's claims about Jesus come to life when read alongside early Jewish texts.

For Further Reading

Additional Ancient Texts

Daniel 7:13's "one like a son of man" also appears in 4 Ezra 13; 2 Bar. 29–30; 39–40; 53:1–3; 70–74. For early Jewish texts that describe angelic figures like the angel in Daniel 10, see Apoc. Zeph. 6:11–15; Apoc. Abr. 17:1–4; Joseph and Asenath 14:7–10; 15:11–12. Jesus refers to himself as *"the* Son of Man" on over eighty occasions in the Gospels, including Matthew 8:20; 16:27–28; 25:31; Mark 2:10; 2:28; 8:31; 13:26; 14:62; Luke 12:8; 17:24; 22:48; 24:7; John 1:51; 3:13; 8:28; 9:35; 13:31. See also Acts 7:56.

English Translations and Critical Editions

Bertalotto, Pierpaolo, Ken M. Penner, and Ian W. Scott, eds. "1 Enoch." Edition 1.5. In *The Online Critical Pseudepigrapha*. Edited by Ian W. Scott, Ken M. Penner, and David M. Miller. Atlanta: Society of Biblical Literature, 2006. www.purl.org/net/ocp/1En.

Knibb, Michael A. *The Ethiopic Book of Enoch*. 2 vols. Oxford: Clarendon, 1978.

Nickelsburg, George W. E., and James K. VanderKam. *1 Enoch: The Hermeneia Translation*. Minneapolis: Fortress, 2012.

Olson, Daniel C. *Enoch: A New Translation*. North Richland Hills, TX: BIBAL, 2004.

Secondary Literature

Baynes, Leslie. "Introduction to the Similitudes of Enoch." Pages 256–63 in vol. 2 of *Early Jewish Literature: An Anthology*. Edited by Brad Embry, Ronald Herms, and Archie T. Wright. Grand Rapids: Eerdmans, 2018.

Boccaccini, Gabriele, ed. *Enoch and the Messiah Son of Man: Revisiting the Book of Parables*. Grand Rapids: Eerdmans, 2007.

Bock, Darrell L., and James H. Charlesworth, eds. *Parables of Enoch: A Paradigm Shift*. London: Bloomsbury, T&T Clark, 2013.

Hannah, Darrell D. "The Throne of His Glory: The Divine Throne and Heavenly Mediators in Revelation and the Similitudes of Enoch." *ZNW* 94 (2003): 68–96.

Nickelsburg, George W. E., and James C. VanderKam. *1 Enoch 2: A Commentary on the Book of 1 Enoch, Chapters 37–82*. Hermeneia. Minneapolis: Fortress, 2012.

Rowland, Christopher. "The Vision of the Risen Christ in Rev. i. 13ff.: The Debt of an Early Christology to an Aspect of Jewish Angelology." *JTS* 31 (1980): 1–11.

VanderKam, James C. "Righteous One, Messiah, Chosen One, and Son of Man in 1 Enoch 37–71." Pages 169–91 in *The Messiah: Developments in Earliest Judaism and Christianity*. Edited by James H. Charlesworth. Minneapolis: Fortress, 1992.

CHAPTER 2

The Epistle of Enoch and Revelation 2:1–3:22: Poverty and Riches in the Present Age

Mark D. Mathews

John's message to the churches in Asia Minor displays several distinguishing features. The stylistic pattern that persists throughout indicates his strategy was to streamline the messages into a single literary form that would cohere with the apocalyptic section (chs. 4–22).[1] While seven real churches are addressed, the circular nature of the letter implies that the seven messages function to provide a comprehensive picture of the state of the church in Asia Minor. At the same time, the formulaic pattern of the seven messages reveals two distinct anomalies.

First, the call to repentance is absent in only two messages, both of which are addressed to churches experiencing similar circumstances. The church at Smyrna is experiencing "poverty" ("I know your afflictions and your poverty," 2:9) while Philadelphia likewise has few resources ("I know that you have little strength," 3:8). These two churches share a situation of social and economic marginalization. To the contrary, those who are called to repent are adhering to the "teaching of Balaam" (2:14), which likely includes what John regarded as an excessive interest in wealth and could be a reference to greed, as shown in other traditions.[2] In addition, the church

---

1. Seven lampstands, stars, seals, angels, trumpets, bowls, crowns, etc. Likewise, the language of repentance (Rev 9:20–21; 16:9–11), conquering (5:5; 6:2; 11:7; 12:11; 13:7; 15:2; 17:14; 21:7), nakedness and shame (16:15), the tree of life (2:7; 22:14, 19), the second death (2:11; 20:6, 14; 21:8), Jezebel's adultery (2:22; 14:8; 17:2; 18:3; 19:2), Satan (2:9, 13, 24; 3:9; 12:9), and the New Jerusalem (3:12; 21:2) come into play in the apocalyptic section (chs. 4–22) that ties the visions to the churches.

2. 2 Pet 2:15; Jude 11; Philo, *Mos.* 1:294–99; Josephus, *Ant.* 4:126–30; m. 'Abot 5:19–22;

is warned to avoid the teaching of Jezebel, which is also related to concerns over riches and affluence. This can be seen in Jezebel's linguistic connection with the rich prostitute Babylon through the language of sexual immorality and deceit, which in chapters 17–18 is associated with economic activity (cf. 2:22–23; 13:14–17; 18:3–4, 23).

The second anomaly, found in the message to Laodicea, is a rhetorical device referred to as imputed or attributed speech. In it, members of the church are said to boast in their accumulated wealth: "You say, 'I am rich; I have acquired wealth and do not need a thing'" (3:17). This is found elsewhere in the Apocalypse only in John's harsh critique of Babylon's riches: "In her heart she boasts, 'I sit enthroned as queen. I am not a widow; I will never mourn'" (18:7). The presence of these two instances, taken together with the praise of poverty, suggests that the author's concern with the churches is twofold. First, there exists a disconnect between John's expectations of hostility for the people of the kingdom (cf. 1:9) and the present experience of many in the church. Second, he is grappling with how Christians can accumulate wealth, on the one hand, and remain faithful to God, on the other.[3] This concern over the accumulation of wealth among the people of God finds significant parallels in the Second Temple literature, especially those works that are apocalyptic in nature. The most obvious parallels are found in the Epistle of Enoch.

The Epistle of Enoch

"WOE TO YOU SINNERS FOR YOUR RICHES"

The Epistle of Enoch (1 En. 92:1–5; 93:11–105:2) is part of a multiauthored work commonly referred to as 1 Enoch.[4] The body of the epistle (94:6–104:8) consists of eight woe oracles situated within three prophetic discourses. The first discourse (94:6–100:6) contains six woe oracles pronouncing judgment against rich sinners, alongside words of encouragement for the righteous. The second discourse (100:7–102:3) deals with divine judgment, while the third (102:4–104:8) attempts to answer the question of theodicy. The epistle

Tg. Pal. Num 24:14; Num. Rab. 20:23.

3. Mark D. Mathews, *Riches, Poverty, and the Faithful: Perspectives on Wealth in the Second Temple Period and the Apocalypse of John*, SNTSMS 154 (Cambridge: University Press, 2013), 172.

4. For more information about 1 Enoch, see chapter 1 in this volume by Benjamin E. Reynolds ("The Parables of Enoch and Revelation 1:1–20: Daniel's Son of Man"). For a related comparison with the Epistle of Enoch and Revelation, see chapter 18 by Cynthia Long Westfall ("The Epistle of Enoch and Revelation 18:1–24: An Economic Critique of Rome").

can be dated in the early to mid-second century BC, just prior to the **Maccabean revolt**.

Wealth and the Wicked, Poverty and the Pious. The epistle fits within a larger tradition of Enoch literature concerned with the origins of evil and the question of theodicy.[5] What is notable about the epistle, however, is its unique emphasis on how evil persons are referred to in terms of the rich and powerful, and how these evil persons prosper while the righteous suffer at their hands. Within the epistle, the rich are categorically deemed wicked. Any expectation of material blessing for the righteous is pushed into the future eschatological age. Within the Deuteronomic pattern (cf. Deut 28–30), this casts doubt on the piety of the righteous and serves to validate the wicked who have gained their wealth by unjust means.[6] For example, 1 Enoch 96:4 says: "Woe to you sinners for your riches give you the appearance of righteousness but your hearts convict you of being sinners, and this fact will serve against you—a testament to your evil deeds!"[7]

These denouncements of the wicked are further expressed in terms of their oppression of the faithful (94:7; 96:5), their trusting in riches (94:8–9), their decadence (98:2–3), and their independence of God's authority to live however they wish (97:8–10). These sinners are presented with a series of woe oracles that not only denounce their activity but serve as formal, irreversible pronouncements of judgment that they will not escape punishment.

A Future Reversal of Fortunes. This seeming turn in the promises of blessing for covenant obedience and cursing for disobedience in the Deuteronomic tradition is then offset by an explanation of a future reversal of fortunes in the final discourse (102:4–104:8). In this discourse, these ideas are expressed in the form of imputed speech, a rhetorical device common in ancient Jewish and early Christian texts.[8] In such cases, the speech is not simply a historical account of what someone said, but it assigns to a person a belief or viewpoint that the writer regards as their defining characteristic.

> [5] Woe to you sinners who have died! Whenever you die in the wealth
> of your sins, your peers will say this concerning you: "Blessed are

---

5. The Book of the Watchers, chs. 1–36; The Parables of Enoch, chs. 37–71; The Astronomy Book, chs. 72–82, and The Dream Visions, chs. 83–90.

6. The blessings and curses in Deuteronomy 28–30 promise material abundance for obedience and poverty and persecution for disobedience. This is a core issue that the righteous who suffered at the hands of the wicked rich attempted to reconcile.

7. Daniel C. Olson, *Enoch: A New Translation* (North Richland Hills, TX: BIBAL, 2004), 231.

8. Isa 29:15; 47:8; Jer 2:23; Ezek 18:25; Amos 7:16; Hab 2:6; Mal 1:4; 2:17; 3:8; Sir. 5:1; 11:18–19; Wis 2:1–11; 2 Esd. 10:12–13; Luke 12:16–21.

the sinners! They have seen all their days, [6] and now they have died prosperous and wealthy. They saw no trouble or slaughter during their lifetimes, and they have died in honor. During their lives, judgment did not occur against them." [7] Know this! Your souls will be taken down to Sheol, and there they will be in great distress— [8] in darkness, in snares, and in blazing fire—and your souls will enter into the Great Judgment, and this great judgment will last all the generations of eternity. Woe to you! You will have no peace. (103:5–8)

This displays a more categorical rejection of riches than previous Enoch traditions and escalates the language of rich and poor into categories of wicked and faithful, respectively.

Revelation 2:1–3:22

"I KNOW YOUR AFFLICTIONS AND YOUR POVERTY—YET YOU ARE RICH"

John presents a crisis that deals with false teaching in the church and the consequences for following that teaching. This is evident in the prophetic rivalry between John and three other teachers in the church—those identified as "Jezebel" (2:20), "Balaam" (2:14), and "the Nicolaitans" (2:6, 15). The latter two likely refer not to actual persons but to kinds of teaching that John opposes. His main rival is Jezebel, which can be seen in his confrontation with her (2:21) and by the linguistic associations that link her to other passages.

The Greek term *porneia* ("fornication") and its cognates occur 19 times in the Apocalypse. Three occur in the messages to the seven churches (2:14, 20, 21) and 10 in the visions of the whore and Babylon ("prostitutes," "adulteries," 17:1–2, 4–5, 15–16; 18:3, 9; 19:2 [x2]). The term in chapters 17–18 refers not to sexual immorality but to the economic activity of the kings of the earth and the merchants who have grown rich from the luxurious lifestyle of Babylon (18:3). The imagery of the whore drinking her immoral wine from a golden chalice and the name on her forehead all evoke the economic language John has adopted in previous passages (13:16–17; 14:8–10). It is here that John's critique of the churches comes to its climax and is coupled with a call to the faithful: "Come out of her, my people" (18:4).

Wealth and the Wicked, Poverty and the Pious. Given the economic language in these texts and the linguistic connections to Jezebel, one can see in the message to the church (chs. 2–3) that John intends to undermine her view of wealth in relation to the faithful community. That is, John opposes the idea that the pious and faithful can accumulate individual wealth through activity with the immoral Roman Empire while remaining faithful to God. And this not simply because he sees the Roman world as evil, but because of his apocalyptic worldview that understands the present age as one in which the wicked flourish while the righteous suffer.

A Future Reversal of Fortunes. The mark of covenant faithfulness to God, then, is not affluence in the present age, but hostility and conflict, even persecution—a situation that will be reversed in the coming age when the righteous receive their blessing in Christ along with his consummated kingdom (cf. Rev 21:1–22:5). Hence, the angel lauds the Smyrnans, "I know your afflictions and your poverty—yet you are *rich*!" (2:9), but the Laodiceans, who find security in their wealth, he chides, "You are wretched, pitiful, *poor*, blind and naked" (3:17). The accumulation of riches, with its implied eventual reversal of fortunes, is what John's language of conquering points to.

While only five churches are called to repent, all seven are admonished to "conquer." Thus, the comprehensive solution to the various circumstances mentioned in the messages finds its resolution in "conquering" or obtaining "victory." Two paradoxical ways of conquering are represented throughout the Apocalypse: (1) the evil cosmic forces of the present age make war against the faithful to conquer and kill them (6:2; 11:7; 13:7); (2) the faithful are admonished to conquer or be victorious and are given specific promises for doing so ("To the one who is victorious, I will give . . . ," 2:7, 11, 17, 26; 3:5, 12, 21; 21:7). The realization of these promises are depicted in scenes where the faithful have "conquered" the dragon (12:11) and the beast (15:2), while enigmatically, they too have been conquered. In each of these situations, the death of the faithful is in view. Their triumph is bound up with that of the faithful Lamb who also conquered through death (3:21; 5:5–6). And it is through his death that he is said to be worthy "to receive power and *wealth* and wisdom and strength and honor and glory and praise!" (5:12). This does not mean that John is asking his readers to become martyrs. What he is demanding is that they separate themselves from the evil world system in the present age and its promises of peace and prosperity, and that they instead follow the slaughtered Lamb wherever he may lead.

Parallels and Contrasts. We find both parallels and contrasts when we compare the Apocalypse with the apocalyptic worldview of the epistle. First, like the epistle, John does not view wealth and affluence as a feature of the present age for the Christian community. Rather, he presupposes a postponement of the Deuteronomic promise of material blessing to the coming age. John envisions the world in the present age as irretrievably evil and ruled temporarily by Satan. This follows the same pattern developed in the Second Temple period in which external evil forces deceive humankind (1QS 3:20–21; 1QM 14:9) and lure them into a life of affluence and away from worshiping God (CD 4:13–17).

Second, like antecedent apocalyptic traditions (the epistle in particular), John utilizes the rhetorical device of imputed speech that labels rich sinners and exposes their perverted worldview, while also revealing the consequences for their alliances (3:17; 18:7). He also utilizes the prophetic woe oracle to provide formal, irreversible indictments against rich sinners, thus assuring them of their punishment (8:13; 9:12; 11:14; 12:12).[9] John includes in the judgment of Babylon woe oracles placed in the mouths of her rich cohorts, which assumes the realization of the judgment promised in traditions like the epistle (18:10, 16, 19).

However, unlike the epistle, which makes no accommodation for repentance for rich sinners, John calls for both repentance and conquering. This reveals a marked difference. John is dealing with the church in which some of the people of God are demonstrating wicked behavior. Nonetheless, they are among the people of God. Yet, the remainder of the Apocalypse, which portrays the world not as it is but as it should be, suggests that unless God's people repent and conquer, they will prove themselves to be as false as the teachers they are following. They will find themselves aligned with the dragon and his beasts. John's discourse is not set against the social injustices of the Roman Empire; Rome is not the enemy of the church *per se*. John's worldview is based on his apocalyptic understanding that the present age is irredeemable because the eschatological age has been inaugurated and Satan and his angels have been cast down to the earth (12:7–17).

The very nature of the eschatological age, as John sees it, is that people will be lured into seeking affluence in order to find some sense of false security and establish their self-sufficiency. This pursuit of wealth bears upon them the mark of Satan. The righteous, however, follow the example of the slaughtered Lamb and elect a position of marginalization to establish their identity visibly within the dominant discourse of power, greed, and luxurious living. This correlates with John's admonition to the rich that they "buy" from Christ gold refined by fire so that they might become rich (3:18), traditional language that alludes to God testing his people. Thus, John is

---

9. Loren T. Stuckenbruck, *1 Enoch 91–108*, CEJL (Berlin: de Gruyter, 2007), 216.

encouraging the rich in the church to reject riches in the present age and receive the reproof and discipline of God (3:19), which reflects an alternative, otherworldly economic system.

For Further Reading

Additional Ancient Texts

One should read the epistle in conversation with other Second Temple texts such as the Wisdom of Ben Sira. The latter provides a view of riches from a Deuteronomic perspective. Wisdom of Solomon provides both sapiential and apocalyptic views on the plight of the faithful and the wicked, and how they relate to suffering and wealth, respectively.

English Translations and Critical Editions

Bertalotto, Pierpaolo, Ken M. Penner, and Ian W. Scott, eds. "1 Enoch." In *The Online Critical Pseudepigrapha*. Edited by Ian W. Scott, Ken M. Penner, and David M. Miller. 1.5 ed. Atlanta: Society of Biblical Literature, 2006. www.purl.org/net/ocp/1En.

Isaac, E. "1 (Ethiopic Apocalypse of) Enoch: A New Translation and Introduction." Pages 13–89 in vol. 1 of *The Old Testament Pseudepigrapha*. Edited by James H. Charlesworth. New York: Doubleday, 1983.

Knibb, Michael A. "1 Enoch." Pages 184–319 in *The Apocryphal Old Testament*. Edited by H. F. D. Sparks. Oxford: Clarendon, 1984.

———. *The Ethiopic Book of Enoch*. 2 vols. Oxford: Clarendon, 1978.

Nickelsburg, George W. E., and James C. VanderKam. *1 Enoch: A New Translation*. Minneapolis: Fortress, 2004.

Olson, Daniel C. *Enoch: A New Translation*. North Richland Hills, TX: BIBAL, 2004.

Secondary Literature

Mathews, Mark D. *Riches, Poverty, and the Faithful: Perspectives on Wealth in the Second Temple Period and the Apocalypse of John*. SNTSMS 154. Cambridge: Cambridge University Press, 2013.

Newsom, Carol A. *The Self as Symbolic Space: Constructing Identity and Community at Qumran*. STDJ 52. Leiden: Brill, 2004.

Schüssler Fiorenza, Elisabeth. *Revelation: Vision of a Just World*. Minneapolis: Fortress, 1991.

Stuckenbruck, Loren T. *1 Enoch 91–108*. CEJL. Berlin: de Gruyter, 2007.

CHAPTER 3

The Testament of Levi and Revelation 4:1–11: Ascent to the Heavenly Throne

DAVID A. DESILVA

J ohn's fantastic images have always more readily invited decoding than visualizing. While some of his images must indeed be decoded, since the text itself moves in that direction (see, for example, Rev 17:9, 18), Christians from the late second century on have sought to decode nearly *all* of John's images as if John sought to have an impact only at an intellectual level attained through a symbolic reading and not at the visceral level as he invited people to "see" as *he* "saw" heavenly realities.

During the second and third centuries, Christians interpreted the heavenly beings who inhabit the spaces around God's throne as symbolic representations of what was of concern to them as they gave shape to their faith and canon. Thus, the four living creatures with the faces of a lion, an ox, a man, and an eagle were seen as symbols for the four Gospels, each presenting a different face of the one Jesus (Irenaeus, *Haer.* 3.11.8; Origen, *Comm. Joh.* 5.6; Victorinus, *In Apoc.* 4.4; Augustine, *Tract. Ev. Jo.* 36.5.2). Irenaeus found here a warrant for the church's embracing of a fourfold Gospel canon, as opposed to voices that promoted a single Gospel or a conflated harmony of the four Gospels. The twenty-four elders were decoded as the twelve patriarchs of Israel and the twelve apostles of the Lord (Origen, *Comm. Joh.* 5.6; Tyconius, *Exposition of the Apocalypse* 2.4.4) or as the twenty-four books of the law and the prophets (Victorinus, *In Apoc.* 4.3). The seven lamps, which John himself explains as "the seven spirits of God," were taken to represent the one Holy Spirit (Primasius, *Commentary on the Apocalypse* 4.5).

Reading certain comparative texts, however, might lead us in another direction for experiencing John's visions of the enthroned deity and his entourage. The tradition of the mystical visualization of these spiritual realities has its roots in Isaiah 6 and Ezekiel 1, but by the Hellenistic and Roman periods, one finds more detailed, more involved, and more densely populated visions of God's heavenly realm. One such report of an ascent into the divine realm and observation of its varied inhabitants is to be found in the Testament of Levi.

The Testament of Levi

"THE ANGEL OPENED TO ME THE GATES OF HEAVEN"

A popular literary genre during the late **Second Temple period** was the "testament," a writing that purported to preserve the dying words of a Jewish patriarch to his children and grandchildren. These appear to have been inspired by deathbed speeches in Scripture like Jacob's blessing of nine of his twelve sons (having passed over Reuben, Simeon, and Levi!) in Genesis 49:1–33. Testaments were vehicles for the imaginative and interpretive expansion of the scriptural narratives concerning the characters who give their "testament," for ethical instruction of their spiritual heirs (the actual audience of the testaments), and, in many instances, otherworldly revelations and end-time predictions. Examples include the Testament of Abraham, Testament of Moses, Testament of Job, and the Testaments of the Twelve Patriarchs (the twelve sons of Jacob). Within the last collection we find the Testament of Levi, distinctive among the twelve for including Levi's ascent through the heavens and their various inhabitants to the very throne of God.

A Jewish or Christian Composition? The Testaments of the Twelve Patriarchs were preserved and handed down not in Jewish circles, but in Christian circles. The oldest complete manuscripts were produced by Christian scribes. They bear the unmistakable mark of *Christian* convictions about Jesus as the promised heir of Judah and Levi through whom God's deliverance would come to God's people. Scholars are divided concerning the extent to which the Testaments offer a window into pre-Christian Judaism. Were the Testaments originally Jewish compositions that were lightly edited by Christian scribes, such that, after eliminating their commentary, we are essentially able to read the pre-Christian document, or are they a Christian composition that makes heavy use of Jewish traditions?

I believe the former position to remain the stronger one: (1) the manuscripts give evidence of progressively greater "Christianization" of the Testaments; (2) the distinctively Christian material is, for the most part, easily identified and isolated from its context (within which it often sits awkwardly); (3) distinctively Jewish interests and convictions permeate the Testaments; (4) the Testaments regularly echo many traditions found in early Jewish texts but they do not echo early Christian literature, with which the authors seem entirely unfamiliar.[1] The Testaments thus remain an important witness to pre-Christian Jewish exegesis, ethics, and eschatology.

A Journey to a Heavenly Throne. After a brief prologue, the Testament of Levi opens with a dramatic ascent: "The heavens opened, and an angel of the Lord said to me, Levi, come in" (T. Levi 2.6).[2] The angel escorts Levi on a tour through the seven heavens, a typical number for the levels of the heavens in Jewish visionary literature. The lowermost heaven is gloomy, as it witnesses human sins and injustice (T. Levi 3.1). The second contains natural elements (including fire, ice, and winds) held in readiness for the day of vengeance (T. Levi 3.2). In the third are stationed the angelic armies that will combat and destroy the hosts of Beliar (a common name for Satan) on the day of judgment (T. Levi 3.3).

The upper four heavens are of a different character, all focused on God who sits "upon a throne of glory" in the highest heaven, notably in the "holy of holies" of the heavenly temple (T. Levi 3.5; 5.1). God seated upon a throne and adored by angels is a familiar image from the **canonical** Jewish Scriptures (see 1 Kgs 22:19; Isa 6:1–3; Ps 103:19–22). God's dwelling place is pictured here as a heavenly temple, the author sharing in the fairly widespread notion that the wilderness tabernacle was a model of the heavenly prototype (see Wis. 9:8; Heb 8:1–5). In the three intervening heavens, Levi sees various angelic orders, whose actions are conceived largely in priestly and Levitical terms. Next to the highest heaven are the "angels of the presence," an elite order of angels who "make expiation to the Lord for all the sins committed unwittingly by the righteous" (T. Levi 3.5–6).[3] In the next heaven below them Levi is shown a lower order of angels "who bear the answers to the angels of the Lord's presence" (T. Levi 3.7). Another celestial

---

1. David A. deSilva, *The Jewish Teachers of Jesus, James, and Jude: What Earliest Christianity Learned from the Apocrypha and Pseudepigrapha* (New York: Oxford University Press, 2012), 194–222.

2. Quotations are from the translation by Marinus de Jonge, "Testaments of the Twelve Patriarchs," in *The Apocryphal Old Testament*, ed. H. F. D. Sparks (Oxford: Clarendon, 1984), 505–600.

3. See Lev 5:18 on sins committed in ignorance.

order, the "thrones and powers," sit in the fourth heaven, "in which praises are offered to God continually" (T. Levi 3.8). Levi's angelic guide contrasts the deep reverence with which these heavenly forces give God proper glory with the ignorant irreverence of the majority of human beings, who "do not perceive these things, and they sin and provoke the Most High" (T. Levi 3.10). Even after God's judgments begin to be revealed, Levi's angelic guide predicts, human beings "will be unbelieving and persist in their iniquities" (T. Levi 4.1; cf. Rev 9:20–21; 16:9, 11).

The heavenly ascent, culminating in an encounter between Levi and the enthroned God, set the stage for the "interpretive expansions" of the biblical story found in the Testament of Levi, which center on Levi and Simeon's brutal massacre of the male inhabitants of Shechem in reprisal for the prince of the city's rape of their sister Dinah (Gen 34:1–31). Scripture is ambiguous concerning the justice of this act—accomplished through deception and earning Jacob's curse (Gen 34:13–15, 25–31; 49:5–7). In the Testament of Levi, however, the angel himself equips Levi with sword and shield and commissions him to take vengeance against Shechem (T. Levi 5.3–4). Levi would indeed act against his father's will, but in obedience to the divine will (T. Levi 6.1–7.4). The Testament also focuses on God's personal commissioning of Levi as the ancestor of the line of priests that would serve God on earth (T. Levi 5.2; 8.1–9.14), about which Genesis is silent.

Revelation 4:1–11

"THEY NEVER STOP SAYING: 'HOLY, HOLY, HOLY IS THE LORD GOD ALMIGHTY'"

Angelic Attendants in the Heavenlies. Reading John's account of the entities and activities around the heavenly throne of God alongside Testament of Levi's account of the patriarch's ascent leads us away from symbolic readings of the various figures around the throne (which replace the strange images with more familiar realities, like the four Gospels or the twelve patriarchs plus the twelve apostles) and allow the images to stand, in all their strangeness, as precisely what John presents them to be—the otherworldly staff of God's heavenly temple and throne room. John's images are admittedly stranger than those presented in Testament of Levi, but this is due to John's weaving in significant elements from the more colorful visions of God's throne and God's heavenly attendants in the older vision reports of Ezekiel 1 and Isaiah 6.

In both texts, the heavens must first be opened before the visionary can perceive what lies beyond the visible sky (Rev 4:1). In Revelation, Christ himself (and not an angel) issues the invitation to the prophet John to "come up" into the divine realm. John dispenses with the enumeration of the heavens and begins in God's throne room itself. John gives a prominent place to four beings whose appearance is inspired by Ezekiel's four-faced "living creatures" and whose activity is informed by Isaiah's vision of the seraphim who cry "Holy, holy, holy" before God's throne (Ezek 1:5–10; Isa 6:2–3). These four beings have no counterpart in Testament of Levi, but the latter (along with Isaiah) still leads us first to think of them as one of the angelic orders stationed in their concentric circles around (or, in Testament of Levi, in successive heavens below) God's throne.

There are "seven spirits" before God's throne in both Revelation and Testament of Levi. Although it has been popular to identify these "seven spirits of God" in Revelation as the Holy Spirit, no doubt because of the winsomeness of finding the Trinity visually represented in Revelation 4–5, the prominence of "the angels of the Presence" in Testament of Levi (as well as texts like Tobit) should give us pause. John himself will shortly speak (again) of "the seven angels who stand before God" in 8:2 in a manner that assumes that the hearers have prior acquaintance with this group. The only available antecedent within Revelation would be the "seven spirits" of Rev 4:5 who are "before the throne."[4] "Angels" and "spirits" are used interchangeably in other texts (Ps 104:4 and Heb 1:7 explicitly equate the two). "Thrones" surround the enthroned God in both Rev 4:4 and Testament of Levi (see also Col 1:16). John's twenty-four enthroned elders may provide a more detailed representation of this angelic order.

Temple Imagery. Another prominent point of contact between Revelation and Testament of Levi, shared with other Second Temple Jewish texts as well, is the temple imagery that dominates descriptions of God's realm. This is not yet explicit in Rev 4:1–5:11, but quickly emerges as the primary spatial frame for the unseen realm. The souls of martyrs cry out from below a sacrificial altar in heaven (6:9–11). An angel comes to this same altar to offer up incense with the saints' prayers and then to cast his censer, filled with fire from the altar, down to the earth (8:1–6). The heavenly temple will later be opened, revealing the ark of the covenant (11:19). Two angels will come out

---

4. Cf. Tob. 12:15; David E. Aune, *Revelation 1–5*, WBC 52A (Dallas: Word, 1997), 34–35. Several Greek manuscripts of 1 En. 20:7 also enumerate the angels of the Presence as a group of seven.

from this temple calling for the reaping and harvesting of the earth (14:15, 17), and seven will emerge to deliver the seven last plagues (15:5–8). Seeing the heavenly throne room as a heavenly temple, the twenty-four elders' accoutrements are even more directly suggestive of priestly activities—their harps recall Levitical duties and their bowls of incense the priestly duties in the earthly temple.[5] The white robes and wreaths of these celestial priestly worshipers (which also make them resemble the multitude of the redeemed standing before God's throne and the Lamb) are details that contrast them with the white-robed, wreathed priests and worshipers celebrating, in counterfeit adoration, the emperor and the Greco-Roman pantheon in the cities of the seven churches.[6]

Contrasting Commissions. Perhaps the most dramatic *difference* between these two texts lies in the action that the heavenly ascent foregrounds. Here it is not the commissioning of Levi for priesthood (and for vengeance against Shechem for its violation of the proper boundaries between Israel and the nations), but the commissioning of the Lamb, who has purchased for God an expanded priestly kingdom "from every tribe and language and people and nation" (Rev 5:9), to initiate God's final judgments of the world and summon all of its inhabitants to account—a role for which he alone has proven worthy (Rev 5:1–6). This reflects the radical redefinition of the "holy" people of God emerging within early Christian culture, no longer a matter of bloodline, as well as the emergence of Christ as the focal figure of God's redemptive and judging activity.

FOR FURTHER READING

Additional Ancient Texts

As in Testament of Levi, angels also play an intercessory role in Tobit (cf. 3:1–17; 12:1–22). A principal character is Raphael, who identifies himself as "one of the seven angels who stand ready and enter before the glory of the Lord" (Tob 12:15). First Enoch 1–36 is another apocalypse that laments how humans alone do not align with the cosmic order in honoring God and relates a heavenly ascent and otherworldly journey.

---

5. John may well have set the number of these elders at twenty-four because he conceived of this order of angels as the heavenly archetype for the twenty-four orders of priests and Levites in the earthly temple (1 Chr 24:4–6). See Ben Witherington, III, *Revelation* (Cambridge: Cambridge University Press, 2003), 117.

6. Craig R. Koester, *Revelation*, AYBC 38A (New Haven: Yale University Press, 2014), 368–69.

English Translations and Critical Editions

de Jonge, Marinus. "Testaments of the Twelve Patriarchs." Pages 505–600 in *The Apocryphal Old Testament*. Edited by H. F. D. Sparks. Oxford: Clarendon, 1984.

de Jonge, Marinus et al. *The Testaments of the Twelve Patriarchs: A Critical Edition of the Greek Text*. Leiden: Brill, 1997.

Kee, Howard C. "Testaments of the Twelve Patriarchs (Second Century BCE)." Pages 775–828 in vol. 1 of *The Old Testament Pseudepigrapha*. Edited by James H. Charlesworth. New York: Doubleday, 1983.

Secondary Literature

deSilva, David A. "The *Testaments of the Twelve Patriarchs* as Witnesses to Pre-Christian Judaism: A Re-Assessment," *JSNT* 22 (2013): 21–68.

Himmelfarb, Martha. *Ascent to Heaven in Jewish and Christian Apocalypses*. New York: Oxford University Press, 1993.

Hollander, Harm W., and Marinus de Jonge. *The Testaments of the Twelve Patriarchs. A Commentary*. Leiden: Brill, 1985.

Kugler, Robert. *The Testaments of the Twelve Patriarchs*. Sheffield: Sheffield Academic, 2001.

Slingerland, H. Dixon. *The Testaments of the Twelve Patriarchs: A Critical History of Research*. Atlanta: Scholars Press, 1977.

CHAPTER 4

4 Ezra and Revelation 5:1–14: Creaturely Images of the Messiah

DANA M. HARRIS

One of the most intriguing and challenging aspects of Revelation is its use of symbolic language. Rather than *depicting* truth as a correspondence between a proposition and reality (e.g., the proposition "today is Tuesday" is true only if, in fact, the day is Tuesday), symbolic language *describes* truth in ways that are evocative and suggestive. Symbolic language (especially in Revelation) is frequently allusive, recalling images and symbols from both the Old Testament and Second Temple literature.

Revelation 5 continues the throne room vision begun in Revelation 4, which draws heavily on images from the Roman Empire and critiques Caesar's throne. In Revelation 4, the One on the throne—presented in unbelievable splendor—is worshiped by the twenty-four elders and the four living creatures. In Revelation 5, John sees a scroll, written on both sides, in the right hand of the One on the throne. This scroll likely symbolizes the final events (cf. 4:1) that result in Satan's ultimate judgment, the eradication of evil, and the new creation. But no one in the totality of creation is found worthy to open this scroll and thereby culminate God's plans for history. John weeps, lamenting the horrific possibility that God's redemption (later celebrated in 5:9–10) might not be effected. In response, one of the elders commands John to behold "the Lion of the tribe of Judah, the Root of David" (5:5)—the only one worthy to open the scroll.

The "Lion of Judah" alludes to Gen 49:8–9 and Jacob's final blessing of his sons: "Judah . . . your hand will be on the neck of your enemies; your father's sons will bow down to you. You are a lion's cub, Judah; you return from the prey." This image is of a powerful warrior who defeats his enemies. The lion also portrays the strength and power associated with royalty (e.g., 1 Kgs 10:19–20). God is frequently presented with lion imagery in the Old Testament (e.g., Job 10:16; Isa 31:4; Jer 50:44; Hos 5:14; Amos 3:8), but such imagery was not understood in messianic terms in the OT or in Jewish writings prior to the first century AD. The second designation, "Root of David," alludes to Isaiah 11:10 (cf. 11:1): "In that day the Root of Jesse will stand as a banner for the peoples." The banner associates the root with militaristic power. This image was understood messianically in both the OT and in later Jewish writings, such as 4 Ezra. Although 4 Ezra was likely composed about the same time as Revelation (or even later), it appears to reflect some traditions and messianic expectations also reflected in Revelation.

4 Ezra

"THE LION . . . WHO WILL ARISE
FROM THE POSTERITY OF DAVID"

Destruction and Theodicy. Fourth Ezra is extant only in Latin translations, from which the designation "4 Ezra" derives (*Esdrae liber IV*).[1] By the time of the King James translation, 4 Ezra was included in the Apocrypha as part of 2 Esdras. Although 4 Ezra purports to contain visions given to a seer named Salathiel (or Ezra) 30 years after *Babylon's* destruction of Jerusalem (587/6 BC), the text clearly indicates that *Rome's* destruction of Jerusalem (AD 70) is in view, with AD 100 as the likely composition date.[2]

Fourth Ezra presents seven visions that offer a general theodicy and a more specific attempt to explain why God has (apparently) forsaken his covenant and people to the pagans. The first three visions concern the fate of the righteous and wicked in the age to come. The fourth vision presents a woman, ostensibly mourning the loss of her only son, suddenly transformed into the glorious, heavenly Zion. The fifth vision describes an eagle rising from the sea, purportedly depicting future events. The sixth vision presents a human figure who rises from the sea and leads a heavenly army that vanquishes his enemies. The seventh vision presents Ezra's commissioning

---

1. It is unclear if the original was written in Greek, Aramaic, or Hebrew.

2. Richard Bauckham comments that people whose worldview depended upon the "biblical narratives" would naturally seek to understand current events "by putting themselves imaginatively within the story of the closest analogy in Israel's history: the fall of Jerusalem to the armies of Nebuchadnezzar." Richard Bauckham, "Apocalypses," in *Justification and Variegated Nomism: Volume 1—The Complexities of Second Temple Judaism*, ed. D. A. Carson et al. (Grand Rapids: Baker, 2001), 135–87, at 160.

to reproduce the (lost) twenty-four canonical books and to write seventy additional books to remain hidden.

The Lion Who Challenges Rome. The sixth vision, the "eagle vision," suggests some parallels with Revelation 5. The vision itself (4 Ezra 11) describes a great eagle (a frequent symbol for the Roman Empire), with twelve wings and three heads (symbolizing Roman rulers), arising from the sea. This eagle subjugates the entire world without opposition. As the vision unfolds, various wings gain power but eventually disappear. Finally, the smaller two of the three heads conspire to form a joint rule, but are temporarily defeated by the largest head. When this third head disappears, the smaller heads regain power, but the right head eventually devours the left one. Toward the vision's end, a voice like a man is heard, but Ezra sees a creature like a lion who rebukes the eagle for its oppression, deceit, and terrorizing. The lion links the eagle to the four beasts that have gone before (4 Ezra 12:11), an allusion to Daniel (e.g., Dan 7:7). After the lion speaks, the eagle's remaining wings disappear, and the body of the eagle is burned up. In 4 Ezra 12, the vision is explained to Ezra. Of particular relevance is 12:31–36:

> [31] And as for the lion that you saw rousing up out of the forest and roaring and speaking to the eagle and reproving him for his unrighteousness, and as for all his words that you have heard, [32] this is the Messiah whom the Most High has kept until the end of days, who will arise from the posterity of David, and will come and speak to them; he will denounce them for their ungodliness and for their wickedness, and will cast up before them their contemptuous dealings. [33] For first he will set them living before his judgment seat, and when he has reproved them, then he will destroy them. [34] But he will deliver in mercy the remnant of my people, those who have been saved throughout my borders, and he will make them joyful until the end comes, the day of judgment, of which I spoke to you at the beginning. [35] This is the dream that you saw, and this is its interpretation. [36] And you alone were worthy to learn this secret of the Most High.[3]

Most significant for Revelation 5 is the surprising fact that the lion is the messiah—an allusion to the "Lion of Judah" in Genesis 49:8–9. The image of the messiah arising from the line of David alludes to Isaiah 11:1, 10.

---

3. Translation from Bruce M. Metzger, "The Fourth Book of Ezra: A New Translation and Introduction," in *Old Testament Pseudepigrapha*, ed. J. H. Charlesworth, vol. 1 (Garden City, NY: Doubleday, 1985), 517–59, at 550.

Several aspects of this messiah are noteworthy, especially its depiction as a lion. Surprisingly, given the lion imagery, this messiah achieves justice without the clear use of political or military force. Instead his rebuke and judgment alone appear to defeat the eagle,[4] unlike other Jewish writings (e.g., 1QSb 5:29), where the lion depicts a messianic military warrior who destroys Israel's enemies and conquers the nations.[5] Finally, the messiah (following the eagle's defeat) ushers in a joyful time until "the end" (4 Ezra 12:34). Given that the lion is not an OT messianic image, it is plausible that John knew of a later Jewish depiction of the messiah as a lion, possibly as presented in 4 Ezra, and may have drawn upon it in Revelation 5.

Revelation 5:1–14

"SEE, THE LION . . . HAS TRIUMPHED"

The Lion Who Is the Lamb. Revelation 5 opens with the One sitting on the throne holding a scroll that none (apparently) can open. As John weeps over this, one of the twenty-four elders commands him: "See, the Lion of the tribe of Judah, the Root of David, has triumphed" (Rev 5:5), an allusion to both Genesis 49:8–9 and Isaiah 11:1, 10. Given that lion imagery used to portray the messiah was uncommon in Jewish writings, its use in Revelation 5 is striking. Assuming that John drew upon a common tradition that also lay behind 4 Ezra, the command to *look* for a *lion* sets up the expectation of a victorious warrior come to defeat God's enemies.[6] The contrast between what John expected to see (a victorious lion) and what he actually saw could not be more shocking: "Then I saw a Lamb, looking as if it had been slain" (Rev 5:6). This contrast would be even more powerful if an allusion to the lion who conquered the eagle (the Roman Empire) in 4 Ezra were clearly intended.

The Lamb of the New Exodus. The lamb imagery draws on the Old Testament, likely the sacrificed Passover lamb, whose blood was spread on the doorposts of Israelite houses in Egypt. By virtue of this blood, Israelites were spared during the plague of the firstborn (Exod 11:1–12:30). The slaughtered lamb was associated with divine deliverance. This image may also allude to

---

4. The avoidance of a militaristic messiah is likely due to the failed Jewish revolt (AD 66–73) that caused the destruction of Jerusalem. Bauckham, "Apocalypses," 165–66.

5. Richard Bauckham, *The Climax of Prophecy: Studies on the Book of Revelation* (Edinburgh: T&T Clark, 1993), 181.

6. Bauckham, *Climax of Prophecy*, 182.

the Suffering Servant in Isaiah 53:7, who is likened to a slaughtered lamb. Both images were later understood as pointing to Jesus in the Christian tradition (e.g., John 1:29, 36; Acts 8:32; 1 Cor 5:7; 1 Pet 1:19). This lamb imagery is significantly developed in Revelation, where "Lamb" is the title used most frequently for Jesus (28 times), and the Lamb's blood is repeatedly associated with redemption (5:9; 7:14; 12:11; 22:14).

This juxtaposition between the Lion and the Lamb could not be more powerful. At one level, this reverses nature, where lambs are vulnerable and lions are powerful (cf. Isa 11:6–7; 65:25). At a more significant level, however, this reverses popular Jewish expectations of the messiah as a conquering warrior who would defeat the Roman Empire. Such hopes aligned with the messiah depicted as a lion, not a lamb! Yet just as the Passover Lamb was the means by which God defeated Pharaoh and delivered his people in the exodus, so too the Lamb's blood is the means by which God defeats Satan and delivers his people from sin and death, thereby effecting a new exodus. In this way, imagery associated with the messiah as a conquering Lion is transformed into the unexpected imagery of the slaughtered Lamb who now reigns because of his submission, death, and resurrection. The Lamb, not the Lion, is the victorious, divine warrior in Revelation (e.g., 17:14; cf. 6:16). The marriage feast of the Lamb in Revelation 19:1–10 juxtaposes with the triumphant arrival of the (warrior) rider on the horse in Revelation 19:11–21, whose victory has already been won before the "battle" begins. Notice that despite the militaristic imagery, the rider who is called "Faithful and True" conquers by his *word* (19:15), *not* by his physical prowess. This suggests another parallel with 4 Ezra (12:32; cf. 11:39–46), namely that the Messiah conquers evil with his authoritative word, not military might.

The Power of the Lamb. Revelation 5:6 further describes the slaughtered Lamb as having seven horns and seven eyes. The horn was a common symbol of power, frequently depicting kings or kingdoms (e.g., Dan 7:7–8, 11–12). The Lamb is the all-powerful King. The seven eyes allude to Zechariah 4:10 and are further specified as the seven spirits of God sent out into the world. As a result, the Lamb is all-seeing, or omniscient. That the seven spirits were previously presented in conjunction with the One on the throne (Rev 4:5) and are now associated with the Lamb underscores the Lamb's divinity and indicates the presence of the Trinity in the throne room.

Drawing on messianic imagery from the OT and later Jewish traditions reflected in 4 Ezra, John radically redefines popular messianic hopes and expectations. The power and strength (political, military, or other) of a lion is not what is needed to defeat evil kings or kingdoms. Instead, it is the surprising vulnerability and weakness of a Lamb, who was slaughtered and resurrected, that vanquishes evil and ushers in the new creation. Because the Lion of Judah, who is the Lamb, has conquered, he is *able* to open the scroll; because the Lamb was slain and resurrected, he is *worthy* to open the scroll.[7] Whereas Ezra the seer was worthy to receive secrets from the Most High (4 Ezra 12:36), the Lamb is worthy to receive worship from all creation—the same worship given to the One on the throne—because he was willing to offer up his very life to accomplish God's redemptive purposes. Amen!

FOR FURTHER READING

Additional Ancient Texts

Like Revelation 5, both 4Q Patriarchal Blessing and 4Q Florilegium 1:11–12 draw upon Genesis 49:8–9 and Isaiah 11:1, 10. A close parallel to 4 Ezra 12:31–26 (cf. 4 Ezra 13:37–38) occurs in 2 Baruch 39:8–40:3, with a somewhat similar idea of the Messiah's victory found in Sibylline Oracle 3:652–656. Psalms of Solomon 17:21–25 depicts the Messiah destroying the ungodly with his word. In contrast, 1QSb 5:29 presents the Messiah as a military warrior. Additionally, 1 Enoch 89:45–46 and 90:6–19 present a militaristic (messianic) lamb figure who conquers the wicked.

English Translations and Critical Editions

NETS (2 Esdras)

NRSV (2 Esdras)

Longenecker, Bruce W. *2 Esdras*. GAP. Sheffield: Sheffield Academic, 1995.

Metzger, Bruce M. "The Fourth Book of Ezra: A New Translation and Introduction." Pages 517–59 in vol. 1 of *The Old Testament Pseudepigrapha*. Edited by James H. Charlesworth. Garden City, NY: Doubleday, 1983.

Stone, Michael E. *Fourth Ezra*. Hermeneia. Minneapolis: Fortress, 1990.

Wong, Andy, with Ken M. Penner and David M. Miller, eds. "4 Ezra." Edition 1.0. In *The Online Critical Pseudepigrapha*. Edited by Ken M. Penner and Ian W. Scott. Atlanta: Society of Biblical Literature, 2010. www.purl.org/net/ocp/4Ezra.

---

7. John D'Souza, *The Lamb of God in the Johannine Writings* (Allahabad, India: St. Paul, 1968), 63.

Secondary Literature

Bauckham, Richard. "Apocalypses." Pages 135–87 in *The Complexities of Second Temple Judaism*. Edited by D. A. Carson, Peter T. O'Brien, and Mark A. Seifrid. Vol. 1 of *Justification and Variegated Nomism*. Baker: Grand Rapids, 2001.

——. *The Climax of Prophecy: Studies on the Book of Revelation*. Edinburgh/ New York: T&T Clark, 1993.

D'Souza, John. *The Lamb of God in the Johannine Writings*. Allahabad, India: St. Paul, 1968.

Johns, Loren L. *The Lamb Christology of the Apocalypse of John: An Investigation into Its Origins and Rhetorical Force*. WUNT 2/167. Mohr Siebeck: Tübingen, 2003.

CHAPTER 5

2 Maccabees and Revelation 6:1–17: Martyrdom and Resurrection

IAN PAUL

The book of Revelation opens with apocalyptic and prophetic elements set within an epistolary framework, communicating unambiguously that John is writing to particular people in a particular time and place. But the cosmic vision he has of Jesus in the second half of chapter 1, which identifies him not only with God but also as both the angelic messenger of God and priestly mediator between God and humanity, shows that John's message has transcendent significance. After recording the messages that he hears for the assemblies of Jesus-followers in seven of the cities in Asia (western Turkey), the vision report resumes as he enters the heavenly throne room in chapters 4 and 5 and he both sees and hears the worship of God and Jesus (now depicted as the slain but raised Lamb) without rival in all of creation. This sets the scene for the unsealing of the scroll, best understood as the will of God for the world, and the sequence of seven seals, with images of death, destruction, and judgment, represent for many readers the beginning of the truly apocalyptic section of the book—and is often the place where they stop reading.

In chapter 6 we encounter the explicit use of numerical structuring. John has used "seven" spatially, selecting some cities in Asia to stand for the whole (seven being the number of completeness). Now he uses it temporally, with the breaking of the successive seals culminating, after an interlude in chapter 7, with the rabbinic notion of eschatological silence before God in 8:1.[1]

---

1. The seven messages are structured into two halves of 3 + 4, marked by the switch of the final exhortations "the one having ears/the one conquering"; the seven seals are in two halves of 4 + 3.

We also encounter the cascade of vivid, emotive, and archetypal imagery; the four horsemen are perhaps the most widely known image from the whole book, occurring frequently in film, political cartoon, and cultural comment.[2] But, like all the images in Revelation, the *vehicles* of the metaphors (lamb, horsemen, beasts) are deployed without any explicit mention of the *subjects* of the metaphors (Jesus, natural disasters, empires), which makes them both vivid *and* ambiguous, able to be interpreted in a wide range of later contexts.

The introduction of the martyrs under the altar into the narrative disrupts the structure of the opening of the seals, raising questions about why they are introduced here and how martyrdom was viewed in the ancient world. To help fill out the picture of martyrdom, comparison can be made with a famous martyrdom story in 2 Maccabees 7.

2 Maccabees

"THE KING OF THE UNIVERSE WILL RAISE US UP TO EVERLASTING LIFE MADE NEW"

The four books with the title "Maccabees" all relate to the crisis precipitated by the Seleucid ruler **Antiochus IV Epiphanes** and his desecration of the temple by sacrificing pigs and erecting pagan statues in 167 BC. This provoked the revolt led by the Hasmonean priest-ruler Judas Maccabeus, and his reconsecration of the temple in 164 BC is still celebrated in the Jewish festival of Hanukkah. "Maccabeus" is commonly understood to mean "hammer," but it is also the acronym of the battle-cry—"Who is like you among the gods Yahweh?" (Exod 15:11).[3]

First and Second Maccabees are in the Apocrypha of the Roman Catholic and Eastern Orthodox canon, while 3 and 4 Maccabees are part of the Old Testament pseudepigrapha. First Maccabees appears to be a translation into Greek from a Hebrew or Aramaic original, while 2 Maccabees is written in *koine* (common) Greek and offers more detail. The text articulates some key theological ideas of Second Temple Judaism that are essential background to reading the New Testament. Third Maccabees recounts legendary material from the preceding period, while 4 Maccabees is a treatise on the virtue of pious reason over passion reflecting on the martyrdom of the seven sons.

---

2. The publicity posters for Francis Ford Coppola's Vietnam war film *Apocalypse Now* (1979), for example, feature a sequence of four US Army helicopters as an echo of the four horsemen.

3. Compare the meaning of Michael ("Who is like God?") in Rev 12:7 and the exclamation "Who is like the beast?" in Rev 13:4.

The account of the martyrdoms is detailed and gruesome, and came to be admired and emulated in medieval Christian devotions to martyred saints; it gives rise to the English term "macabre."[4] The story begins:

> They were being tortured by the king with whips and thongs to force them to eat pork, contrary to the law. But one of them, speaking for all, said: "What do you expect to learn by interrogating us? Rather than break our ancestral laws we are prepared to die." In fury, the king ordered great pans and cauldrons to be heated. This was attended to without delay; meanwhile he gave orders that the spokesman's tongue should be cut out and that he should be scalped and mutilated before the eyes of his mother and six brothers. A wreck of a man, but still breathing, he was taken at the king's direction to the fire and roasted in one of the pans. (2 Macc 7:1b–5a)[5]

There are five things to note about the way the martyrdoms are described.

Faithfulness to God's Laws. First, the proximate reason for the suffering of the brothers is their adherence to their "ancestral laws" (2 Macc 7:2) which are the laws of the "King of the universe" (7:9). Faithfulness to God's laws, and in particular the food laws, is worth suffering and dying for: "When the question was put to [the third brother], he at once showed his tongue and courageously held out his hands. 'The God of heaven gave these to me, but his laws mean far more to me than they do'" (7:10–11). The importance of food laws as *the* point of testing loyalty lies behind controversies we find in the New Testament (Mark 7:17–23; Acts 10:9–16; Rom 14:17).

Sin, Judgment, and Atonement. Second, the explanation for their suffering goes beyond a simple question of loyal resistance to forces that might make them compromise. The oppression of Antiochus Epiphanes has been brought about (by God?) as a just punishment against the Jewish people for their sins. In the words of the seventh brother: "It is for our own sins that we are suffering, and, though to correct and discipline us our living Lord is angry for a brief time, yet he will be reconciled with his servants" (2 Macc 7:32–33). This theological interpretation of what is happening is in line with the theological shape of the Deuteronomistic history, beginning with the blessings and curses for obedience and disobedience in Deuteronomy 28,

---

4. From the Latin term *Machabaeorum chorea*, meaning Dance of the Maccabees.
5. Translations of 2 Maccabees are from the *Revised English Bible* (Oxford: Oxford University Press, 1989).

and ending with the destruction of Jerusalem and the people carried off to exile in 2 Kings 25.

Third, the brothers' death has further significance—not just coming as a result of the sin of the people, but because their faithfulness and suffering even atones for these sins and in some sense satisfies and brings to an end God's anger: "May the Almighty's anger, which has justly fallen on all our race, end with me and my brothers!" (2 Macc 7:38). The importance of the death of these seven, and the faithfulness of their mother (whose cause of death in 7:41 is unexplained) is that, in some sense, they have died *for* the people, an idea echoed in the words of Caiaphas about Jesus: "Better . . . that one man die for the people" (John 11:50; 18:14).

Hope and Vindication. Fourth, all of this is framed in a quite explicit articulation of the hope of bodily resurrection for those who have kept faith. With his final breath, the second brother declares: "The King of the Universe will raise us up to everlasting life made new" (2 Macc 7:9). The language here of "everlasting" or "eternal life" is the same as what we find in the Fourth Gospel (John 3:15, 16, 36; 4:14, 36, and so on) but with an indication of life "made new," which corresponds to the distinction between "this age" and the "age to come" (Matt 12:32; Mark 10:40; Luke 20:34–35). In the resurrection, the brothers' bodies, now dismembered and disfigured, will be healed and restored (2 Macc 7:11), and the mother will receive her sons back (7:29). However, in contrast to the universal resurrection described in Daniel 12:2 in which some rise to eternal life and others to judgment, the expectation is that Antiochus, as one of the wicked, will die and not be raised (2 Macc 7:14).

Fifth, the hope of the brothers is that God will avenge them by raising up a leader who will punish Antiochus through violent opposition and warfare, and the following chapters narrate just that outcome. Martyrdom here is paired with a willingness to resist through combat; in chapter 8 the preparation for the conflict includes praying that God will "give ear to the blood that cried to him for vengeance" (2 Macc 8:3).

Revelation 6:1–17

"THOSE WHO HAD BEEN SLAIN BECAUSE OF THE WORD OF GOD AND THE TESTIMONY THEY HAD MAINTAINED"

Judgment and Atonement. The catastrophes unleashed with the breaking of the first four seals have an ambiguous status in relation to the sovereignty of

God. On the one hand, they are released at the instigation of Jesus-as-lamb, but the four horsemen mediate the catastrophes, and they in turn are called forth by one of the four living creatures around the throne. In contrast to the direct sovereignty of God expressed in 2 Maccabees, the action of God in bringing disaster seems here to be at least qualified or in some sense mediated. God's first unmediated action in Revelation is to "wipe away every tear from their eyes" (Rev 7:17; 21:4). The catalog of conquest, violent warfare, famine and food shortages, and early death and disease represented by the horsemen are experiences with which John's readers would have been very familiar—as have many later generations.[6]

Opening the fifth seal does not lead to further action, but allows John a vision of the "souls who had been slain." The term "soul" might suggest a nonbodily existence, so it is unclear in what sense John can "see" them. But the term "slain" links them with the image of the lamb "looking as if it had been slain" (Rev 5:6); where the martyrs of 2 Maccabees receive suffering at the hand of God (justly) punishing his people, here the martyrs share the suffering that their Lord himself has experienced. Although John sees these souls "under the altar," there is no suggestion that their suffering has atoning value, since the heavenly temple has only one altar, for the offering of incense (see Rev 8:3), whereas the earthly temple which it parallels has two, one for incense and one for sacrifice. It is the slaying of the lamb which alone has atoning power, his blood "purchasing" his people for God (5:9); it is as though the throne of God itself has become the altar of atoning sacrifice.

Faithful Witnesses. The brothers were killed for their devotion to the law, but the martyrs here suffer because of the "word of God and the testimony they had." The "word of God" appears to refer to the message about Jesus, not least because at one point it is given as his title (19:13), and is twice paired with the "testimony of Jesus" (1:2, 9) which in turn is linked with the prophetic word of the Spirit (19:10).[7] "Testimony" and "witness" both translate the same word in Greek, from which our word "martyr" derives, and it is a key theological idea in the book. Jesus is described as the "faithful and true witness" (3:14) and his name occurs 14 times in the text, the product of 2 (the biblical number of witness; see Deut 17:6; 19:5) and 7 (the number of completeness). His followers are also called to be faithful witnesses like

---

6. The Black Death (fourteenth century) killed a third of Europe; the Spanish flu of 1918–19 infected a third of the world's population. Freedom from such experiences is a relatively rare phenomenon in human history.

7. The speech of Jesus and the speech of the Spirit are closely identified throughout Revelation, not least in the seven messages in chapters 2 and 3, where the proclamation of Jesus is each time offered as "what the Spirit is saying to the assemblies."

him: "They triumphed over [Satan] by the blood of the Lamb and by the word of their testimony; they did not love their lives so much as to shrink from death" (12:11). Indeed, the "word of God and the testimony of Jesus" is identified by John as the reason for the "tribulation" that he himself was suffering along with his brothers and sisters to whom he writes (1:9). In this sense, the martyrs under the altar are archetypal of what it means to be a follower of the lamb.

The idea that these martyrs are suffering because of the sins of the people of God is entirely absent; the cause is the opposition of "the inhabitants of the earth," a term used ten times to designate those who follow the beast and receive his mark (13:8), contrasted with the heaven-dwelling followers of the Lamb. God's final judgment will be against all who have "shed the blood of [his] holy people" (16:6; cf. 17:6; 18:24). But God's just judgment is postponed "a little time," during which the devil vents his fury (12:12) and God's people must patiently endure (1:9). Revelation here follows the quietist ethic in the face of oppression articulated in Daniel.

The "white robes" signify purity in the presence of God (4:4) granted by means of the atoning death of Jesus as the slain lamb (7:14). Though bodily resurrection is not mentioned in this episode, it looms large on the eschatological horizon of the narrative as a whole (20:12–13).

Patient Endurance. The depiction of martyrs in Revelation clearly shares a number of assumptions with the account in 2 Maccabees—the virtue of suffering at the hands of an evil oppressor, the justice of the sovereign God, and the certainty of judgment. But at key points Revelation offers a radically different theological understanding. God's judgment will come after eschatological delay, and will be effected by God alone and not by military or political action. Atonement is achieved by the suffering of Jesus alone, yet the suffering of his people follows his example of patient endurance. Their response to evil oppression is therefore not to take up arms in resistance, but to continue in their faithful testimony as they look to The End when God will make all things new (Rev 21:5).

FOR FURTHER READING

Additional Ancient Texts

The story of the seven martyred brothers is expanded in 4 Maccabees 8–12 and appears to have been retold in a different form in the Mishnah Gittin 57b (and the later Seder Eliahu Rabbah 30). The earliest rabbinical account of martyrdom is found in the Sifra Emor 9.5, part of the Halakhic midrash to Leviticus, in which Pappus and Julian are martyred during the reign of Trajan (AD 98–117). Another important example of Jewish martyrdom in the period is the group of rabbis known as "The Ten Martyrs," referred to in the haggadic literature as '*Asarah Haruge Malkut*. Though they are collected together in the liturgies of *Tisha B'Av* (the commemoration of the destruction of the temple) and *Yom Kippur*, their deaths occurred at different times and are mentioned in the Talmud (Avodah Zarah 17b, 18a; Berakhot 61b; Sanhedrin 14a) and the Mishnah Rabbah (Lam. Rab. ii. 2; Prov. Rab. i. 13, Sotah 13.4) and the minor tractates Semahot 8.8 and Avot of Rabbi Nathan 38A and 41B. The Martyrdom of Polycarp is the earliest account of Christian martyrdom outside the New Testament.

English Translations and Critical Editions

NETS

NRSV

Hanhart, R. *Maccabaeorum Liber II*. Septuaginta 9.2. Göttingen: Vandenhoeck & Ruprecht, 1976.

Secondary Literature

Boyarin, Daniel. "Martyrdom and the Making of Christianity and Judaism." *JECS* 6.4 (1998): 577–627.

Doran, Robert. *2 Maccabees: A Critical Commentary*. Hermeneia. Minneapolis: Fortress, 2012.

Lander, Shira. "Martyrdom in Jewish Traditions." Paper for Bishops Committee on Ecumenical and Interreligious Affairs and the National Council of Synagogues (December 11, 2003). www.bc.edu/content/ dam/files/research_sites/cjl/texts/cjrelations/resources/articles/ Lander_martyrdom/index.html#_ftnref15.

Middleton, Paul. *The Violence of the Lamb: Martyrs as Agents of Divine Judgement in the Book of Revelation*. LNTS 586. New York: T&T Clark, 2018.

Schwartz, Daniel R. *2 Maccabees*. CEJL. Berlin: de Gruyter, 2008.

CHAPTER 6

Psalms of Solomon and Revelation 7:1–17: The Sealing of the Servants of God

RONALD HERMS

R evelation is popularly known for its repeating cycles of judgment and (apparent) destruction. Some readers are convinced there is little else to the book. However, Revelation 7 is noteworthy among John's visions for providing readers (or hearers) with a rhetorical (even psychological!) "pause" or "interlude" from the barrage of plagues and disasters. Readers are offered assurance amid—even respite from—the building tension of judgment cycles; the intended effect is to engender confidence in God's mindfulness and protection of those who are faithful to the Lamb despite hostile circumstances. A key feature of this strategically positioned interlude is the promise that God's seal of authentication and protection rests on those who participate in his kingdom work (7:2–3; cf. 1:6; 5:10).

Ironically, many readers of Revelation associate the concept of a "mark" or "seal" on a person's forehead with the threatening scenario in Revelation 13—the dreaded specter of the "mark of the beast."[1] A common misconception is that this is the dominant reference to such an idea in Revelation and, as such, represents a potential (even deceptive) snare that is entirely ominous and to be avoided at all costs by those who are faithful to Jesus. Unfortunately, such a reading of Revelation misses the wider conceptual point that this is actually a familiar image in the Apocalypse introduced well before the (in)famous chapter 13. The image of sealing the servants of

---

1. See any number of sources on popular interpretations of Revelation 13:16–18 but, especially, Richard G. Kyle, *Apocalyptic Fever: End-Time Prophecies in Modern America* (Eugene, OR: Cascade, 2012), 82–86, 123–28.

God (on the forehead) will be the focus of this short essay; in particular, a comparative analysis will be made between Revelation 7:2–4 and Psalms of Solomon 15:6–9. In both texts the people of God are positively described as being "sealed" or "marked" with divine protection and their security is set in contrast with those "marked" for destruction because they antagonize and actively oppose God's purposes.

Psalms of Solomon

"GOD'S MARK IS ON THE RIGHTEOUS FOR THEIR SALVATION"

In the history and memory of the Jewish people, the invasion of Jerusalem in 63 BC under the Roman general Pompey effectively introduced foreign political control to the region the Romans eventually called Judaea.[2] The Psalms of Solomon, (likely) written in response to these events, represents the collected efforts of at least one Jewish community to come to terms with this loss of national independence and threat to socioreligious identity. From this perspective, the annexation and scandalizing of Jerusalem was God's just response to failing temple leadership (2:3–5), for "because of our sins, sinners rose up against us" (17:5; cf. 2:11–13; 8:8–13). Further, there was the disorienting state of affairs that Jewish rulers were believed to have colluded with invading foreigners (mixed allegiances) who then made peace with, but ultimately betrayed and annihilated, them (8:16–20). At the same time, these experiences of judgment and upheaval were tangible reminders that the foreign enemy's arrogance and corrupting influence would also earn God's righteous judgment (17:12–14). These psalms contain, in turn, expressions of grief (8:1–5), (righteous) anger (4:1–8), acceptance of the Lord's discipline (3:3–8), exhortations to faithful purity (6:1–6), and hope for the arrival of God's messianic agent—the heir to David's throne who would prove capable of enacting God's righteous rule and toppling the structures of wickedness (17:21–43).

---

2. The identification of Pompey and Roman forces with "a warrior who arrives from the west" (Pss. Sol 17:12–14) is widely accepted, with Psalms of Solomon 2:26–27 serving as an acknowledgement of his death in Egypt in 48 BC: "And did I not wait long until the Lord showed me his [dragon's] insolence, having been pierced upon the mountains of Egypt, held in greater contempt than the least upon the earth or sea, his body being carried by waves of great insolence. There was no one to bury him, for he despised his shame." All translations are from Brad Embry, "The Psalms of Solomon," in *Early Jewish Literature: An Anthology*, vol. 2, eds. B. Embry, R. Herms, and A. T. Wright (Grand Rapids: Eerdmans, 2018), 563–84.

Communicating Certainty. It is not surprising then that, in the face of such imposed Greco-Roman influence aided by the (apparent) collusion of Jewish leaders, it became a critical task of the Psalms of Solomon to communicate the certainty of God's refining judgment—purification and restoration of his people, the temple, and the land. But how could such a compromised people embrace that certainty? What guarantee of God's faithful judgment could this author offer the righteous ones? It is here that Psalms of Solomon 15:6–9 employs the motif of a divine "mark" on the people of God (the same image that the author of Revelation later also takes up as both a "seal" and a "mark"):

> [15:4] The one who does these things will never be disturbed by evil; the flame of fire and anger against the unrighteous shall not touch him [5] when it goes out from the Lord's presence against sinners to destroy the sinners' every assurance. [6] *For God's mark is on the righteous for (their) salvation.* [7] Famine and sword and death shall be far from the righteous; for they will retreat from the devout like those pursued by famine. [8] But they shall pursue sinners who overtake them, for those who act lawlessly shall not escape the Lord's judgment. [9] They shall be overtaken as by those experienced in war, *for on their forehead (is) the mark of destruction.*

In a sudden pivot away from the reflections of chaos, critique, and disorientation leading up to Psalms of Solomon 15, the opening lines of this psalm contain several elements of a traditional "thanksgiving song": the reference to hardship ("I was persecuted"), the recollection of a prior act of salvation ("I was saved"), and the affirmation that God is mindful of the oppressed ("the hope and refuge of the poor"). Further, the psalm then celebrates the power of confession and singing ("the fruit of lips") as the posture for those who are reassured that God's vindicating protection is surely on the way—evidence that they do, indeed, carry "God's mark" of protection. The contrast with "sinners" could not be more striking in that they cannot escape damning judgment, "for on their forehead (is) the mark of destruction." The psalm's frequent use of symbolic, colorfully descriptive language suggests that, in both instances, the "mark" is likely not physically visible but is, rather, known (obvious) in view of "the day of the Lord's judgment" (15:12). Thus, Psalms of Solomon 15 represents an eschatological appropriation of those traditions (see below) which may well have assumed a more tangible understanding of being marked.

Biblical Antecedents. As background to the use of the "mark" image in Psalms of Solomon 15:6–9, it is helpful to note that biblical traditions of sealing or marking influenced how later authors employed the image in early Jewish texts. According to Genesis 4:15, in response to Cain's fear of retaliatory vengeance for the murder of his brother Abel, "the Lord put a mark on Cain so that no one who found him would kill him." Here the "mark" is clearly a positive sign of protection—assurance that, in the face of uncertainty, the Lord would look after Cain in his vulnerable state. This must surely be seen as an act of mercy in light of Cain's violence. Further development of this image in biblical traditions is evident in Ezekiel 9:4–6 where the Lord gives instructions to "put a mark on the foreheads" of those who are identified as a remnant (minority) of the righteous. This mark is said to provide protection from impending trial and judgment which the prophet expects to come upon the people of Judah for their abominations. Conversely, the prophet Habakkuk, in the face of an ominous Chaldean threat, can also claim, "O Lord, you have marked them [the arrogant, violent Chaldeans] for judgment" (Hab 1:12, NRSV).

Taken together, these biblical texts witness to a familiar motif wherein God's awareness and protective action on behalf of his faithful people is presented as a seal or mark guaranteeing security amid hardship and hostility. At the same time, there appear to be equally effective positive and negative applications of this image; in other words, the image alone does not carry a value judgment of the recipient of a "mark" or "seal"—that determination is made by the Lord (or the respective author, as the case may be).

Revelation 7:1–17

"WE PUT A SEAL ON THE FOREHEADS OF THE SERVANTS OF OUR GOD"

Adapting this familiar theme from Israel's scriptural traditions, Revelation 7 serves as the symbol-laden response to the cry of despair and question raised by the opening of the sixth seal on the seven-sealed scroll in 6:17 ("For the great day of their wrath has come, and who can withstand it [lit., who is able to stand]?"). John answers with two parallel, complementary visions of the people of God: first, the scene of the 144,000 suggests they are fully accounted and known (7:1–8); second, the vision of the innumerable multitude communicates overwhelming responsiveness to the Lamb's work of restoring earth's peoples (7:9–17; cf. 5:9–10). Two scenes, one message: these are the people who "can stand" as a result of God's faithfulness to them. That message is what the description of the sealing of God's faithful servants anticipates.

> [7:1] After this I saw four angels standing at the four corners of the earth, holding back the four winds of the earth to prevent any wind from blowing on the land or on the sea or on any tree. [2] Then I saw another angel coming up from the east, *having the seal of the living God.* He called out in a loud voice to the four angels who had been given power to harm the land and the sea: [3] "Do not harm the land or the sea or the trees *until we put a seal on the foreheads of the servants of our God."*

Biblical Antecedents. John's strategy for communicating assurance and comfort to his fellow followers of the Lamb includes constructing a collection of images associated with divine protection from several OT traditions and early Jewish sources. In the opening lines of Revelation 7 alone the following three images of assurance are deployed: angelic restraint of the four winds of the earth (7:1); seals for judgment and protection of God's people (7:2–3); and organization of the people of God according to ancient Israel's tribal traditions (7:4–8). Individually, each image draws upon biblical and traditional sources to contribute a distinctive element to John's overall message (see Figure 6.1).

Figure 6.1: Images Drawing on OT and Early Jewish Traditions

Revelation 7:1–4	OT Traditions	Early Jewish Traditions
"the four winds of the earth"	Ezek 37:9; Dan 7:2; Zech 6:5–6	1 En. 18:1–4; 76:1–14; 4 Ezra 13:5
"the seal of God"	Gen 4:15; Exod 28; Ezek 9:2–6	Pss Sol 15:6–9; 4 Ezra 6:5; 8:53; CD 19.12
"the 144,000"	Num 1; 10	1QM 3.13–14; 5.1–3

In the case of the seal image, this is only the first of multiple references to this tradition through the use of two main terms: (1) "seal/sealed" (Gk. *sphragis/sphragizō*), used exclusively as a positive term for the faithful (7:2, 3, 4, 5, 8; 9:4)[3]; and, (2) "mark" (Gk. *charagma*), used exclusively as a negative term for those who resist God (13:16, 17; 14:11, 14; 16:2; 19:20; 20:4). Readers

---

3. The most common association of this image in the ancient world was with the signet ring of a ruler as a sign of authority and authentication (often applied with a wax seal); see David E. Aune, *Revelation 6–16*, WBC 52B (Nashville: Thomas Nelson, 1998), 453. For good reasons

would be expected to identify with this "sealed" group only to discover later that another "marked" group also exists.

Assurance of Protection. In Revelation 7 the promise to seal God's servants comes in response to the successive descriptions of destruction at the opening of the scroll (6:1–17). Assurance that faithful witness will be vindicated is critical. But, while Psalms of Solomon 15:6–9 poignantly applied *both* positive and negative expressions of "marking," John follows the tradition from Ezekiel 9 more closely in that he only refers to sealing the faithful "servants of God."[4] Ultimately, the dual application of this image emerges later in John's rhetorical agenda in Revelation; so chapter 7 plays a critical role in preparing readers for the later introduction of the "mark of the beast" in Revelation 13. In John's cosmology, sealing (or marking) is presented as an inevitable, universal human experience—and yet, the final outcome of which group readers (and others) might find themselves among is more an open question in Revelation than in Psalms of Solomon or Ezekiel.

With the entire narrative of Revelation in mind, it is possible to observe that readers only fully learn the significance of the seal when they hear, in 14:1–5, that it is actually "his [the Lamb's] name and his Father's name written on their foreheads." Now the Ezekiel 9 vision may well have been merged with the Israelite high priest's practice of wearing a signet inscribed "holy to the LORD" on the forehead (Exod 28:36). This makes clear that such a "sealing" was already anticipated in Revelation 3:12 with the promise of a new name, and ultimately realized by the faithful in the final vision of the New Jerusalem and the garden of God (Rev 22:3–4). All these elements of a coherent theme in John's narrative were initiated with the announcement of a seal for God's servants in Revelation 7. That this traditional image also appeared in Psalms of Solomon 15 suggests that Ezekiel's vision of a grieving remnant who are promised the assurance of protection became singularly formative for some early Jewish and Christian communities. This should not be altogether surprising when we consider that both texts were composed in times of (real or perceived) crisis. In their respective settings, both texts sought to find ways to encourage the faithful to remain so, while also insisting that the one who sealed them would invariably thwart even the darkest hostility of their opponents.

---

as to why this should not be seen as reflecting the practice of branding or tattooing slaves, see Craig R. Koester, *Revelation*, AYB 38A (New Haven: Yale University Press, 2014), 416–17.

4. This primary concern for the faithful is confirmed in Revelation 9:4 where locust-like creatures "were told not to harm the grass of the earth or any plant or tree, but only those people *who did not have the seal of God on their foreheads*" (emphasis added).

For Further Reading

Additional Ancient Literature

There are further sources that could be explored, such as CD 19:12 and 4 Ezra 6:5 for their use of the tradition of God's seal. Some commentators have noted the language of "sealing" used to describe the role of the Holy Spirit in the life of a believer (2 Cor 1:22; Eph 1:13); however, those settings seem only indirectly related, if at all, to the eschatological vindication communicated in both Psalms of Solomon 15 and Revelation 7.

English Translations and Critical Editions

Kim, H. C. *Psalms of Solomon: A New Translation and Introduction.* Highland Park, NJ: Hermit Kingdom, 2008.

Wright, Robert B. *Psalms of Solomon: A Critical Edition of the Greek Text.* London: T&T Clark, 2007.

———. "*Psalms of Solomon*: A New Translation and Introduction." Pages 639–70 in vol. 2 of *The Old Testament Pseudepigrapha*. Edited by James H. Charlesworth. Garden City, NY: Doubleday, 1985.

Secondary Literature

Atkinson, Kenneth. "Enduring the Lord's Discipline: Soteriology in the *Psalms of Solomon*." Pages 145–66 in *This World and the World to Come: Soteriology in Early Judaism*. Edited by Daniel M. Gurtner. New York: Bloomsbury, 2011.

Bons, Eberhard and Patrick Pouchelle, eds. *The Psalms of Solomon: Language, History, Theology*. Early Judaism and Its Literature. 40. Atlanta: SBL Press, 2015.

Embry, Brad. "Psalms of Solomon." Pages 563–84 in vol. 2 of *Early Jewish Literature: An Anthology*. Grand Rapids: Eerdmans, 2018.

Gordley, Matthew E. "Creating Meaning in the Present by Reviewing the Past: Communal Memory in the Psalms of Solomon." *Journal for Ancient Judaism* 5 (2014): 368–92.

Hill, Wesley. "*Psalms of Solomon* and Romans 1:1–17: The 'Son of God' and the Identity of Jesus." Pages 31–37 in *Reading Romans in Context: Paul and Second Temple Judaism*. Edited by Ben C. Blackwell, John K. Goodrich, and Jason Mason. Grand Rapids: Zondervan, 2015.

CHAPTER 7

The Testament of Adam and Revelation 8:1–13: Heavenly Silence

JASON MASTON

Revelation 8 concludes the series of "seals" and begins the "trumpets," shifting from one eschatological judgment scene to another. The chapter begins with the silencing of heaven when the seventh seal is opened, followed by God distributing the seven trumpets to seven angels (8:1–2). Before the trumpets are sounded, John relates a scene in which an angel places "on the golden altar in front of the throne" some "incense" along with "the prayers of all God's people," which ascend before God (8:3–4). At this point the angel fills the censer with "fire from the altar" and flings it toward the earth, bringing about "peals of thunder, rumblings, flashes of lightning and an earthquake" (8:5). After the cosmic signs of judgment in 8:5, the narrative returns to the seven angels with the seven trumpets. In 8:7–9:21, John describes what happens when the first six angels blow their trumpets (the seventh appears in 11:15–18 after a long interlude). The final three trumpets are set off from the rest by the statement in 8:13, which identifies them each as a "woe!"

Revelation is a book replete with awe-inspiring imagery, and yet the message of chapter 8 is conveyed by stressing not so much the visual as the aural. From beginning to end, we are bombarded with "peals of thunder," cosmic "rumblings," "trumpets," "an eagle . . . call[ing] out in a loud voice," and "the prayers of all God's people." Over against all this noise stands the opening line of the chapter: "When he opened the seventh seal, there was silence in heaven for about half an hour" (8:1). In a scene filled with sounds, the opening silence is deafening. This statement raises several questions: Why is there silence? Why does it last for "about half an hour"? How does the silence relate to the following scene of the angel before the altar?

Why, in fact, is this altar scene included between the distribution of the trumpets and their sounding? John provides no clear answers to these questions, assuming probably that his readers would know the purpose of the silence. In fact, Jewish writers often discuss silence in heaven. To help better understand John's comment, comparison can be made with the Testament of Adam, a complex but intriguing text of Jewish and Christian origin.

The Testament of Adam

"SILENCE IS IMPOSED ON ALL THE RANKS OF FIRE AND WIND"

A "testament" is a record of a person's last words of advice and instruction to his children. In the Hebrew tradition, the genre appears as early as Jacob's final words to his twelve sons (Gen 49). In the Second Temple period many adopted and adapted this genre, the most well-known being the Testament of the Twelve Patriarchs. A lesser known example is the Testament of Adam.

The Testament of Adam consists of three sections. The first section, the Horarium (chs. 1–2), records the praises of creation according to the hour in which they occur. The second section, the Prophecy (ch. 3), records Adam's words to his son Seth about future events in the world. The last section, the Hierarchy (ch. 4), describes the nine orders of heavenly beings.

The Testament of Adam has been transmitted through several languages, and our passage (1:10–12) has survived in Greek, Syriac, and Armenian. It is unclear what the original language was; scholars have proposed Hebrew, Greek, and Syriac. More important for our purpose are questions about its original date and Christian influence. There is no doubt that the Testament of Adam has been heavily influenced by Christian beliefs, particularly in the Hierarchy, which explicitly mentions "our Lord Jesus the Messiah" (4:1, 8), and the Prophecy, which refers to the incarnation and the Virgin Mary (3:3).[1] The Christianized form of the Testament of Adam probably comes from the third century AD. The Horarium, however, may have originated much earlier. It does not appear to have any Christian elements, and most studies consider it to be Jewish in origin. Richard Bauckham contends that 1:12 must reflect the practices of the priests before the destruction of the

---

1. Translations from S. E. Robinson, "Testament of Adam," in *The Old Testament Pseudepigrapha, Vol. 1: Apocalyptic Literature and Testaments*, ed. James H. Charlesworth (Garden City, NY: Doubleday, 1983), 989–95.

second temple (AD 70).[2] This means that at least this part, but most likely the whole Horarium, was composed in the first century and testifies to beliefs and practices current around the time Revelation was written.

The Horarium describes the worship patterns of creation according to the hour of each day in which they occur. Of particular interest are the events happening in the tenth through the twelfth hours of the night. The text reads:

> The tenth hour is the praise of human beings, and the gate of heaven is opened through which the prayers of all living things enter, and they worship and depart. And at that hour whatever a man will ask of God is given to him when the seraphim and the roosters beat their wings. The eleventh hour there is joy in all the earth when the sun rises from Paradise and shines forth upon creation. The twelfth hour is the waiting for incense, and silence is imposed on all the ranks of fire and wind until all the priests burn incense to his divinity. And at that time all the heavenly powers are dismissed. (T. Adam 1:10–12)

Offering Incense. Following the Jewish practice of beginning a day at sunset, the Horarium begins by describing the events that happen overnight. The night's activities close with silence in preparation for the offering of incense. This most likely refers to the morning activity of the priest offering incense as prescribed in Exodus 30:7: "Aaron must burn fragrant incense on the altar every morning when he tends the lamps." The altar of incense sat directly in front of the curtain that separated the Holy Place from the Most Holy Place in the tabernacle and later the temple (Exod 30:6).

The Silence of Angelic Hosts. The time of preparation for the offering of the incense is marked by the silence of "all the ranks of fire and wind" (1:12). Two pieces of evidence suggest that "fire and wind" refer to the angelic host, not cosmic elements. First, the Horarium consistently describes the actions of the angelic hosts. For example, hours four and nine of the evening describe the actions of the seraphim and cherubim, respectively (1:4, 9). The hours of the day contain even more activities of the angels (2:1, 2, 6, 9). Second, the author may be alluding to Psalm 104:4: "He makes winds his messengers, flames of fire his servants" (NIV). The idea is that God uses the winds or the flames of fire as his messengers. With a slight altering of the grammar and by understanding the word "messengers" as "angels" (which is how the

---

2. Richard Bauckham, *The Climax of Prophecy: Studies on the Book of Revelation* (Edinburgh: T&T Clark, 1993), 79–81.

word is translated in other texts), the identification of the angels as wind or flaming fire becomes even clearer. For example, the epistle to the Hebrews quotes the LXX: "He makes his angels spirits [or winds], and his servants flames of fire" (1:7). The Horarium may have the same idea.

In preparation for the offering of incense, the angels cease all activities. The previous eleven hours contain a variety of actions, including the singing of praises by both angels and the rest of creation. However, in this hour all activity stops and silence "is imposed" (T. Adam 1:12). The question is, why must there be silence?

The Prayers of Israel. There is no specific reason given for the silence of the angelic host, but there is a tradition within Judaism that says that the angels will be silent in order for the prayers of Israel to rise to God's throne. Bauckham points to several rabbinic texts that describe the angels becoming silent so that God can hear the prayers of his people.[3] While these texts are later than the first century AD, they provide some additional material that helps to explain the silence of the angels in the Testament of Adam. In our passage, the tenth hour of the evening "is the praise of human beings" (1:10). It may be that the act of the "seraphim and the roosters beat[ing] their wings" points to the idea of the angels bringing the prayers of Israel up to God's throne.

The Testament of Adam is, unfortunately, hazy on many points, but a general picture begins to emerge. The night's activities conclude with Israel's praise and prayers. After these are offered, the angels, who had been worshiping God, now become silent so that God can listen to the prayers of his people. The prayers of God's people are more important than the praises of the angels or other created things, so the latter become silent in order for God to attend to his people, "for whatever a man will ask of God is given to him" (1:10; cf. 2:12).

Revelation 8:1–13

"THERE WAS SILENCE IN HEAVEN FOR ABOUT HALF AN HOUR"

In the Horarium, Adam describes what happens each hour of the day as the heavenly powers praise God. The setting is heaven itself. In Revelation 8, John describes what he sees in heaven. As noted above, Revelation 8 ends

---

3. Bauckham, *Climax of Prophecy*, 70–76.

the description of the seals and begins the account of the trumpets. The chapter is filled with aural language, which makes the opening silence stand out. Also like the Testament of Adam, John does not describe the purpose of the silence. He assumes instead that his readers will know what it signifies. The Testament of Adam helps to break the silence.

The Silence of Angelic Hosts. John does not explain who is silent. As discussed above, the Testament of Adam indicates that the angelic host becomes silent, and it seems likely that John is implying the same. Revelation 4 indicates that the praises of angelic beings are constantly sounding forth in God's throne room. Revelation 4:8 tells us about the four living creatures— "Day and night they never stop saying: 'Holy, holy, holy is the Lord God Almighty,' who was, and is, and is to come" (cf. Isa 6). Yet, at the end of time, silence holds forth in heaven. The angels that have sung forever are now quiet.[4]

Offering Incense. After the trumpets are distributed, another angel enters the scene and comes to stand at "the golden altar in front the throne" (Rev 8:3). The angel holds "much incense" and "the prayers of all God's people." The angel serves a cultic role and probably should be understood as a counterpart to an earthly priest. In the ancient Jewish context, events that happen on earth are mirrored in heaven. There is a correspondence. So the burning of incense on the altar of incense in the tabernacle or temple is matched by the offering of incense in the heavenly temple of God's throne room. John seems to be suggesting that the incense and prayers are intermingled, and as with sacrifices, the incense gives the prayers a sweet aroma that is pleasing to God.

The Prayers of the Martyrs. Whose prayers are these and what is prayed for? The last altar mentioned in Revelation was in 6:9. At the opening of the fifth seal, John sees "under the altar the souls of those who had been slain because of the word of God and the testimony they had maintained." These martyrs cry out, "How long, Sovereign Lord, holy and true, until you judge the inhabitants of the earth and avenge our blood?" (6:10). They are given white robes and promised justice, but not "until the full number of their fellow servants, their brothers and sisters, were killed just as they had been" (6:11). It seems likely that John intends his readers to draw a connection between the scenes described in 8:3–5 and 6:9–11.[5] "The prayers of all God's

---

4. The expression "for about half an hour" (Rev 8:1) is unusual. One might have expected a less precise time, such as "about an hour." Commentators discuss the significance of the half hour, but there is no obvious reason why John is this specific.

5. Commentators debate whether the altar in Revelation 8:3 is identical to that of

people" (8:3) are specifically the martyrs' appeals for justice.[6] The silence of the angels implies that God hears only these prayers at this time.

The silence indicates the solemn nature of the situation. Whereas God had previously delayed acting, now he will delay no longer. The angel who had offered up the incense and the prayers of the martyrs now fills the censer "with fire from the altar" and proceeds to throw "it on the earth" (Rev 8:5). This act results in judgment, as indicated by the cosmic signs of "peals of thunder, rumblings, flashes of lightning and an earthquake." God has now vindicated his people.[7]

Theologically, this connection between God's judgment and the prayers of his people is important. God does not judge like a tyrant, nor is his judgment comparable to a toddler's irrational tantrum. Rather, God judges precisely to bring justice, to restore what is right and vanquish evil. God's judgment is his response to the prayers of the faithful who have suffered "because of the word of God and the testimony they had maintained" (6:9).

The Testament of Adam offers us one possible explanation for the silence in heaven and how it relates to the burning of incense and the offering of the saints' prayers. Not all commentators are convinced by this explanation, which reminds us of the complexity of interpreting Revelation. Reading Revelation alongside the Testament of Adam helps us to see potential connections in John's vision that might otherwise have gone unnoticed. The silence of the heavenly beings allows the prayers of the martyrs to sound forth. The silence tells us that God hears our prayers and will act to vindicate his people.

FOR FURTHER READING

Additional Ancient Texts

Several rabbinic texts mention the angels becoming silent: b. Ḥagigah 12b; Genesis Rabbah 65:21; Targum Ezekiel 1:24–25. The Dead Sea Scroll 4QShirShabb (4Q405) 20–22 is also relevant. These and other texts are

---

6:9. However one understands John's view of sacred space, it seems likely that he intended some connections to be drawn between these two scenes.

6. Some commentators suggest that the prayers are not specifically those of the martyrs, but instead prayers offered by all Christians. This is certainly possible, but the content of the prayers should be limited to requests for divine judgment as indicated by the cosmic signs of judgment in 8:5.

7. The trumpets should probably not be interpreted as God's response to the prayers in 8:3–5. The trumpets indicate a different aspect of judgment. How the trumpets relate to the seals and bowls is one of the most disputed issues in the study of Revelation.

discussed by Bauckham in his *Climax of Prophecy*. Another view of the angelic silence links it with a return to primeval creation; see 4 Ezra 7:30 and 2 Baruch 3:7.

English Translations and Critical Editions

Robinson, S. E. "Testament of Adam." Pages 989–95 in vol. 1 of *The Old Testament Pseudepigrapha*. Edited by James H. Charlesworth. Garden City, NY: Doubleday, 1983.

Stone, Michael Edward. *Armenian Apocrypha Relating to the Patriarchs and Prophets*. Jerusalem: Israel Academy of Sciences and Humanities, 1982.

Secondary Literature

Bauckham, Richard. *Climax of Prophecy: Studies on the Book of Revelation*. Edinburgh: T&T Clark, 1993.

Hansen, Ryan Leif. *Silence and Praise: Rhetorical Cosmology and Political Theology in the Book of Revelation*. Emerging Scholars. Minneapolis: Fortress, 2014.

Robinson, Stephen E. "The Testament of Adam: An Updated Arbeitsbericht." *JSP* 5 (1989): 95–100.

———. *The Testament of Adam: An Examination of the Syriac and Greek Traditions*. SBLDS 52. Chico, CA: Scholars, 1982.

Stone, Michael E. *A History of the Literature of Adam and Eve*. SBLEJL 3. Atlanta: Scholars Press, 1992.

CHAPTER 8

The Animal Apocalypse and Revelation 9:1–21: Creaturely Images during the Great Tribulation

IAN BOXALL

Trumpets evoke many things in the biblical tradition. Trumpets are blown to proclaim victory in battle, announce a fast or a festival, or herald the eschatological Day of the Lord.[1] The appearance of seven angels with trumpets (Rev 8:2) in the heavenly sanctuary, immediately following the Lamb's opening of the seventh seal, heightens expectation that a crucial moment has been reached. The eschatological aspect is to the fore: judgments ensue in rapid succession as the first four angels blow their trumpets. At Revelation 9:1–21, however, John's narrative description slows as he describes the effects of the fifth and sixth trumpets in greater detail. Unlike the first four trumpet plagues, these latter directly target the human world, specifically "the inhabitants of the earth" (8:13).

What John now describes is nightmarish in the extreme. The unlocking of the Abyss, or "bottomless pit," by a fallen star allows a terrifying army of locusts to emerge onto the earth (9:3–11). Their hybrid character reinforces the sense of revulsion and fear at their appearance. The massive army John sees at the sixth trumpet blast reinforces this sense of the world's worst nightmare. The locusts' horse-like appearance has been replaced by a vast army of actual cavalry, whose horses are fearsome hybrids with leonine heads and serpentine tails (9:17–19). Yet the wider literary context of this section provides reason for hope. The blowing of the trumpets is directly connected with the Lamb's opening of the sealed scroll (6:1–8:1) containing

---

1. On the latter, see, e.g., Zeph 1:14–16; Joel 2:1; Matt 24:31; 1 Cor 15:52; 1 Thess 4:16.

the divine plan for salvation. Mention of locusts recalls the locust plague of Exodus 10:1–20, as well as Joel's locust vision heralding the Day of the Lord (Joel 1:4–7). The unfolding of these judgments raises expectations that this Lamb too will be central to a new Passover, and a new exodus, whereby God will liberate his people.

Revelation 9 presupposes a tripartite cosmology (heaven, earth, the Abyss) and regular movement between its realms (fall, ascent). This interaction between different levels of the cosmos, as well as this chapter's creaturely imagery, would have been familiar to early Christian audiences shaped by the Jewish apocalyptic tradition. The visionary world presupposed in 1 Enoch is especially illuminating for our passage.

The Animal Apocalypse

> "AND BEHOLD A STAR FELL FROM
> HEAVEN, AND IT AROSE AND ATE AND
> PASTURED AMONGST THOSE BULLS"

First Enoch is the common title for a "library" of traditions about the antediluvian patriarch Enoch (Gen 5:21–24), comprising five books dating from different periods, which was highly influential in the New Testament period (e.g., Matt 25:31–46; Jude 6, 14–15) and beyond (e.g., Ep. Barn. 4.3; Apoc. Pet. 4; 13; Tertullian, *Cult. fem.* 1.2; *Idol.* 4; Origen, *Princ.* 1.3.3; 4.4.8).[2] Most of the traditions were originally written in Aramaic (fragments from all but one of the book's five sections survive from **Qumran**), translated into Greek, and thence into Ethiopic, becoming an important **canonical** text for the Ethiopian Orthodox Church. The fourth book, known as the Book of Dreams (1 En. 83–90), contains two dreams purportedly received by Enoch prior to his marriage: a dream predicting Noah's flood (1 En. 83–84) and the so-called Animal Apocalypse (1 En. 85–90), which encompasses the broad sweep of human history. The identification of the ram with the "big horn" (1 En. 90:9) as Judas Maccabeus leads to a consensus date c. 163 BC, at the height of the crisis provoked by the Greek **Seleucid Antiochus IV**.

The Animal Apocalypse is an **allegory** of the human story, from the creation of Adam through Israel's history to the **eschaton**, in which humans are symbolized by nonhuman animals, angels by human figures, and fallen

---

2. For more information about 1 Enoch, see chapter 1 in this volume by Benjamin E. Reynolds ("The Parables of Enoch and Revelation 1:1–20: Daniel's Son of Man").

angels by stars. The creaturely imagery has a logical pattern: the patriarchs from Adam to Isaac are bulls, Jacob/Israel is a ram, and the people of Israel are sheep. Gentile nations, who often oppress Israel, are differentiated according to species (e.g., asses = Ishmaelites; wolves = Egyptians; lions = Babylonians/Chaldeans). The restoration of Israel in the messianic age results in the re-emergence of the white bulls, i.e., a return to the beginning. This visionary sweep of history, written at a time of crisis for Israel under foreign oppression, offers prophetic reassurance that the historical process remains firmly under divine control.

Fallen Stars. The story of human history is interrupted, following the description of Adam and his immediate descendants (1 En. 85), by that of the Watchers, or fallen angels. The Animal Apocalypse presupposes the myth founded in the earlier Book of the Watchers (1 En. 1–36, specifically 6–11), a more developed version of Genesis 6:1–4. According to the Book of the Watchers, rebellion by some of the angels resulted in a transgression of the boundary between heaven and earth. The fallen Watchers, led by Semihazah, took human wives and fathered a hybrid race of destructive giants. Interwoven with this is a parallel tradition, which attributes the earth's plight to a group of angels, led by Asael or Azazel, teaching humans forbidden heavenly secrets.

In the Animal Apocalypse, Enoch sees a star falling from heaven (1 En. 86:1), followed by many other stars, which "came down and were thrown down [*or* and threw themselves down] from heaven to that first star" (1 En. 86:3).[3] Angels are commonly likened to stars (e.g., Dan 12:3; Rev 1:20; 3:1; 8:10–11). A falling star is an appropriate image for a fallen angel. The first star probably is to be identified not as Semihazah, but as Asael, given that he will later be bound hand and foot and thrown into the Abyss, or bottomless pit (1 En. 88:1; see the similar fate of Asael in 1 En. 10:4–8). The Abyss serves the function of a temporary prison, where Asael resides until the final judgment, when all the fallen stars will be thrown into a fiery abyss (1 En. 90:24). According to Enoch's description, the prison-abyss was "narrow, and deep, and horrible and dark" (1 En. 88:1), a vivid description of the prison environment that reflects the character of its prisoners.

Warring Creatures. But the damage has already been done for the earth by the time Asael is confined. Creation's order has given way to chaos due to the crossbreeding between angels and humans, spirit and flesh. Paralleling

---

3. The translation used is that of M. A. Knibb, "1 Enoch," in *The Apocryphal Old Testament*, ed. H. F. D. Sparks (Oxford: Clarendon, 1984), 184–319.

its animal symbolism for human players in history, the Animal Apocalypse also depicts the half-human offspring of the Watchers and their human wives in creaturely terms:

> And I looked at them [the fallen stars] and saw, and behold all of them let out their private parts like horses and began to mount the cows of the bulls, and they all became pregnant and bore elephants and camels and asses. (1 En. 86:4)

Elephants and camels, if not asses, are strange-looking creatures, suitable symbols for angelic-human hybrids.[4] Their attacks on the bulls (= humans) foreshadows the ongoing attacks on God's people (the sheep) by varieties of wild animals in the subsequent review of Israel's story (1 En. 89–90). For example, different animal species are used to describe the attacks of pagan nations (the Chaldaeans, Syrians, Egyptians, Moabites, and Ammonites, see 2 Kgs 23:28–35; 24:2–3) in the last days of the kingdom of Judah[5]: "And he gave them into the hands of the lions and the tigers and the wolves and the hyenas, and into the hands of the foxes, and to all the animals; and those wild animals began to tear those sheep in pieces" (1 En. 89:55). History is prone to repeat itself.

Revelation 9:1–21

"THE STAR WAS GIVEN THE KEY TO THE SHAFT OF THE ABYSS"

Fallen Stars. John's vision of a star falling from heaven (Rev 9:1) recalls Enoch's vision of the fallen star Asael. In contrast to the Animal Apocalypse, however, emphasis is less on angelic rebellion than on divine sovereignty. This star is "given" or "granted" the key to unlock the shaft of the Abyss, signifying divine permission (9:1; also 9:3, 5). The star-angel can now let the forces of evil and chaos, in the guise of terrifying locusts, out of their subterranean prison. Yet paradoxically, these same forces function as God's agents. Commentators are divided over whether the angel with the key is to be identified with the angel of the Abyss, called Abaddon ("Destruction") or Apollyon ("Destroyer"), who rules as king over the locusts (9:11).

---

4. George W. E. Nickelsburg, *1 Enoch 1*, Hermeneia (Minneapolis: Fortress, 2001), 374.
5. Nickelsburg, *1 Enoch 1*, 385.

Most probably the two are separate characters: the fallen angel opens the door from outside, whereas Abaddon rules over those inside.

The Prison-Abyss. The "shaft" of the Abyss, or "bottomless pit," suggests a narrow and possibly long passage leading to the depths below. In the three-tiered cosmology that John describes in this vision, the Abyss refers to the watery deep (Hebrew *tehōm*, Gen 1:2; Isa 51:10; Ezek 31:15; Amos 7:4) and dwelling place of demons. Its evil occupants are evident from the acrid smoke emerging from the shaft, which darkens sun and air. This stands in sharp contrast to the sweet-smelling incense smoke ascending to the divine throne in heaven, mingled with the prayers of the saints (Rev 8:4). That the entrance to the Abyss is kept under lock and key highlights its prison status. Here it is opened to let its prisoners out. Later, the door will be opened again to imprison the dragon Satan for a thousand years (20:1–3).

Warring Creatures. Revelation also employs creaturely imagery. Yet whereas in the Animal Apocalypse it is largely used of human nations, in this passage the monstrous hybridity of the locusts and horses places them firmly on the side of the dragon Satan, as does the fact that they emerge from the Abyss. The nearest Enochic equivalents are the violent offspring of the Watchers, symbolized as elephants, camels, and asses. Hybrid creatures stand on the wrong side of the boundary between order and chaos, clean and unclean. Revelation's locusts combine the destructive energy of a locust swarm with the painful effects of scorpion stings. Similarly, the vast phalanx of fire-breathing horses unleashed at the River Euphrates ("twice ten thousand times ten thousand," 9:16) are a potent mixture of warhorse, lion, and snake.

The demonic character of the locusts is not in doubt. However, there is also a more familiar dimension to these devilish creatures. Their faces resemble human faces (9:7). They have women's hair, a probable reference to its length (9:8). This is a disturbing reminder of the close collaboration between the superhuman forces unleased from the Abyss and their human agents. The Parthians, Rome's greatest threat on its eastern border, were famous for the long hair of their warriors (Plutarch, *Crass.* 24:2; cf. Suetonius, *Vesp.* 23:4). Moreover, according to certain tales circulating when John wrote, the supposedly deceased Nero had actually escaped to Parthia, only to return with a Parthian army (Sib. Or. 4.119–124, 137–139; cf. Suetonius, *Nero* 47; Tacitus, *Hist.* 2.9). Like the millions of cavalry John sees (Rev 9:16–19), the Parthians will come from the River Euphrates. Some commentators detect a further Neronian allusion in the Greek name of the king of the locusts, Apollyon ("Destroyer"), given Nero's frequent identification with the god Apollo (Suetonius, *Nero* 53; Tacitus, *Ann.* 14.14.1).

Yet divine control constrains what these demonic creatures can achieve. Unlike earthly locusts, which can devastate the food supply, these locusts are forbidden to harm any vegetation. Instead, their target is humanity: specifically, tormenting those lacking the seal of God, though only for the limited period of five months. The horsemen are able to wreak far more havoc through their association with the angels released at the Euphrates, who are permitted to kill a third of humanity (9:15). The judgment is harsh. But it is limited, and it functions as a wake-up call to repentance, even if it fails to have the desired effect (9:20–21).

Both Revelation and the Animal Apocalypse describe in nightmarish terms a world that is out of kilter, marked by demonic forces and human rebellion. For the Animal Apocalypse, hybridity unbalanced creation at the beginning. For Revelation, it only intensifies in the lead-up to the end. The Abyss can serve as a temporary prison for fallen angels and their associates, but ultimately a more permanent solution is required. In the Animal Apocalypse, the crucial victory of the ram (= Judas Maccabeus, 1 En. 90:9) over the wild animals is not yet the final resolution. That will come with the emergence of a white bull (possibly the **Messiah**) after the judgment (1 En. 90:37). In Revelation, God is already in control, severely constraining the destructive power of the demonic hybrids through another animal, acting as divine agent. The slaughtered Lamb has broken the seven seals, enabling God's salvific plan to be put into effect. Passover has arrived. The New Exodus has begun.

FOR FURTHER READING

Additional Ancient Texts

Angels as wayward, falling, or descending stars also appear at 1 Enoch 80:6–7, Sibylline Oracles 5.158–61, and Jude 13. Among ancient texts viewing the abyss as a place of imprisonment or punishment, one might compare 1 Enoch 18–21, and Luke 8:31. Abaddon, generally a synonym for Sheol (e.g., Job 26:6; Prov 15:11), appears to be personified at 1QH^a 11:19 and 4Q286, Frag. 7, as an alternative name for Belial.

English Translations and Critical Editions

Bertalotto, Pierpaolo, Ken M. Penner, and Ian W. Scott, eds. "1 Enoch."
   In *The Online Critical Pseudepigrapha*. Edited by Ian W. Scott, Ken
   M. Penner, and David M. Miller. 1.5 ed. Atlanta: Society of Biblical
   Literature, 2006. www.purl.org/net/ocp/1En.

Isaac, E. "1 (Ethiopic Apocalypse of) Enoch." Pages 13–89 in vol. 1 of *The Old Testament Pseudepigrapha*. Edited by James H. Charlesworth. Garden City, NY: Doubleday, 1983.

Knibb, Michael A. "1 Enoch." Pages 184–319 in *The Apocryphal Old Testament*. Edited by H. F. D. Sparks. Oxford: Clarendon, 1984.

———. *The Ethiopic Book of Enoch*. 2 vols. Oxford: Clarendon, 1978.

Nickelsburg, George W. E., and James C. VanderKam. *1 Enoch: The Hermeneia Translation*. Minneapolis: Fortress, 2012.

Olson, Daniel C. *Enoch: A New Translation*. North Richland Hills, TX: BIBAL, 2004.

Secondary Literature

Collins, John J. *The Apocalyptic Imagination: An Introduction to Jewish Apocalyptic Literature*, 3rd ed. Grand Rapids: Eerdmans, 2016.

Lupieri, Edmondo F. *A Commentary on the Apocalypse of John*. Translated by M. Poggi Johnson and A. Kamesar. Grand Rapids: Eerdmans, 2006.

Nickelsburg, George W. E. *1 Enoch 1*. Hermeneia. Minneapolis: Fortress, 2001.

Ryan, Sean M. *Hearing at the Boundaries of Vision: Education Informing Cosmology in Revelation 9*. LNTS 448. London: Continuum, 2012.

Stuckenbruck, Loren T. "The Book of Revelation as a Disclosure of Wisdom." Pages 347–60 in *The Jewish Apocalyptic Tradition and the Shaping of New Testament Thought*. Edited by Benjamin E. Reynolds and Loren T. Stuckenbruck. Minneapolis: Augsburg Fortress, 2017.

CHAPTER 9

Jubilees and Revelation 10:1–11: Heavenly Beings Bearing Heavenly Books

JOHN K. GOODRICH

Near the end of Revelation 9, the sixth trumpet is sounded and various disasters ensue: angels are released (9:14–15), an army is mounted (9:16–17), and a third of the world's population is destroyed (9:18–19). All of this represents God's punishment of unrepentant humanity. But the judgment is not yet complete, for John has already reported that there are not six but seven angels with trumpets (8:2, 6). Whether these trumpets are inaugurating judgments altogether different from those triggered by the seals, or John is merely recapitulating the same series of seven events in different terms, the reader is under no illusion that the trumpet calls are over. A seventh and final trumpet blast awaits.

The trumpets, however, are not about to reach their finale. A chapter-long interlude separated the sixth and seventh seals, and so it will be with the final two trumpets.

As John waits for the seventh trumpet to sound, he receives a fresh vision. He encounters "another mighty angel" holding a "little scroll" (10:1–2). In time, the angel is instructed to pass the scroll to John, who does not read it, but eats it, causing his stomach to turn sour (10:8–10). The honest reader is thinking, "Well, that's why you don't eat scrolls," which is a fair point.

Figure 9:1 Seals, Trumpets, and Interludes

6:1–17	7:1–17	8:1–5	8:6–9:21	10:1–11:14	11:15–19
Seals 1–6	Interlude	Seal 7	Trumpets 1–6	Interlude	Trumpet 7

But we should also be wondering why the angel delivers John the scroll in the first place. This essay seeks to illuminate this strange episode by showing how heavenly beings and heavenly books function, both independently and in tandem, within another Jewish apocalyptic work—the book of Jubilees.

Jubilees

"AND THE ANGEL OF THE PRESENCE SPOKE TO MOSES . . . SAYING: 'WRITE THE COMPLETE HISTORY OF THE CREATION'"

The book of Jubilees is a second-century BC retelling of Genesis and the first half of Exodus. The 50-chapter work seeks to clarify the meaning of these earliest parts of the Bible, particularly the significance of the Mosaic legislation for the Hebrew patriarchs, that is, prior to its receipt at Sinai. For according to Jubilees, "This law is for all the generations forever" (15:25).

Although Hebrew manuscripts of Jubilees were discovered in Qumran, the book has survived primarily in Ethiopic. Jubilees does not include any visions, heavenly journeys, or large-scale rehearsals of sacred history, so it is not an apocalypse by genre—rather, it is *rewritten Scripture*. However, the book contains many themes shared by the apocalypses (esp. 1 Enoch), so it is widely considered apocalyptic in its theological orientation.[1] For our purposes, we will focus on two apocalyptic subjects that occur prominently in Jubilees—the activity of heavenly beings and the function of heavenly books.

Heavenly Beings. Angels appear early and often in Jubilees, even in the book's retelling of the creation narrative.[2] The account commences with the creation of the heavens, the earth, and the waters, but is followed immediately by the creation of the heavenly host, including no less than nineteen different classes of angels (2:2).[3] Preeminent among them are "the angels of the presence." These are high-ranking spirits who primarily serve before God "in his sanctuary" (31:14) and who together with "the angels of sanctification" form the "two great [angelic] classes" (2:18).

In Jubilees, however, angels are not restricted to heaven, for they also

---

1. Cf. Todd R. Hanneken, *The Subversion of the Apocalypses in the Book of Jubilees,* SBLEJL 34 (Atlanta: SBL, 2012).

2. For a brief summary, see James C. VanderKam, "The Angel of the Presence in the Book of Jubilees," *DSD* 7 (2000): 378–93, at 378–80.

3. Adapted from R. H. Charles, ed., *The Apocrypha and Pseudepigrapha of the Old Testament in English: With Introductions and Critical and Explanatory Notes to the Several Books,* 2 vols. (Oxford: Clarendon, 1913), 2:13–14.

carry out errands on earth. For example, the angels known as the Watchers, who eventually receive divine punishment for disobedience (5:1–5), were originally sent to earth to "instruct the children of men, and . . . [to] do judgment and uprightness on the earth" (4:15). Other angelic groups are also highlighted for their involvement with various people groups. One especially instructive section reads:

> [27] Before the angels of the presence and the angels of sanctification he has sanctified Israel, that they should be with him and with his holy angels. . . . [31] And he sanctified [Israel], and gathered [them] from amongst all the children of men; for there are many nations and many peoples, and all are his, and over all has he placed spirits in authority to lead them astray from him. [32] But over Israel he did not appoint any angel or spirit, for he alone is their ruler, and he will preserve them and require them at the hand of his angels and his spirits, and at the hand of all his powers in order that he may preserve them and bless them, and that they may be his and he may be theirs from henceforth forever. (15:27–32)

According to this extraordinary passage, various celestial beings have been assigned specific responsibilities in relation to particular people (cf. Deut 32:8 LXX; Dan 10:13–21; 12:1). On the one hand, demonic beings ("spirits in authority")—"those which were put under [the] hand" of prince Mastema, "the chief of the spirits" (10:7; 11:5)—rule over the nations "to lead them astray" (15:31). Good angels, on the other hand, provide a protective service for God's people (15:32), though none of these beings, strictly speaking, rules over Israel, because God himself rules the nation.

Heavenly Books. One other service provided by angels in Jubilees is worth noting—the mediation of heavenly books. Although the concept of heavenly books originates early in Israel's sacred writings (Exod 32:32–33), the notion becomes a recurring apocalyptic motif during the Second Temple period. Several kinds of heavenly tablets receive mention in Jubilees, including the book of life (30:19–23), the book of destruction (36:10), and the book of deeds (4:17–23; 39:6). These books serve various purposes in Jubilees and related literature. Yet regardless of what kind of heavenly document an author has in view, "the heavenly book motif," as Leslie Baynes explains, "always functions to grant divine authority to whatever claim is asserted by the text that appeals to it."[4]

---

4. Leslie Baynes, *The Heavenly Book Motif in Judeo-Christian Apocalypses 200 B.C.E.–200 C.E.*, JSJSup 152 (Leuven: Brill, 2012), 206.

At least one additional kind of heavenly book surfaces in Jubilees, what Baynes labels "the book of fate."[5] This is a record of historic events, from creation to new creation, presented in advance to a special recipient. The book of Jubilees itself purports to be a copy of this very document, which was given to an angelic mediator who then dictated it to Moses on Mount Sinai:

> [27] And [God] said to the angel of the presence: "Write for Moses [the history] from the beginning of creation till my sanctuary has been built among them for all eternity." . . . [29] And the angel of the presence who went before the camp of Israel took the tables of the divisions of the years—from the time of the creation . . . [until][6] the day of the [new] creation when the heavens and the earth shall be renewed and all their creation according to the powers of the heaven. . . . [2:1] And the angel of the presence spoke to Moses according to the word of the Lord, saying: "Write the complete history of the creation . . ." (1:27–2:1)

According to Jubilees, Moses is presented through angelic mediation a record of human history. This he transcribes and must impart to stiff-necked Israel (1:7), so that despite their rebellion and eventual exile the nation "will recognize that [God is] more righteous than they" and "that [he will be] truly with them" (1:6). The implications of such a claim are astonishing. This suggests not only that God is unswervingly faithful to his covenant promises, but that the book of Jubilees itself reliably and authoritatively attests to God's predetermined cosmic plan. As James VanderKam explains, "What could be more authoritative than a book written by Moses, dictated to him by an angel of the very face of God, based on the unimpeachable contents of the heavenly tablets, and mandated by God himself?"[7] This revelation, promising as it does both joy and anguish for Israel, has been entrusted to a single human being, Moses, who thereby possesses not only the heavenly tablets of fate but also the supreme authority they convey. The reader's mandate is clear: take heed of the authoritative word of Moses.

---

5. Baynes, *The Heavenly Book Motif*, 109–34.

6. For the restoration of this puzzling verse, see O. S. Wintermute, "Jubilees," in *The Old Testament Pseudepigrapha*, vol. 2, ed. James H. Charlesworth (Garden City, NY: Doubleday, 1985), 35–142, at 54n1.

7. VanderKam, "The Angel of the Presence," 393.

Revelation 10:1–11

"I TOOK THE LITTLE SCROLL FROM THE ANGEL'S HAND AND ATE IT"

Heavenly Beings. Jubilees and Revelation employ many of the same apocalyptic themes, not least the angelic activity and heavenly writing. Indeed, angels are as equally pervasive in Revelation as they are in Jubilees. Just as Jubilees locates angels in God's heavenly presence, so John refers to the heavenly angelic host who, "numbering thousands upon thousands, and ten thousand times ten thousand," surround the throne in order to praise the Lamb and worship God (Rev 5:11–12; 7:11–12; cf. 8:2–3). And just as Jubilees reports angels rebelling against God and deceiving the nations, so Revelation narrates the exile of angels from heaven and their leading people into evil (9:11; 12:7–9; 16:13–14; 18:2). Finally, just as Jubilees describes angels protecting Israel, so Revelation casts angels superintending churches (1:20; chs. 2–3). Beyond these parallels, God's angels in Revelation fulfill additional acts of divine service. John sees angels communicating with and guiding him (1:1; 19:9; 21:9; 22:1, 6–11, 16), proclaiming important messages (5:2; 14:6–9; 18:1–3; 19:17), executing divine judgment (7:1–2; 9:14–15; 14:15–19; 15:1; 15:6–16:12; 16:17; 17:1–18; 18:21), even directly combating Satan and his demons (12:7–9; 20:1–3).

Yet one of John's most striking episodes involving celestial beings concerns his own angelic encounter in Revelation 10:1–11. John reports:

> [1] Then I saw another mighty angel coming down from heaven. He was robed in a cloud, with a rainbow above his head; his face was like the sun, and his legs were like fiery pillars. [2] He was holding a little scroll, which lay open in his hand. He planted his right foot on the sea and his left foot on the land, [3] and he gave a loud shout like the roar of a lion. When he shouted, the voices of the seven thunders spoke. (10:1–3)

This is an impressive angel. In addition to evoking the previous "mighty angel" in 5:1–2, this being resembles the enthroned human-like figure who appears in the opening of Ezekiel: "from what appeared to be his waist up he looked like glowing metal, as if full of fire, and . . . *from there down he looked like fire*, and brilliant *light* surrounded him. Like the appearance of a *rainbow in the clouds* on a rainy day, so was the radiance around him" (Ezek 1:27–28). If this enthroned figure is, as it would seem, the Lord himself, then John is describing the angel he encounters in the very likeness of God.[8] But what is the significance of the "little scroll, which lay open in his hand" (Rev 10:2)?

Heavenly Books. As observed in Jubilees, heavenly documents are a common apocalyptic theme, so it is not surprising for them to surface in Revelation as well. Just as Jubilees refers to the book of life and the book of deeds, so does John's Apocalypse (3:5; 13:8; 17:8; 20:12, 15; 21:27). The "little scroll" in the hand of the mighty angel is a different sort of document, yet a heavenly book nonetheless (Gk. *biblaridion* = little book [10:2, 9, 10]; *biblion* = book [10:8]).

The scroll receives greater prominence as the chapter continues. Following the angel's announcement of the impending completion of God's eschatological plans (10:4–7), a heavenly voice commands John to take possession of the scroll:

> [8] Then the voice that I had heard from heaven spoke to me once more: "Go, take the scroll that lies open in the hand of the angel who is standing on the sea and on the land." [9] So I went to the angel and asked him to give me the little scroll. He said to me, "Take it and eat it. It will turn your stomach sour, but 'in your mouth it will be as sweet as honey.'" [10] I took the little scroll from the angel's hand and ate it. It tasted as sweet as honey in my mouth, but when I had eaten it, my stomach turned sour. [11] Then I was told, "You must prophesy again about many peoples, nations, languages and kings." (10:8–11)

This is a bizarre scene, but clarity comes when one realizes that John is once again echoing the earliest parts of Ezekiel, where the prophet receives a similar commissioning from the enthroned figure: "'Son of man, eat this scroll I am giving you and fill your stomach with it.' So I ate it, and it tasted as sweet as honey in my mouth. He then said to me: 'Son of man, go now to the people of Israel and speak my words to them'" (3:3–4). There are obvious parallels between Ezekiel's episode and Revelation 10:8–11. Both scenes involve prophets consuming honey-flavored scrolls delivered by heavenly beings and then receiving instructions to speak to rebellious people. Equally significant, however, are their differences. Ezekiel is commanded to speak to Israel in exile, while John "must prophesy again about many peoples, nations, languages and kings" (Rev 10:11). And whereas both scrolls are sweet to the taste, John's scroll embitters his stomach. John's adverse reaction

---

8. See also the similarities with Rev 5:1–2.

probably echoes Ezekiel 3:14, where the prophet is taken away by the Spirit "in *bitterness* and in the anger of my spirit." Because Ezekiel tells us how "on both sides of [the scroll] were written words of lament and mourning and woe" (2:10), it is probably the content of Ezekiel's message, together with the resistance he anticipates from obstinate exiles, that causes him bitterness and anger. We are never told the precise content of John's scroll, but the same probably is true in his case, since John must prophesy to and about unrepentant nations and kings (cf. 9:20–21). This is why the mighty angel directs John to eat the scroll in the first place: the scroll must be ingested so John receives God's message, experiences its effects—both the joy (sweetness) of salvation and the anguish (bitterness) of judgment—and thus is able more vividly to portray its content in the chapters to follow.

John's visionary experience, however, is similar not only to Ezekiel's commissioning but also parallels Moses's encounter with the angel of the presence in Jubilees. In both works, a heavenly being imparts to God's prophet a hidden message through a heavenly book. While John is tasked not simply with inscribing his message but also with ingesting it, both he and Moses are thereby authorized to declare salvation and judgment to rebellious people. In both episodes, receipt of a heavenly book from a heavenly mediator conveys remarkable authority, causing the message and its messenger to become barely distinguishable. The reader should therefore take heed.

For Further Reading

Additional Ancient Texts

Various angels and heavenly books surface in Second Temple Jewish literature, especially in the apocalypses (see the Secondary Literature below). Otherworldly mediators appear in 1 Enoch 17–36, the Apocalypse of Abraham 12–17, Testament of Levi 2–5, Testament of Abraham 10–14, as well as throughout 4 Ezra and 2 Baruch. Angels are said to participate in heavenly writing in 1 Enoch (10:8; 33:4; 72:1; 81:1–2), and Testament of Abraham 12:1–18. In 1 Enoch 69:8–11, a fallen angel is given credit for teaching humanity to write. For the consumption of heavenly food in the process of transmitting divine information, see 4 Ezra 14:38–41.

English Translations and Critical Editions

VanderKam, James C. *The Book of Jubilees: A Critical Text.* Corpus Scriptorum Christianorum Orientalium 510; Scriptores Aethiopici 87. Leuven: Peeters, 1989.

Wintermute, O. S. "Jubilees." Pages 35–142 in vol. 2 of *The Old Testament Pseudepigrapha*. Edited by James H. Charlesworth. Garden City, NY: Doubleday, 1985.

Secondary Literature

Baynes, Leslie. "Revelation 5:1 and 10:2a, 8–10 in the Earliest Greek Tradition: A Response to Richard Bauckham" *JBL* 129 (2010): 801–16.

Davidson, Maxwell J. *Angels at Qumran: A Comparative Study of 1 Enoch 1–36, 72–108 and Sectarian Writings from Qumran*. JSPSup 11. Sheffield: Sheffield Academic, 1992.

VanderKam, James C. *Jubilees: A Commentary in Two Volumes*. Hermeneia. Minneapolis: Fortress, 2018.

———. *The Book of Jubilees*. GAP 9. Sheffield: Sheffield Academic, 2001.

van Ruiten, Jacques. "Angels and Demons in the Book of *Jubilees*." Pages 585–609 in *Angels: The Concept of Celestial Beings—Origins, Development and Reception*. Deuterocanonical and Cognate Literature Yearbook 2007. Edited by F. V. Reiterer, T. Nicklas, and K. Schöpflin. Berlin: de Gruyter, 2007.

Warren, Meredith J. C. "Tasting the Little Scroll: A Sensory Analysis of Divine Interaction in Revelation 10.8–10." *JSNT* 40 (2017): 101–19.

CHAPTER 10

4 Ezra and Revelation 11:1–19: A Man from the Sea and the Two Witnesses

GARRICK V. ALLEN

Revelation 11 represents a classic interpretive crux, both in the deciphering of the specific locations and characters it mentions and in its narrative ambiguity as an interlude in the close of the seven trumpets cycle. After eating a sweet, yet bitter, scroll from the hand of one of his angelic guides (10:10–11), the seer is handed a "measuring rod like a staff" and commanded by an anonymous voice to "come and measure the temple of God, the altar, and those worshiping in it" (11:1).[1] He is forbidden from measuring the outer courts because it has been given over to the nations to trample for 42 months (11:2). Before the seer can act on these commands, the voice moves into the future tense, introducing two characters: "my two witnesses" who will prophesy for 1,260 days wearing sackcloth (11:3). The length of their prophetic activity corresponds to the length of time that the nations trample the outer courts of the temple that the seer is commanded to measure, connecting the unfulfilled command to measure to the actions of the witnesses. The voice opaquely identifies them as "the two olive trees and the two lampstands which are before the Lord of the earth" (11:4), alluding to the "sons of oil" in Zechariah 4. The witnesses are able to expel fire from their mouths and devour potential enemies, drawing on traditions of confrontational prophetic speech, and Elijah in particular (Jer 5:14; Sir 48:1).

---

1. There are multiple ways to interpret this voice as either divine or angelic, but the most provocative is put forth by Ian Boxall, *The Revelation of Saint John* (London: Continuum, 2006), 163, who argues that John takes on a prophetic divine persona.

The witnesses also have authority to stop the rain (like Elijah in 1 Kgs 17:1), turn water to blood, and strike the earth with plagues (Exod 7:17–24).

Despite their authority during the period of their prophetic activity, the beast from the abyss makes war with the witnesses, conquering and killing them (11:7).[2] Their bodies lie in the streets of the great city—Sodom and Egypt, where the Lord was crucified (11:8)—and they are marveled at by many peoples for three and a half days, the same people who gloat over their corpses and exchange gifts because of the prophets' tormenting of the inhabitants of the world. After three and a half days, a spirit of God enters them and they are summoned to heaven (11:12). Following their departure, an earthquake occurs, destroying a tenth of the city and killing seven thousand people; those who survived are terrified and worship God (11:13). And just in time because the seventh trumpet sounds in 11:15, instigating a heavenly proclamation of God's kingdom and a report of the worship of the twenty-four elders around his throne. The heavenly temple opens, the ark of the covenant appears, and a list of disturbances rock the cosmos. This is the end.

The two witnesses play an enigmatic but crucial role in the eschatological scenario that unfolds in Revelation 11. This period is characterized by a conflict between God's prophetic witnesses and the inhabitants of the earth, which only becomes violent with the rising of the beast. Their ministry culminates in a victory (resurrection and ascension) snatched from the jaws of defeat that leads to the reign of God. But what traditions contextualize the eschatological role of the witnesses and help us to understand their failure to use their advantageous powers?

While numerous connections between this chapter and Second Temple Jewish literature could be mustered, I focus on the eschatological implications of the actions of the two witnesses and their relationship to 4 Ezra 13, the Man from the Sea Vision. Reading 4 Ezra with the two witnesses narrative heightens the eschatological tension of the passage and contextualizes the strange behavior and abilities of these prophets.

4 Ezra

"THE MAN FROM THE SEA"

Fourth Ezra 3–14 uses the destruction of the temple by the Babylonians as a literary construct in an effort to grapple with issues surrounding the

---

2. Cf. the sea and land beasts that appear in Rev 13:1, 11.

destruction of the Second Temple by the Romans in AD 70. It contains seven highly symbolic visions received by Ezra. These visions culminate in the end of the age using exodus language and Ezra's prophetic restoration of inspired scriptural works (14:1–48).[3]

Violent Resolution. In the sixth vision of 4 Ezra—"the Man from the Sea" (13:1–58)[4]—Ezra sees a man arise from the sea, who flies with the clouds, and whose voice melts those who hear it as if exposed to flame.

> After seven days I dreamed a dream in the night; and behold, a wind rose from the sea and stirred up all its waves [cf. Dan. 7:1–2]. And I looked, and behold, this wind made something like the figure of a man come up out of the heart of the sea. And I looked, and behold, that man flew with the clouds of heaven; and wherever he turned his face to look, everything under his gaze trembled, and whenever his voice issued from his mouth, all who heard his voice melted like wax melts when it feels the fire. (4 Ezra 13:1–4)[5]

In opposition to him, an innumerable multitude gathers to make war; in response, the man carves a mountain and flies to it (13:5–7). The tension boils into open conflict when the multitude advances against him. They are routed by a stream of fire from his mouth that leaves only ashes and the smell of smoke in the place of the hostile multitude (13:8–11; cf. Isa 11:4; Hos 10:10–11): "and from his tongue he shot forth a storm of sparks. All these were mingled together, the stream of fire and the flaming breath and the great storm, and fell on the onrushing multitude which was prepared to fight and burned them all up, so that suddenly nothing was seen of the innumerable multitude but only the dust of ashes and smell of smoke" (13:10b-11). Following the victory, the man descends the mountain and calls forth a peaceful multitude (13:12–13).

Immediate Judgment. After an extended request (13:14–24), the vision is interpreted, identifying the man from the sea as God's son (13:26, 32) whose appearance will bring bewilderment upon the earth and rouse military conflict. In addition to national conflicts (13:31–32), the man unites these

---

3. For more information about 4 Ezra, see chapter 4 in this volume by Dana M. Harris ("4 Ezra and Revelation 5:1–14: Creaturely Images of the Messiah").

4. The imagery of this scene is closely related to preceding visionary material in 4 Ezra (the "Eagle Vision" in 11:1–12:51) and indebted to Daniel 7. Cf. Stone, *4 Ezra*, 384.

5. Translation from Bruce M. Metzger, "The Fourth Book of Ezra: A New Translation and Introduction," in *The Old Testament Pseudepigrapha*, ed. J. H. Charlesworth (Garden City, NY: Doubleday, 1985), 551.

forces against him (13:33–34). The mountain upon which he stands is Zion, and it is the platform from which he judges the nations (13:35–38). In his judgment he gathers the "peaceful multitude" (13:39), identified as ten tribes who were taken across a river to another land by Shalmaneser (13:40–41; cf. 2 Kgs 17:1–23). Shalmaneser's plans, however, were scuttled, as the exiles decided to "leave the multitude of the nations" to sojourn to an uninhabited land where they might keep the law (13:41–43; cf. Josephus, *Ant.* 11.133; Sib. Or. 2.170–173; T. Mos. 3:4–9; 4:9). These tribes dwell in this land until "the last times," and they are about to come again (13:46–47).

Revelation 11:1–19

"MY TWO WITNESSES"

The militaristic and triumphant messiah of 4 Ezra 13 and the two witnesses in Revelation 11 share a number of thematic similarities.

Figure 10.1: Shared Features in 4 Ezra 13 and Revelation 11

4 Ezra 13	Revelation 11
Unexplained appearance of the man from the sea (13:1–3)	Unexplained appearance of witnesses (11:13)
Flying with the clouds (13:3)	Heavenly journey on a cloud (11:12)
Victory in battle through violence and fire (13:10)	Ability to kill with fire those who wish them harm (11:5)
Standing upon Zion (13:35–36)	Located in Jerusalem (11:8)
Expectation of Zion's future coming (13:36)	Temple imagery anticipates the New Jerusalem (11:1–2, 19; 21:1)
Eschatological opposition from the frightened multitude (13:5)	Eschatological opposition and the nations (11:7)

Both of these scenes describe events that immediately precede the end, narrating the roles of eschatological figures who travel via clouds. The narrated events occur in Jerusalem (at least figuratively), and both the witnesses and the man from the sea are opposed by large groups. Connecting the actions of Revelation's witnesses to an eschatological figure in a nearly contemporaneous work unburdens the witnesses from the hegemony of the unfamiliar in ways that help us comprehend what is at the outset a challenging text.

Passive Resistance. The relationship between 4 Ezra and Revelation 11 is not direct, as their many differences indicate, differences that also backlight our understanding of one of Revelation's dramatic visions of the end. The primary difference between these traditions is the way in which their respective conflicts play out. In 4 Ezra 13, the man, perched upon the high ground of a mountain, roundly defeats the vast multitude gathered against him, reducing them to dust and smoke. The man then calls to himself a peaceable multitude, symbolically reconstituting Israel around Zion and decisively ending exile in its most seemingly irreversible form. He is a victorious conqueror who enacts the long-awaited end of exile. The two witnesses in Revelation 11, in contrast, are entirely passive despite their enumerated abilities. The narrator indicates that they *can* kill their enemies, but there is no report that they do so. They have authority to shut the heavens, but they never do. Even in their conflict with the beast from the abyss they are easily conquerable passive objects (11:7). Their resurrection too is enacted by an outside force, through their corpses' passive acceptance of a spirit of life from God (11:11). The witnesses model Revelation's response to eschatological violence and the consequences of cosmic warfare: passive resistance despite aggressive options leads to eventual victory wrought through the agency of God. The militaristic messiah of 4 Ezra differs from the passive models of resistance inherent in Revelation's messiah (a slain lamb) and its construal of effective prophetic witness.

Deferred Judgment. This idea controls also how the stories differ in their conceptions of the end. The vision in 4 Ezra 13 concludes with the graphic destruction of the man's enemies and the gathering of a peaceable multitude, acts which are interpreted as the messiah's prophetic judgment of ungodly nations (13:37–38) and the end of exile. In this text, it is the messiah who efficiently enacts judgment and reconstitutes God's people following militaristic conflict. The story in Revelation 11 is more nuanced, focusing instead on two prophetic figures who follow a messianic model based on Jesus's actions, but who are not messiahs themselves. The end is authorized by the seventh angel's trumpet blast (11:15), not the direct actions of the witnesses, which leads to the in-breaking of the kingdom of God, worship in heaven, the opening of the heavenly temple, and cataclysms. The book as a whole is leading up to the advent of the New Jerusalem in chapters 21–22, but chapter 11 gives the impression that the end is characterized by a sudden fit of judgment (11:18), the blurring of lines between heaven and earth, and the reign of God and his Messiah (11:15). The mechanics of the end differ in these traditions.

Despite the lack of direct literary relationships between Revelation 11 and 4 Ezra 13, these texts share a number of conceptual similarities that contextualize the acts of the two witnesses and the consequences of their actions. The similarities explain their powerful abilities and highlight the unexpectedness of their unwillingness to use them, as well as the surprise that they are defeated by the beast. Their experience of resurrection, leading to the coming of the kingdom, is influenced, however, not by a scenario similar to 4 Ezra 13 but by the life of Jesus, who is also snatched to heaven away from the red dragon in chapter 12 and who returns as a conquering rider in chapter 19. Even though he is identified only in an oblique way once in the chapter (11:15), Jesus remains a central figure that determines the contours of the narrative and eschatological scenario of which the witnesses are a part, even if their prophetic ministry is closely connected to Elijah as the prototypical eschatological prophet.

FOR FURTHER READING

Additional Ancient Texts

A number of other meaningful parallels between Revelation 11 and Second Temple Jewish literature exist. The most obvious are heavenly measurement traditions deriving from Ezekiel 40–48, located also in the *New Jerusalem* text from Qumran (1Q32, 2Q24, 4Q554, 4Q554a[?], 4Q555, 5Q15, 11Q18),[6] Temple Scroll, and 1 Enoch 61:1–5. These traditions focus on boundedness and protection, although there is functional diversity within the deployments of this tradition. Another more obscure tradition relates to the ark of the covenant, most obviously observed in texts like 2 Maccabees 2:6–8 and 2 Baruch 6:1–9. This tradition is mainly concerned with the end of exile and the recovery of the heritage of pre-exilic Israel. More concretely, Revelation 11:4 alludes to Zechariah 4:14, a locution that is also alluded to in a fragmentary manuscript from Qumran—4QCommentary on Genesis C (4Q254 4). Elijah traditions (cf. 1 Kgs 17:1–19:18) are also connected to shared traditions in Revelation 11 and 4 Ezra. See, for example, examples of Elijah as an eschatological prophet par excellence in early Judaism and Christianity (e.g., Mark 9:9–13; 15:35; Luke 1:17; 4:25–27; 9:8; cf. Deut 18:18; Mal 4:5–6).

---

6. Cf. Lorenzo DiTommaso, *The Dead Sea* New Jerusalem *Text*, TSAJ 110 (Tübingen: Mohr Siebeck, 2005).

English Translations and Critical Editions

NETS (2 Esdras)

NRSV (2 Esdras)

Metzger, Bruce M. "The Fourth Book of Ezra: A New Translation and Introduction." Pages 517–59 in vol. 1 of *The Old Testament Pseudepigrapha*. Edited by James H. Charlesworth. Garden City, NY: Doubleday, 1985.

Wong, Andy, with Ken M. Penner and David M. Miller, eds. "4 Ezra." In *The Online Critical Pseudepigrapha*. Edited by Ken M. Penner and Ian W. Scott. 1st ed. Atlanta: Society of Biblical Literature, 2010. www.purl .org/net/ocp/4Ezra.

Secondary Literature

Allen, Garrick V. *The Book of Revelation and Early Jewish Textual Culture*. Cambridge: Cambridge University Press, 2017.

———. "The Reuse of Scripture in 4QCommentary on Genesis C (4Q254) and 'Messianic Interpretation' in the Dead Sea Scrolls." *RevQ* 27 (2015): 303–17.

Herms, Ronald. *An Apocalypse for the Church and for the World: The Narrative Function of Universal Language in the Book of Revelation*. BZNW 143. Berlin: de Gruyter, 2006.

Stone, Michael E. *Fourth Ezra*. Hermeneia: A Critical and Historical Commentary on the Bible. Minneapolis: Fortress, 1990.

CHAPTER 11

The Life of Adam and Eve and Revelation 12:1–17: The Rebellion of the Satan Figure

ARCHIE T. WRIGHT

There are only a few possible instances in biblical and early Jewish literature where one reads about the fall of the Satan figure. Scholars have proposed that Ezekiel 28:11–19 and Isaiah 14:3–20 describe the fall of Satan due to his pride, but the exegetical evidence suggests on both occasions the authors are talking about a human king. A third text that is thought to describe the fall of Satan is Luke 10:18, though a case may be argued this is a prophetic announcement by Jesus of an eschatological event (perhaps Rev 12) or other possible interpretations. The Satan/devil figure is mentioned several other times in the New Testament, but as noted, rarely is anything said about his so-called fall from glory. Revelation 12 is one of those occasions.

Another text that describes the fall of Satan is the Life of Adam and Eve 12:1–17. The Life of Adam and Eve offers significant parallels—concepts, vocabulary, imagery—to Revelation 12. As we will see, these parallels not only provide significant context for the study of Revelation but also suggest the author of Revelation was likely aware of the tradition used in this early Jewish account of Adam and Eve.

The Life of Adam and Eve

"BECAUSE OF YOU I WAS CAST OUT ONTO THE EARTH"

The Life of Adam and Eve is primarily a midrashic interpretation of Genesis 3–5 that provides readers with a vision of the post-garden experiences of

Adam and Eve.[1] Although Slavonic and Armenian manuscripts exist, the earliest known accounts of the stories have been transmitted in a Greek text (LAE or Apoc. Mos.) and a Latin text (*Vita*). *Vita* survives in several manuscripts, the earliest of which dates to the ninth century AD and others from the fourteenth and fifteenth. Several scholars suggest there was an original Hebrew text from the first century BC from which a Greek translation was written in the first century AD.[2] The Latin text is likely translated from the Greek, but possibly also from the Hebrew, between the second and fourth centuries AD.[3] However, the significant differences between the content of the Greek and Latin versions suggest a complicated translation process.

The Function of Angels. Both versions of the Life of Adam and Eve describe the events in the garden with significant details not present in Genesis. There are noteworthy references to angelic beings, including four archangels[4] and the leader Michael.[5] Michael performs important functions, including escorting the body and soul of Adam after his death (*Vita* 22:2). He also serves as the primary messenger between God and humanity (LAE 2:1; 3:2; 49:2). He appears to follow a similar role of the chief angelic being seen in Revelation 12.

The Function of Satan. In addition to describing good angels, LAE and *Vita* also refer numerous times to the Satan/devil figure. One of this figure's main functions or tasks is to inspire humanity to sin through "his evil poison, which is his covetousness" (LAE 19:3; 25:4; 28:3; *Vita* 15:3; 17:1). He is also responsible for various sicknesses in the natural world, along with death (LAE 2:4; 14:2; 8:2; 10–12; 20:3; *Vita* 34–35; 37–39).[6] *Vita* 17:1 points out that one other function of Satan, at least according to the cry of Adam, is that he seeks to destroy the souls of humanity. Deception is clearly his primary mode of operation, for we are told Satan disguises himself with the brilliance of an angel in his second effort to entice Eve to turn from the path of the Lord (*Vita* 9:1–5; cf. "messenger of light," 2 Cor 11:14).

---

1. The term "midrash" suggests an exegesis of a biblical text more deeply than in the mere historical-critical sense. The author endeavors to comprehend the spirit of the Scriptures, while examining the passages from various angles and offering an interpretation not immediately apparent.

2. M. D. Johnson, "Life of Adam and Eve," in *The Old Testament Pseudepigrapha*, vol. 2, ed. James H. Charlesworth (New York: Doubleday, 1985), 251.

3. *Vita* 29:8 refers to a Jewish second temple without any discussion of its destruction, which suggests the base text may have been pre-AD 70 and the destruction of the Jerusalem Temple by the Romans. It should be noted, though, that this is not the most reliable Latin manuscript.

4. LAE 32; 40:2; *Vita* 21:2; 22:2; 41:1; 46:3.

5. LAE 2:1; 3:2; 7:2; 17:1; 22; 33:3; 36:1, 3; 37:3–6; 49:2.

6. All translations of the Life of Adam and Eve are mine.

The Fall of Satan. One of the major content differences between the two versions is the inclusion of the account of the fall of Satan in the Latin *Vita* (12:1–17:3), which is missing in the Greek LAE. The Satan account in *Vita* affirms Satan is a preexistent fallen angel, but preexistent only in relation to humanity, not necessarily in relation to the creation event itself. In this account the devil himself describes the reason for his fall from heaven—he blames Adam for this catastrophe ("because of you I was cast out onto the earth," 12:1). In *Vita* 13:2, the devil explains that when humanity (Adam) was created, God blew into Adam the breath of life, and he was created in the image of God. Michael, the chief archangel in heaven, brought Adam before all the angels and made the angels worship Adam in the presence of God (13:3). Michael sets the example for the angels as he "worships the image of the Lord God" and then calls on the devil to "worship the image of God, YHWH."

The devil, however, refuses Michael's instruction, stating, "I do not worship Adam." Nevertheless, Michael continues to compel him and others to do so (14:2–3). The devil then states his reason for refusing: "I will not worship one who is inferior to me, who was created after me; therefore, he should worship me." The author states that the devil has angels who operate under him (15:1), and they too refuse to worship Adam. Michael gives them another opportunity to worship Adam or face the wrath of the Lord (15:2). The devil responds with a threat of utter rebellion in which he states he "will set his throne about the stars of heaven and will be like the Most High" (15:3). This may allude to a tradition of rebellion expressed in Isaiah 14:13–14 in which the king of Babylon sets his throne above the throne of God. In *Vita* 16:1, the devil states that because of this rebellion, the Lord sent the devil and his angels out from the glory of heaven, which had been theirs until that day, and cast them on the earth (cf. Rev 12:8–9). As we will see, this account provides potential background for the vision reported in Revelation 12.

Revelation 12:1–17

"THE GREAT DRAGON WAS HURLED DOWN"

The Story of the Woman and the Dragon. Our passage appears to springboard off of Revelation 11:19 rather than beginning at 12:1.[7] In 11:19, the author

---

7. Revelation 11:19 is read in the lectionary of the Catholic Church along with 12:1–6, 10 during the feast of the Assumption of the Blessed Virgin Mary.

creates a setting for the first great sign to emerge in heaven through the opening of God's heavenly temple and the appearance of the ark of the covenant. At this point, there are great rumblings in the heavens and an earthquake, and the "great sign" was seen in heaven, which was of a woman described in apocalyptic terminology—she is clothed with the sun, with the moon under her feet, and upon her head is a crown of twelve stars (12:1), and she was about to give birth (12:2). The woman represents the protagonist in the story.

The author then states that a second great sign was seen in the heavens, that of the antagonist in 12:3. This figure is described as a great red dragon with seven heads, ten horns, and seven crowns upon his heads. The great dragon is identified in 12:9 as "the ancient serpent called the devil, or Satan."[8] In 12:4, we are told that "its tail swept a third of the stars out of the sky and flung them to the earth." The author then states that the woman of the first great sign gives birth to a male child who will rule over the nations with an iron scepter (12:5). But the child is "snatched up" and taken to God; we are not told by whom or what.

The Fall of Satan. The most relevant section of this passage for our purposes begins at Revelation 12:7. Although Revelation 12:7–9 seems to be an aside inserted into the story about the woman and the dragon, which is the main story line in Revelation 12, here the fall of Satan is briefly narrated. The author speaks of a war breaking out in heaven between Michael the archangel and his group of angels against the dragon/Satan and his angels (12:7). However, the dragon and his angels are defeated and cast out of heaven: "But he [the dragon] was not strong enough, and they lost their place in heaven. The great dragon was hurled down—that ancient serpent called the devil, or Satan, who leads the whole world astray. He was hurled to the earth, and his angels with him" (12:8–9). The celebratory proclamation of the defeat of the Dragon occurs in 12:10, where the author hears of the arrival of the salvation and power of the kingdom of God and the authority of the Messiah.

The Function of Satan. In this passage we are also told of the function of Satan. He is identified as the one "who leads the whole world astray" (12:9). His function is to deceive humanity, causing them to turn away from God and his will. He is also the accuser of humanity. Interestingly, the author perhaps alludes to the Satan figure in the Old Testament: "the accuser . . . accuses them before our God day and night" (12:10), just as Satan did as a member of the divine court in Job 1–2 and Zechariah 3. Curiously, here in

---

8. "Dragon" is used in the NT thirteen times, and only in John's Apocalypse (12:3, 4, 7 [2x], 9, 13, 16, 17; 13:2, 4, 11; 16:13; 20:2).

Revelation 12 the author switches back and forth between devil, Satan, dragon, and serpent without any clarification as to why, which suggests these are all referring to a similar being with a similar function from several different traditions, representing a chief evil figure.

Fortunately, for the believers in Revelation, they conquered the devil by the blood of Christ on the cross (12:11). Unfortunately for them, the devil has come down to the earth with great wrath because he knows he has little time left in his role (cf. Luke 10:18; John 12:31). The great dragon, seeing that he was now confined to the earth, pursues the woman (Rev 12:13). But she is given two wings of the great eagle and is able to escape from the presence of the serpent, and she appears to be protected for a certain period of time: "a time, times and half a time" (12:14). The serpent attempts to entrap the woman by spewing water like a river from its mouth (12:15). But the earth assists the woman by swallowing the river that the dragon has poured out of its mouth (12:16). As a result, the dragon becomes angry with the woman and goes off to make war against her children (12:17), which the language suggests are the followers of Christ, not the male child previously born.

Key Parallels. In summary, several important parallels between Revelation 12 and the Life of Adam and Eve are worth noting. Revelation 12:9 notes that Satan is the deceiver of the whole world; in *Vita* 9, his function is described as one who deceives (also *LAE* 29.17), for he tricks Eve into believing that God is allowing her to come out of the River Tigris and end her period of repentance. Revelation 12:17 states that the dragon/devil would go out and make war against the children of the woman; we find a possible allusion to this in *Vita* 17:1–2, which states the devil is going out to destroy the souls of humanity because he has been cast out of heaven.

Both texts present the Satan figure as a rebellious angel. This is communicated in the Life of Adam and Eve apparently at the beginning of his mission, and in Revelation 12 it could be understood as the end of his mission. The function of the figure is similar in each of the texts—he is the deceiver of humanity, he is the accuser of humanity, and his goal is to turn people away from God's good plan. Both texts present a hierarchy of angelic beings who work with the sovereignty and authority of God, who resides in the heavenly realm. The anthropology of the Life of Adam and Eve suggests humanity is created in the image of YHWH (clearly in *Vita*) and the same is assumed in Revelation 12 in light of other New Testament passages. The fall of Satan from heaven is given no clear explanation in John's Apocalypse, but the Life of Adam and Eve provides some background as to why the war broke out in heaven and why Satan and his angels are cast down to earth.

FOR FURTHER READING

Additional Ancient Texts

The following texts describe heavenly beings or spirits that have a similar role to that of the Satan figure in early Christianity. Although there are no direct parallels, they demonstrate the developing worldview in which evil spiritual beings function within the human realm: 11Q13 9–15; 1QS I, III; 1QM 15–19; Testament of Levi 3; 18; Testament of Simeon 6:6; Testament of Dan 5; 2 Enoch 29 and 31; 1 Enoch 6–16 and 40; Apocalypse of Zephaniah; Jubilees 10; the Greco-Roman myth of Leto; 3 Baruch 4; Egyptian "Isis-Osiris-Horus-Typhon" myth; Sibylline Oracles 3:396–400; Daniel 7–8.

English Translations and Critical Editions

Dochhorn, Jan. *Die Apokalypse des Mose: Text, Übersetzung, Kommentar.* Tübingen: Mohr Siebeck, 2005.

Johnson, M. D. "Life of Adam and Eve." Pages 249–95 in vol. 2 of *The Old Testament Pseudepigrapha*, edited by James H. Charlesworth. 2 vols. Garden City, NY: Doubleday, 1985.

Miller, David M., and Ian W. Scott, eds. "Life of Adam and Eve." In *The Online Critical Pseudepigrapha*. Edited by Ian W. Scott, Ken M. Penner, and David M. Miller. Atlanta: Society of Biblical Literature, 2006. www.purl.org/net/ocp/AdamEve.

Tromp, Johannes. *The Life of Adam and Eve in Greek: A Critical Edition*. Leiden: Brill, 2005.

Secondary Literature

Anderson, Gary, and Michael E. Stone, eds. *A Synopsis of the Books of Adam and Eve*. 2nd ed. SBL Early Judaism and Its Literature 17. Atlanta: Scholars, 1999.

Harkins, Angela Kim, Kelley Coblentz Bautch, and John C. Endres, S. J. *The Fallen Angel Traditions*. CBQMS 53. Washington, DC: Catholic Biblical Association, 2014.

Heiser, Michael S. *The Unseen Realm*. Bellingham, WA: Lexham, 2015.

Levison, John R. "The Life of Adam and Eve." Pages 445–61 in vol. 1 of *Early Jewish Literature: An Anthology*. Edited by Brad Embry, Ronald Herms, and Archie T. Wright. Grand Rapids: Eerdmans, 2018.

Reed, Annette Yoshiko. *Fallen Angels and the History of Judaism and Christianity*. Cambridge: Cambridge University Press, 2005.

Russell, Jeffrey B. *Satan: The Early Christian Tradition*. Ithaca, NY: Cornell University Press, 1981.

Stone, Michael E. *A History of the Literature of Adam and Eve*. SBLEJL 3. Atlanta: Scholars Press, 1992.

Tromp, Johannes. *The Life of Adam and Eve and Related Literature*. Sheffield: Sheffield Academic, 1997.

CHAPTER 12

4 Ezra and Revelation 13:1–18: Blasphemous Beasts

JAMIE DAVIES

In Revelation 13, we find John's vision of the beast, an image made famous by its presence as a trope in supernatural horror movies and heavy metal music.[1] Though John's is perhaps the most well-known, bestial visions like this are not uncommon in Jewish and Christian apocalyptic literature. In Daniel 7, for example, "four great beasts . . . came up out of the sea," resembling a winged lion, a bear, a leopard, and a terrifying horned creature (7:3–8). Each beast meets its judgment before the Ancient of Days and the "one like a son of man" (7:13), whose dominion is everlasting. Daniel is troubled by his vision, but his angelic guide interprets it for him. The four beasts are depictions of four rulers of earthly kingdoms (usually interpreted as Babylonian, Median, Persian, and Greek) which are met by the authority of the reign of God and his holy ones.

This is how apocalyptic beast visions work: they concern the conflict between oppressive political powers and the kingdom of God. These depictions of political realities, as with all apocalyptic imagery, function not as a coded system of symbols that can be neatly unpacked into prose, but as transformative imagery that changes how we imagine our world and its systems. They are a powerful form of anti-imperial political theology exposing deceptive imperial propaganda.[2] Revelation 13 is no exception, but before we turn to that passage, we shall first consider another text that uses similar beast imagery, 4 Ezra 11.

---

1. E.g., "The Omen" (Richard Donner, 20th Century Fox, 1976); Iron Maiden, "The Number of the Beast" (Steve Harris, EMI Records, 1982).

2. For an excellent discussion of this, see Anathea Portier-Young, *Apocalypse Against Empire: Theologies of Resistance in Early Judaism* (Grand Rapids: Eerdmans, 2011).

4 Ezra

"An eagle that had twelve feathered wings and three heads"

Fourth Ezra is an apocalypse composed after the collapse of the temple in Jerusalem, likely during the oppressive reign of Domitian (AD 81–96).[3] It recounts a series of seven visions as "Ezra" wrestles with the question of God's justice in the face of his people's suffering. The fifth of the seven is the dream-vision of chapters 11 and 12. Like that of his "brother Daniel" (12:11), Ezra's vision concerns the question of world-dominating kingdoms.

The Eagle from the Sea. In 11:1–35, Ezra has a dream and sees "an eagle that had twelve feathered wings and three heads" which "spread his wings over all the earth" (11:1–2).[4] It takes flight "to reign over the earth and over those who dwell in it" (11:5), bringing the whole world into subjugation. The wings and heads of the monstrous bird are described in complex detail, each wing sprouting other wings, large and small, which reign over the earth in succession, some at length and some briefly (11:11–29). One of the three heads, which had been resting, wakes and forms an alliance with the other two, devouring the little wings, and "this head gained control of the whole earth, and with much oppression dominated its inhabitants" (11:32). But then suddenly this head disappears, leaving two. One is then devoured by the other, leaving the remaining head as sole ruler.

Though identifying the historical references behind the bewildering series of wings and heads has been difficult, commentators have not struggled to identify the main referent, for the eagle was (literally) a standard symbol for the Roman Empire.[5] The series of wings and heads indicate the succession of emperors from Julius Caesar to the end of the Flavian dynasty.[6]

The Lion from the Forest. A second creature then enters the scene (11:36–12:3). Looking again, Ezra sees that "a creature like a lion was aroused out of the forest, roaring" (11:37). Its voice, however, is that of a man, and it confronts the eagle with a judicial proclamation from the Most High:

---

3. For more information about 4 Ezra, see chapter 4 in this volume by Dana M. Harris ("4 Ezra and Revelation 5:1–14: Creaturely Images of the Messiah").

4. All English translations of 4 Ezra are from Bruce M. Metzger, "The Fourth Book of Ezra: A New Translation and Introduction," in vol. 1 of *The Old Testament Pseudepigrapha*, ed. James H. Charlesworth (Garden City, NY: Doubleday, 1985), 517–59.

5. Battle standards carried by the Roman legions took the form of an eagle.

6. The three Flavian emperors, identified by many with the three heads of the eagle, were Vespasian (AD 69–79), Titus (AD 79–81), and Domitian (AD 81–96). The last of these was known particularly for his cruelty. See, e.g., Michael Stone, *Fourth Ezra*, Hermeneia (Minneapolis: Fortress, 1990), 10, 361–65.

Are you not the one that remains of the four beasts which I had made to reign in my world, so that the end of my times might come through them? You, the fourth that has come, have conquered all the beasts that have gone before; and you have held sway over the world with much terror, and over all the earth with grievous oppression . . . you have judged the earth, but not with truth; for you have afflicted the meek and injured the peaceable. . . . And so your insolence has come up before the Most High, and your pride to the Mighty One. And the Most High has looked upon his times, and behold, they are ended, and his ages are completed! Therefore you will surely disappear, you eagle . . . so that the whole earth, freed from your violence, may be refreshed and relieved, and may hope for the judgement and mercy of him who made it. (11:38–46)

These words of the lion bring about the disappearance of the eagle's remaining head (12:1), leading to a period of tumult before "the whole body of the eagle was burned" (12:3).

Ezra awakes, perplexed and exhausted from his dream, and asks the Lord for an interpretation. Just as it is not difficult to identify the eagle as Rome, reinterpreting Daniel's "fourth kingdom" (12:11), so the image of the lion has an obvious referent, which the interpretation makes clear. This is the Lion of the tribe of Judah, "the Messiah whom the Most High has kept until the end of days, who will arise from the posterity of David" (12:32). He comes to judge and reprove the eagle, to set it before the judgment seat of the Most High, and finally to destroy it. He comes also to bring mercy and deliverance for the remnant of the people of God who have endured its oppression. Thus the imperial eagle is overthrown by the anointed ruler of God's kingdom, bringing relief to a world ruled by violence.

Revelation 13:1–18

"AND I SAW A BEAST COMING OUT OF THE SEA"

And so we come to Revelation 13, a vision of not one but three beasts. The first, the dragon, has already been introduced and identified as "that ancient serpent, who is called the devil, or Satan" (12:9). As chapter 13 opens, the dragon has been thrown down to earth and has taken his stand "on the shore of the sea" (13:1). He remains in the scene, then, as John witnesses

118

the arrival of the first of two more monstrous beasts, one from the sea and one from the earth, like ancient Leviathan and Behemoth.[7]

The Beast from the Sea. The echoes of the four beasts of Daniel 7 are again clear in the imagery John uses to describe this first beast, which, like the eagle of 4 Ezra, comes up out of the sea (Rev 13:1–10). But unlike the eagle, which is identified as the fourth of Daniel's beasts, John's vision seems to combine aspects of all four. The seven-headed, ten-horned sea-beast is like "a leopard, but had feet like those of a bear and a mouth like that of a lion" (13:2). If this is a depiction of a political kingdom, as we should expect, then it is not merely the latest in a succession of empires but one that embodies the worst of them all.

This beast, we are told, makes war on the saints and conquers them, and receives global authority (13:7). Its power, however, runs deeper than mere political and military victory, for the inhabitants of the earth not only follow the beast, but worship it. This act parodies the rhetorical question reserved, in the hymns of the Old Testament, for God alone: "Who is like the beast? Who can wage war against it?" (13:4).[8] This is a worldview-transforming depiction of the Roman Empire, which, under the promise of a "golden age,"[9] not only conquered the known world by its military and political dominance but was buttressed (especially in its eastern provinces) by the imperial cult: worship offered to the emperor himself.

The Beast from the Earth. The blasphemous nature of the beast, indicated by the names on its heads (13:1) and the words from its mouth (13:5), is further underlined when the second of the two beasts comes on the scene (13:11–18). Rising up from the earth, this beast has the horns of a lamb but speaks like a dragon. Its purpose is religious, enforcing worship, deceiving through the performance of great signs (including, like Elijah in 1 Kgs 18:38, calling fire from heaven), and instructing idolatry (Rev 13:12–15). In ancient Rome, religious practice was not separated from economic and political life. So too with the earth-beast: in order to buy or sell, all people are made to bear the mark of the beast, 666.

This, John tells us, calls for wisdom and understanding. But where is such wisdom and understanding to be found? John gives us a clue—it is

---

7. These two beasts, one from the sea and one from the earth, are commonplace in ancient Jewish literature (e.g., Job 40:15–41:34) and reflect imagery found in many ancient creation accounts. Fourth Ezra 6:49–52 also mentions them.

8. Cf., e.g., Exod 15:11; Ps. 35:10; 89:6.

9. The Latin *aurea saecula* was a widespread motif in Roman literature and propaganda, signifying the promise of a prosperous communal life with peace for all and plenteous supplies of food.

"the number of a man" (13:18)—but beyond that we are in danger of being lost in a swamp of speculation. Some ancient evidence comes to our aid. Preserved on a wall in the ruins of Pompeii is a romantic confession: "I love her whose number is 545." This ancient graffito is an example of a commonly used practice called *gematria*. In ancient Hebrew, Greek, and Latin, letters were used for numbers, and fun could be had in giving numerical values to words and names. The letters of "Caesar Nero" (*nerōn kaisar*), transliterated into Hebrew from Greek and their values added together, gives 666.[10] Most interestingly, the alternative spelling in Greek (*nerō kaisar*) gives 616—precisely the variant we find in some manuscripts of Revelation 13:18. Since the chances of exactly these variations coinciding are very slim, most scholars are convinced the name behind the number 666 is that of Nero, Roman emperor and infamous persecutor of Christians.

Figure 12.1: The Gematria System[1]

Neron Kaisar	Nero Kaisar
N/נ = 50	N/נ = 50
R/ר = 200	R/ר = 200
Ō/ו = 6	Ō/ו = 6
N/נ = 50	
K/ק = 100	K/ק = 100
S/ס = 60	S/ס = 60
R/ר = 200	R/ר = 200
666	616

[1] Adapted from Wilson, *Charts on the Book of Revelation*, 86.

But the point, remember, is not to convert the apocalyptic imagery into prose, like cracking a code, but to consider these historical references while recognizing the power of the images *as images*. The effect of this vision on John's understanding of his world goes beyond the mere identification of the beasts. It reshapes how these powers are imagined, not as the bringers of "peace and security" they claim to be,[11] but as blasphemous beasts. The relationship between them drives this imaginative critique still deeper. The sea-beast's source of power and authority is not merely its own political and military strength but also the satanic dragon's (13:2, 4). The sea-beast shares this authority with the earth-beast, who acts on its behalf (13:12, 14), speaking "like a dragon" (13:11), and making the inhabitants of the earth worship the sea-beast (13:12). Thus the three are closely related, like an unholy trinity, the blasphemous power at the heart of the kingdom of this world.

In conclusion, reading Revelation 13 in the context of 4 Ezra 11 provides

---

10. This is also the result of adding up the values of the transliterated word for "beast," *thērion*. For a chart of the *gematria* system, and many other useful things, see Mark Wilson, *Charts on the Book of Revelation* (Grand Rapids: Kregel, 2007), 85.

11. The Latin *pax et securitas* is possibly an imperial catchphrase. Cf. 1 Thess 5:3.

some interesting insights. Like Daniel before them, they both portray empire in bestial and arrogant imagery, transforming the Christian political imagination. They are excellent examples of how such imagery should be read. Endless decodings and wild speculation have plagued modern interpretation, as interpreters seek to work out which modern political leader is encoded by Revelation's beast. Comparison with other apocalypses, such as 4 Ezra, helps us to see that the primary reference for this imagery is found in the first century, not the twenty-first.

But that is not to say that the meaning of the symbol is consigned to ancient history. Revelation's imagery has a "surplus of meaning" that makes it continually powerful.[12] Any political leader, or system, pronouncing "proud words and blasphemies" (13:5), promising a golden age and demanding allegiance, should be reimagined as a bestial and ungodly power, possibly one whose authority comes from the dragon. When such bestial idolatry is revealed, faithful witness is required in response. "This," as John says in 13:10, "calls for patient endurance and faithfulness on the part of God's people."

For Further Reading

Additional Ancient Texts

In addition to the seminal vision of Daniel 7, there are other ancient apocalyptic writings which contain the use of bestial imagery. For example, animal imagery is deployed to speak of worldly kingdoms and the history of Israel in 1 Enoch 85–90 (often called the "Animal Apocalypse"). The book of 2 Baruch, 4 Ezra's "sister apocalypse," uses a variety of apocalyptic imagery for similar ends. See, for example, the "Apocalypse of the Forest" in chapters 35–43 and the "Cloud Apocalypse" of 53–74. The *Aeneid*, an epic poem by Virgil, is one of the most important texts for exploring the self-understanding of the Roman Empire. The end of Book 6 contains the famous lines telling how the "golden age" will be brought about by the rule of Augustus, the "son of a god."

English Translations and Critical Editions

NETS (2 Esdras)
NRSV (2 Esdras)

---

12. Richard Bauckham, *The Theology of the Book of Revelation* (Cambridge: Cambridge University Press, 1993), 10.

Metzger, Bruce M. "The Fourth Book of Ezra: A New Translation and Intro-
    duction." Pages 517–59 in vol. 1 of *The Old Testament Pseudepigrapha*.
    Edited by James H. Charlesworth. Garden City, NY: Doubleday, 1985.
Wong, Andy, with Ken M. Penner and David M. Miller, eds. "4 Ezra."
    In *The Online Critical Pseudepigrapha*. Edited by Ken M. Penner and Ian
    W. Scott. Atlanta: Society of Biblical Literature, 2010. www.purl.org/
    net/ocp/4Ezra.

Secondary Literature

Bauckham, Richard. *The Theology of the Book of Revelation*. Cambridge:
    Cambridge University Press, 1993.
Blount, Brian K. *Can I Get a Witness? Reading Revelation Through African
    American Culture*. Louisville: Westminster John Knox, 2005.
Gorman, Michael J. *Reading Revelation Responsibly*. Eugene, OR: Cascade,
    2011.
Hays, Richard B., and Stefan Alkier, eds. *Revelation and the Politics of
    Apocalyptic Interpretation*. Waco: Baylor University Press, 2012.
Koester, Craig R. *Revelation and the End of All Things*. 2nd ed. Grand Rapids:
    Eerdmans, 2018.
Kraybill, J. Nelson. *Apocalypse and Allegiance*. Grand Rapids: Brazos, 2010.
Stone, Michael E. *Fourth Ezra*. Hermeneia. Minneapolis: Fortress, 1990.

CHAPTER 13

The Damascus Document and Revelation 14:1–20: Angels Marking Out the Two Ways

BEN C. BLACKWELL

Revelation cycles between a focus on the followers of Jesus and a focus on godless humanity, so chapter 14 does not seem distinct within the flow of the book: we first see the Lamb and the 144,000 (14:1–5) and then various angels who carry out God's judgment on the ungodly (14:6–13). However, rather than the community of the Lamb encountering general opposition from godless humanity, new demonic figures—the dragon, the beast out of the sea, and the beast out of the earth—have just arisen as the kingpins behind this opposition to God and his people (chs. 12–13). The dragon's plan is "to wage war against the [woman's] offspring—those who keep God's commands and hold fast to their testimony about Jesus" (12:17). This raises key questions: what will happen to God's people in the face of this opposition, and what will happen to the mass of humanity who follow the dragon and the beasts?

Revelation 14 explores both questions in an **apocalyptic** framework. God works out his divine plan by setting out two distinct paths: blessing for holiness and punishment for wickedness. While striking to us, this broad approach is not unique in ancient texts. A number of Second Temple Jewish texts use this type of lens as they explain how Jews were to remain faithful to the **covenant** in the face of pagan opposition. Among these texts, the Damascus Document shares some distinctive similarities with Revelation that will help us to understand our text better.

The Damascus Document

"FLAMES OF FIRE BY THE HAND OF ALL THE ANGELS OF DESTRUCTION AGAINST PERSONS TURNING ASIDE"

The Damascus Document is the only **sectarian Qumran** document that we had access to before the **Dead Sea Scrolls** were discovered. This text was found in the Cairo Genizah of the Ben Ezra Synagogue in the late nineteenth century,[1] but its original provenance is that of the Qumran community (or one like it).[2] (Its abbreviation is CD for Cairo Damascus document.) Many of the Qumran texts circulated among a variety of Jewish groups and are thus described as nonsectarian texts. In contrast, the Damascus Document and texts like Community Rule (1QS), the War Scroll (1QM), and the Hodayot (1QH^a) are sectarian texts, in that they point to the distinct identity of separatist Jewish groups like the Qumran community over against other Jewish groups.[3] Set within a larger salvation-historical framework, the Damascus Document explains the theological justification for the covenant community and gives rules on how to live as part of this community.

Contrasting the Two Ways. Drawing from the history of exile and (partial) return detailed in the Old Testament prophets, this community sees themselves as the faithful heirs to the covenants. The wickedness of the nations is a given, so the text focuses on the division between Jews who truly keep the covenant by following the Teacher of Righteousness and those Jews who only do so partially (and thus unfaithfully). The consequence of the unfaithfulness of this latter group is that "the curses of his covenant would adhere to them, to deliver them up to the sword carrying out the vengeance of the covenant" (CD 1:17–18).[4]

The text continues by describing the unfaithful leaders (most likely the Pharisees) and the nature of their community:

For they sought easy interpretations, chose illusions, scrutinized loopholes, chose the handsome neck, acquitted the guilty and sen-

---

1. A genizah is a (temporary) storage area for sacred texts waiting to be buried in a cemetery that have worn out or are no longer in use.

2. Though the Cairo scrolls date from the Middle Ages (tenth–twelfth centuries AD), the original text dates back to the Second Temple period since we have found ten manuscripts from Qumran (4Q266–73; 5Q12; 6Q15).

3. John J. Collins, *Beyond the Qumran Community: The Sectarian Movement of the Dead Sea Scrolls* (Grand Rapids: Eerdmans, 2009).

4. Translations of the *Damascus Document* are from Florentino García Martínez and Elbert J. C. Tigchelaar, eds., *The Dead Sea Scrolls: Study Edition*, vol. 1 (Grand Rapids: Eerdmans, 1997).

tenced the just, violated the covenant, broke the precept, banded together against the life of the just man, their soul abominated all those who walk in perfection, they hunted them down with the sword and provoked the dispute of the people. And kindled was the wrath of God against their congregation, laying waste all its great number, for their deeds were unclean in front of him. (CD 1.18–2.1)

Besides their general immorality, these unfaithful people persecuted the righteous community. As a result, God's wrath in the form of covenant curses was poured out on them and brought their destruction. The Damascus Document contrasts those who experience God's forgiveness and those who will be punished:

God loves knowledge . . .; patience is his and abundance of pardon, to atone for persons who repent from wickedness; however, strength and power and a great anger with flames of fire by the [hand] of all the angels of destruction against persons turning aside from the path and abominating the precept, without there being for them either a remnant or survivor. For God did not choose them at the beginning of the world, and before they were established he knew their deeds, and abominated the generations on account of blood and hid his face from the country, from [Israel], until their extinction. (CD 2.3–9)

God provides forgiveness for those who repent when they break the covenant, but the experience of exile showed that the greater portion of Israel was unrepentant.

Overlapping Agencies: Divine, Angelic, and Human. Damascus Document 2.3–9 highlights a distinct tension between divine and human agency. (By "agency" I mean willing and acting, as in discussions of divine sovereignty and human free will.) Holding out the hope of forgiveness for those who do repent, the text implies that humans have the agency to turn and receive God's pardon. However, we see a more deterministic perspective reflecting wider views in the sectarian documents: the division between the righteous and unrighteous was already in consideration at the "beginning of the world." In addition to the divine and human elements, the Damascus Document also notes how the demonic agent (Belial) "will be set loose against Israel," leading them into fornication, wealth, and defilement of the temple (CD 4.13–19). Accordingly, humans are rightly responsible for their punishment, but there are overlapping agencies involved.

This overlapping of divine, human, and angelic agency also plays a role as God's wrath is poured out through "angels of destruction." Though the text includes these angels, how they will destroy is not explicitly detailed. However, later, when the author is describing the unfaithfulness of those at Kadesh who were unwilling to enter the land (Num 13–14), he writes:

And the wrath of God flared up against their congregation. . . . Through it, the very first to enter the covenant made themselves guilty and were delivered up to the sword, for having deserted God's covenant and having chosen their whims, and having followed the stubbornness of their heart, each one doing (what was) his desire. (CD 3.8–12)

The nature of God's wrath is here described through the means of the sword. That is, God's act is by means of the human act. This is the similar type of destruction that God had just described as the result of "angels of destruction." Accordingly, we see overlapping agencies here with God working through both angelic and human agents.

The Damascus Document thus presents the community as standing against unfaithfulness, an image integrated with its perspective of God's active agency in and through angels and humans, much like we will see in Revelation.

Revelation 14:1–20

"THE ANGEL THREW THEM INTO THE GREAT WINEPRESS OF GOD'S WRATH"

Revelation 14 appeals to a type of dualism similar to what we find in the Damascus Document; however, John's narrative focuses much more on the heavenly realities that shape human events. Both texts set their discussion within a wider salvation-historical structure, which sets out to interpret the present and future through the lens of past events, like covenant formation, redemption through the plagues, and judgment in the exile.

Contrasting the Two Ways. While we may at times think of Christian engagement with culture on a sliding scale, Revelation presents a much more dualistic perspective, envisioning either a full commitment to Christ or an opposition to his kingdom. We clearly see this in Revelation 14: in contrast to those who have followed the demonic beast and taken his mark on their foreheads, the 144,000 have Jesus's and the Father's names written on their foreheads and have kept themselves pure and blameless, even remaining virgins. Undergirding this sharp distinction is the eschatological reality of judgment. All nations are called to "fear God and give him glory, because the hour of his judgment has come" (14:7). Though the apocalyptic fervor of Revelation seems focused on generating fear, it has two purposes—giving hope for the righteous and warnings for the rebellious.

The chapter sets up a picture of reversed fortunes for the righteous and unrighteous. The righteous struggle now but will be blessed later, whereas the unrighteous appear to flourish now but will receive the fullness of God's wrath soon. Turning first to the righteous, the text highlights their unique closeness with God, as they learn a song that only the redeemed know (14:3). However, their need for "patient endurance" and the blessing on those who die show that believers will likely experience persecution and martyrdom (14:12–13). Later chapters in Revelation will more fully explore their eschatological blessings. In contrast to the blessed struggle of the faithful, the angels present a stark warning against those in opposition to God. The second half of the chapter uses the imagery of wine, grape harvests, and the winepress to describe this judgment by angels. This wrath will fall on Babylon (14:8; see further in chs. 17–18) and those who worship the beast and take its mark (14:9–11). We will return to the nature of this judgment below, when we address the agency of the angels.

The dualistic vision presented here is similar to that of the Damascus Document, which also worked from a two-ways tradition. While the Damascus Document establishes a sectarian Jewish identity distinct from the larger Jewish community, in Revelation the distinction is not ethnically focused. The markedly multinational Christian community is set against a world of unbelievers. There are, however, elements of the discourse that reflect intra-Jewish debates similar to that of the Damascus Document. For example, we see the critique of "the synagogue of Satan" (Rev 2:9; 3:9), and there is the possibility that the 144,000 are Jewish believers in distinction to the wider multinational church, though many see the 144,000 as pointing to the whole (multiethnic) church.

Overlapping Agencies: Divine, Angelic, and Human. If Revelation speaks with a two-ways tradition similar to the Damascus Document, we see more differences when we consider the issue of overlapping agencies. The Damascus Document primarily highlighted God's agency while only briefly mentioning angels of destruction and Belial. By contrast, in Revelation the frequency and intensity of angelic action to express divine agency is much more pronounced.

Though the Damascus Document does not highlight angelic action, it is important to note that a unique interest in angelic action is evident among other Second Temple texts, developing the ideas found in the Old Testament (e.g., Gen 18–19; Exod 11–12). In particular, these Second Temple texts speak of angels as divine agents doing things such as revealing messages, carrying out punishment, aiding the righteous, battling evil powers, and attending God in heaven. Revelation follows strongly in that tradition.

Although other chapters in Revelation highlight demonic angels in opposition to God, chapter 14 focuses on angels carrying out God's plan. The text initially emphasizes the positive role of the angels. The four creatures (cf. 4:6–8) and a wider community of thundering angels (cf. 10:3–4; 19:6) attend to the song of the redeemed (14:2–3). Later an angel proclaims "the eternal gospel" to the earth (14:6). The greater focus in the chapter is on the successive angels who proclaim and carry out divine judgment against the wicked.

The unifying image related to this judgment in chapter 14 is wine: John envisions drinking (14:8–10), harvesting a vineyard (14:14–18), and pressing grapes (14:19–20). Though angels are foregrounded, the text is clear that they are carrying out God's plan. For example, the angelic punishment for those with the beast's mark is described as "drink[ing] the wine of *God's fury*, which has been poured full strength into the cup of *his wrath*" (14:10).[5] As the angel uses a sickle to harvest humanity, he "threw them into the great winepress of *God's wrath*" (14:19).[6] Accordingly, we see overlapping agency between God and his angels. The Damascus Document also noted the role of "angels of destruction" but did not provide anywhere near as much description of their activities as we see here and throughout Revelation.

The question of human agency is more in focus in the Damascus Document, and we see an interesting parallel to its determinism in Revelation with its description of names in the book of life "from the creation of the world" (Rev 17:8). In Revelation 14, we see human agency in terms of repentance and opposition to God. First, the call to fear and worship God implies that humans have an opportunity to respond to the grace of the Lamb (14:6–7). This also corresponds to the progressive nature of the judgments, which are revelations of God's patient call to heed his ultimate warning. However, Revelation notes that most will not repent (9:21; 16:11). Second, the wine of Babylon's adulteries initially seems like human freedom in opposition to God (14:8), but it also relates to overlapping agencies. The judgment against

---

5. Emphasis added.
6. Emphasis added.

those who have the mark of the beast comes after an angelic pronouncement against Babylon. Interestingly, the beast worshipers "too, will drink the wine of God's fury" (14:10). The use of "too" indicates that the previous judgment related to the "wine of [Babylon's] adulteries" is also the "wine of God's fury." God passively punishes people by letting them pursue their own destruction (as with Babylon's wine), and he also actively punishes people (as expressed through the winepress imagery).

When we consider the Damascus Document and Revelation 14, we see that both have similar concerns regarding a two-ways tradition and the topic of overlapping agencies. Both describe the nature of God's righteous path as based on one central teacher and how they see God working. In Revelation, engagement with the Lamb shapes how humans experience heavenly realities here on earth.

FOR FURTHER READING

Additional Ancient Texts

Many Jewish texts highlight the distinction between the righteous and wicked. The following texts focus specifically on angels as divine agents related to that distinction. The Similitudes of Enoch (1 En. 37–71), especially 53–57, show blessings for the elect and punishments for the wicked. In other texts, angels are mostly described as agents of destruction and wrath: 4QPseudo-Moses (4Q387–390) and Pseudo-Philo's LAB 15. This angelic torment is set in the afterlife in Testament of Abraham 10–14. Angels play many positive roles as well, such as Raphael helping throughout Tobit. Harvesting imagery is used in Matthew 13:24–30.

English Translations and Critical Edition

Eisenman, Robert. "The Damascus Document." Pages 355–78 in *The Dead Sea Scrolls and the First Christians: Essays and Translations*. Edison, NJ: Castle, 2004.

García Martínez, Florentino, and Eibert J. C. Tigchelaar, eds. *The Dead Sea Scrolls: Study Edition*. Volume One. Grand Rapids: Eerdmans, 1997.

Secondary Literature

deSilva, David A., "A Sociorhetorical Interpretation of Revelation 14:6–13: A Call to Act Justly toward the Just and Judging God." *BBR* 9 (1999): 65–117.

Reiterer, Friedrich V., Tobias Nicklas, and Karin Schopflin, eds., *Angels: The Concept of Celestial Beings—Origins, Development and Reception*.

Deuterocanonical and Cognate Literature Yearbook. Berlin: de Gruyter, 2007.

Sullivan, Kevin P. *Wrestling with Angels: A Study of the Relationship between Angels and Humans in Ancient Jewish Literature and the New Testament.* Leiden: Brill, 2004.

Wise, Michael O. "The Origins and History of the Teacher's Movement." Pages 92–122 in *The Oxford Handbook of the Dead Sea Scrolls.* Edited by Timothy H. Lim and John J. Collins. Oxford: Oxford University Press, 2010.

CHAPTER 14

Words of the Luminaries and Revelation 15:1–16:21: Plague Septets and Deliverance from Exile

BENJAMIN WOLD

Interpreters of John's Apocalypse have long struggled to understand his three plague septets (groups of seven): the opening of seals (chs. 6–8), blowing of trumpets (chs. 8–11), and pouring out of bowls (ch. 16). One thing that is agreed is that these visions evoke the ten plagues unleashed upon Egypt during the exodus. Allusions to the ten exodus plagues appear in the septets of seals, trumpets, and bowls in reference to: blood (Rev 8:8; 16:3–4), frogs (16:13), pestilence (6:8), boils/sores (16:2, 11), hail/fire (9:17–18; 16:8–9, 21), locusts (9:3–5), and darkness (8:12; 9:2; 16:10). But why does John refer to only seven plagues rather than all ten?

In the Old Testament and in early Jewish literature, there are several instances when the recounting of exodus plagues is shortened from ten to seven (Ps 78:44–51; 105:28–36; 3 Bar. 16:3; Wis 11–19). By referring to only seven plagues, John's Apocalypse clearly falls within this tradition. However, the way these exodus-like plagues function theologically and serve John's redemptive vision remains open to question. This chapter is concerned with how motifs related to exile in Egypt and deliverance from exile shaped John's enumeration and narration of these end-time plagues. By reading one Qumran discovery (Words of the Luminaries) alongside John's septets, the theme of exile and return in Revelation comes into sharper focus.

Words of the Luminaries

"WE CAME TO HARDSHIPS, AND PLAGUES, AND TRIALS BY THE WRATH OF THE OPPRESSOR"

Words of the Luminaries is preserved in at least two copies (4Q504, 4Q506) at Qumran and perhaps in a third (4Q505). It dates to the mid-to late-second century BC, is not a product of the Yaḥad (i.e., not "sectarian"), and before its discovery in Cave 4 was previously unknown. Words of the Luminaries is a liturgical composition structured around prayers given on each day of the week.

Echoes of Leviticus 26. This penitential work is shaped by reflection on and interpretation of several biblical passages (i.e., Exod 19; 32–34; Num 14; Ps 78; Deut 8:5; Isa 26:16; 43:24; 48:17–18). Especially notable is the sustained attention given to Leviticus 26, which is the focal point here. Leviticus 26 frames warnings about future judgment within a broader recollection of deliverance from captivity in Egypt (26:13, 45). Punishment and plagues are the result of disobedience (26:18, 25) and there are forewarnings that judgment, even exile, will be visited on Israel if they forsake God's commandments. Indeed, four times Leviticus 26 warns that God "will multiply your afflictions seven times over, as your sins deserve" (26:21; cf. 26:18, 24, 28).

Words of the Luminaries (4Q504 frags. 1–2 col. V) is concerned with interpreting and retelling the exodus, from captivity to wandering in the wilderness. This retelling is for the benefit of the author's community (which he perceives to be in a state of theological exile) and is accomplished in part by echoing Leviticus 26 throughout the passage. The column reads as follows, with the relevant allusions appearing in brackets:

> [3] And they [viz. Israel] worshiped a foreign god in their land [Lev 26:1], and their land also is [4] a desolation [Lev 26:32–33] because of their enemies, for your rage was poured out, [5] and your destroying anger in your zealous fire, to lay it waste [6] from either passing through or dwelling [Lev 26:31–32]. In all this you did not reject [7] the seed of Jacob, nor despise Israel [8] to destroy them, or to invalidate your covenant with them [Lev 26:44]. For you [9] are a living God, you alone, and there is none beside you. Remember your covenant! [10] For you brought us forth in the eyes of the nations [Lev 26:45], and did not abandon us [11] among the nations. You acted mercifully towards your people Israel, among all [12] [the] lands to which you banished them, changing [13] their hearts to return to you again and to listen

to your voice [14] [according] to all that which you commanded by the hand of Moses your servant [Lev 26:46]. [15] F[or] you have poured out your holy spirit upon us, [16] [to br]ing your blessings upon us, to heed you in our trouble, [17] [to wh]isper in the chastening of your instruction, for we came to hardships, [18] [and pl]agues [esp. Lev 26:21; cf. 26:18, 24–26], and trials by the wrath of the oppressor, for we too [19] [wea]ry God with [our] iniquities: we struck the rock in our sin, [20] [but you] forced us to leave [our] ways; in the p[ath] [21] [which we went], [and] paid no attention to yo[ur commandments].[1]

Images of Exile. The reformulation of Leviticus 26 in Words of the Luminaries 1–2 V (esp. ll. 3–9) serves at least two purposes. First, it is an important framework for giving thanks to God. Whereas in Leviticus these oracles are made as a promise by God to Israel, in Words of the Luminaries the author uses the passage to recount God's faithfulness when the people have been unfaithful. Second, and more importantly, Words of the Luminaries 1–2 V serves as a prophetic fulfilment of Leviticus 26:43: "For the land will be deserted by them and will enjoy its sabbaths while it lies desolate without them. They will pay for their sins because they rejected my laws and abhorred my decrees." Leviticus 26 looks to the future on the one hand (anticipating exile and return), while on the other it considers God's redemptive work in the past (remembering the exodus). This is apparent as Leviticus 26:44–45 continues: "Yet in spite of this, when they are in the land of their enemies [viz. exile], I will not reject them or abhor them so as to destroy them completely, breaking my covenant with them. . . . But for their sake I will remember the covenant with their ancestors whom I brought out of Egypt in the sight of the nations to be their God." Words of the Luminaries envisages that everything Leviticus 26 forewarns regarding exile has come to pass (including the Egyptian "plagues" revisited upon Israel; cf. l. 18), but that God will redeem an elect group just as he redeemed Israel from Egypt. The author represents those who undoubtedly enter into the role of those "who are left" (Lev 26:39; cf. CD 1.1–5), who confess their sins and "waste away" because of their iniquities, which caused the desolation of their land.

Throughout Words of the Luminaries 1–2 V, the author recounts the exodus and, significantly, views his own community as participating in the biblical narrative, the main motifs of which include "divine benevolence,

---

1. Author's translation based on the Hebrew in Maurice Baillet, *Qumrân Grotte 4.III (4Q482–4Q520)*, DJD 7 (Oxford: Clarendon, 1982), 14.

judgment, and new beginning."[2] He conceives of his own more recent history not only as a fulfilment of prophecy, but the scriptural passages are formulated with concern about exile and eventual deliverance. Leviticus 26 is of special interest in this scroll because Leviticus 26 frames remembrance of Egypt within a warning against future idolatry, and it promises that even when desolation and plagues have come, God will remember his remnant and covenant.

Revelation 15:1–16:21

"I SAW IN HEAVEN ANOTHER GREAT AND MARVELOUS SIGN: SEVEN ANGELS WITH THE SEVEN LAST PLAGUES"

Echoes of Leviticus 26. Leviticus 26 has also been noted as a passage that exerts influence on the Apocalypse, particularly the series of plague septets (seals, trumpets, bowls), because it forewarns that a sequence of four plagues, each described figuratively as "seven," will be visited upon Israel to turn her away from idolatry should she stray. The final "seven" of Leviticus 26 tells of exile but promises that God will keep his covenant and preserve a remnant. When a connection is drawn between the plagues in Leviticus 26 and Revelation 6–16, it is based on the occurrence of the numbers four and seven in relation to divine punishment. Indeed, seven plagues are not explicitly mentioned anywhere else in the Old or New Testament outside of Leviticus (26:18, 21, 24, 28 = God will punish Israel "seven times over") and Revelation (15:1, 6, 8; 21:9 = "the seven angels with the seven plagues").[3]

Richard Bauckham offers an especially intriguing study on the relationship of John's septets to Leviticus 26. He notes that there are in fact four septets of plagues in Revelation, not just three. In addition to the three septets of seals, trumpets, and bowls, one should also include the septet of thunders (10:3–7), which is found in between the trumpets and bowls. In the case of the thunders, although John is not permitted to write down what he witnesses, it is described as a series of seven plagues.[4] Bauckham convincingly

---

2. Jeremy Penner, "The Words of the Luminaries as a Meditation on the Exile," *RevQ* 28.2 (2016): 175–90, at 180.

3. That the punishments in Leviticus were viewed as a series of "plagues" is evident from other interpreters. E.g., Targums Pseudo-Jonathan and Onkelos, where they are individually and explicitly described as a "plague" (cf. Lev 26:21, describes only the second "punishment").

4. Richard Bauckham, *The Climax of Prophecy: Studies on the Book of Revelation* (Edinburgh: T&T Clark, 1993), 31.

argues that the significance of the plagues' pattern is that it depicts a perfect judgment enumerated as four sets of seven—as in Leviticus 26 where God four times promises to punish Israel "seven times over" (26:18, 21, 24, 28).[5] What, then, are the potential theological implications of such numerical connections with Leviticus 26?

Images of Exile. The use of Leviticus 26 in both Words of the Luminaries and Revelation invites us to consider how Revelation's septets evoke images of exile. Indeed, in Revelation 7:17, just before the seventh seal is opened, an allusion to Jeremiah 31:16 recalls return from exile: the Lamb is a shepherd who will guide the saints to living water and "wipe away every tear from their eyes." In Jeremiah 31:16, the Israelites are exhorted to cease their weeping and shed no more tears, for they will return to their own land. John, therefore, is evoking Israel's return from exile as he envisions the salvation of the great multitude. Further, in the last chapters of the Apocalypse, the destruction of Babylon and establishment of a New Jerusalem also depict return from exile. Exile in the Apocalypse takes place in "Babylon," a cryptogram that evokes memory of captivity, and the new exodus motif is that of being led into the kingdom of Christ. This is made clear when the seventh trumpet sounds (Rev 11:15) and a heavenly voice proclaims: "The kingdom of the world has become the kingdom of our Lord and of his Messiah."

Leviticus 26 promises that a remnant will survive the plagues and God will be faithful to his covenant. As seen in Words of the Luminaries, remnant theology in Leviticus appears to attract Jewish communities who conceived of themselves as theologically in exile. In Revelation 7:5–8, the twelve tribes of Israel are idealized (12 x 12,000) and depict the "true Israel" (= the Christian church) and this, in turn, evokes remnant imagery (cf. Rom 9:27–29; 11:4–6). The twelve tribes of Revelation 7, in light of Ezekiel 48:1–29, suggest that a characteristic of remnant ideology is the reunification of Israel at the time of the eschaton. Elsewhere in early Jewish literature are expectations that the ten northern tribes will return from exile in the east at the end of time (e.g., 4 Ezra 13:39–50; T. Mos. 4:9; 2 Bar. 77:17–26; Sib. Or. 2:171). The numbering of the tribes in Revelation 7 (cf. book of Numbers) may be understood as the gathering of a remnant as they return from exile.

Sparks are produced when these observations are set alongside a wider network of allusions to Exodus throughout the Apocalypse. In 5:9–11, imagery

---

5. Noteworthy is Philo's description of the significance of the numbers three, four, and seven (Philo, *Creation* 97–106). In addition to the correlation of numbers in Leviticus 26 and the Apocalypse, a few other allusions to individual Leviticus plagues may occur in Revelation 6–7 (e.g., Rev 6:5–6 to Lev 26:26; Rev 6:8 to Lev 26:5; Rev 7:15, 21:3–7 to Lev 26:11–12).

of a new exodus sets the scene in the lead-up to the presentation of a series of three plague septets. In Revelation 5, the lamb that has been slain is not only the paschal lamb but also a way of recalling Israel's exodus from Egypt. The non-explicit use of exodus traditions in Revelation 5 depicts the liberation of the faithful from universal enslavement through the death of Christ, who is the Passover sacrifice.[6] Later, when the woman flees from the dragon to the wilderness (Rev 12:6) where she is nourished, this is reminiscent of God's provision of quail and manna (Exod 16). Here too the dragon sends forth a river of water to drown the woman, but the earth swallows it up to save her (12:15–16), reminding one of deliverance at the Red Sea.

The progression of plagues to follow is part of the process of deliverance from exile. Indeed, in the second septet when the angels begin to trumpet (8:6–9:19;Woe 11:15–19), allusions to at least four of the exodus plagues may be identified. The pouring out of bowls in Revelation 16 is even more explicit in its use of exodus plagues.[7] The "song of Moses" in Revelation 15:3 continues the new exodus motif by recollecting the Song of the Sea (Exod 15) that Israel sings after they cross the Red Sea, though here, in the Apocalypse, the Song of Moses is sung alongside a glassy sea in heaven and precedes the final septet of exodus-like plagues.

Words of the Luminaries suggests that John drew upon a wider pastiche of scriptural traditions that includes Leviticus 26 with Exodus, which are used together to reflect on exile. Within these sustained reflections on specific scriptural passages, both compositions consider common theological questions related to divine benevolence, judgment, and new beginnings. They are concerned with how Israel (or the "true Israel") should respond to God's trials and how punishments and plagues are used in relation to how God keeps his covenant with them. The specific directions taken, and the conclusions these respective compositions reach, substantially differ. In both Words of the Luminaries and Revelation, the communities of the respective authors are set within narratives related to the exodus; however, one looks more to the past and the other to the future. Nonetheless, Words of the Luminaries allows us to see subtler themes in Revelation, especially allusions to community living in exile and God's faithfulness to bring about deliverance.

---

6. Elizabeth Schüssler Fiorenza, *The Book of Revelation: Justice and Judgment* (Philadelphia: Fortress, 1985), 73–76.

7. George R. Beasley-Murray, *The Book of Revelation* (London: Marshall, Morgan & Scott, 1974), 238–39, provides a comparative outline of the trumpet and bowl septets with Exodus plagues. He finds an Exodus plague in each of the trumpet blasts.

FOR FURTHER READING

Additional Ancient Texts

There is a well-known Jewish tradition of shortening the ten exodus plagues to seven. See, for example, Psalm 78:44–51; 105:28–36; Atrapanus (frag. 2) 23:28–37; 3 Baruch 16:3; Wisdom of Solomon 11–19.

English Translations and Critical Editions

Baillet, M., *Qumrân Grotte 4.III (4Q482–4Q520)*. DJD 7 (Oxford: Clarendon, 1982).

García Martínez, Florentino, and Eibert J. C. Tigchelaar, eds. *The Dead Sea Scrolls: Study Edition*. 2 vols. Leiden: Brill, 1997–98.

Secondary Literature

Bauckham, Richard. *The Climax of Prophecy: Studies on the Book of Revelation*. Edinburgh: T&T Clark, 1993.

Penner, J. "The Words of the Luminaries as a Meditation on the Exile." *RevQ* 28 (2016): 175–90.

Wold, B. "The Eschatological Application of Exodus Plagues in John's Apocalypse." Pages 249–66 in *Eschatologie/Eschatology: The Sixth Durham-Tübingen Colloquium*. Edited by H. Lichtenberger, H.-J. Eckstein, and C. Landmesser. WUNT 272. Tübingen: Mohr Siebeck, 2011.

———. "Reading Revelation's Plague Septets: New Exodus and Exile." Pages 279–98 in *Echoes from the Caves: Qumran and the New Testament*. Edited by F. García Martínez. STDJ 85. Leiden: Brill, 2009.

CHAPTER 15

Joseph and Aseneth and Revelation 17:1–18: Women as Archetypes of Rebellion and Repentance

EDITH M. HUMPHREY

The book of Revelation's symbolism evokes contrasting reactions and sometimes confusion. John follows the biblical tradition of gendered imagery to suggest the relationship between God and the faithful, as well as believers' sibling relationships. We can understand such symbols by considering figures that are similar in some respects, but different in others: in Proverbs, there are Lady Wisdom and Dame Folly, and in Revelation the "mother-cities" Babylon and the New Jerusalem. But we can also compare Babylon with the heroine of Joseph and Aseneth (hereafter Aseneth), a "para-biblical" book not included in the canon.

Though its dating is debated,[1] the novel Aseneth probably was known when John wrote Revelation. We cannot claim that John intended a contrast between his villainous woman and Aseneth, but the use of symbolic women in ancient writings emboldens us to find helpful connections of Aseneth 14–17 with Revelation 17 (and 18). We will discover how these two works use female figures to highlight purity, humility, and incorporation over against corruption, arrogance, and separation. Each figure personifies a human group: those who repent or those who rebel. Their different paths come to a climax in their respective books, encouraging us to embrace or eschew their actions and attitude.

---

1. For the question of dating, see Edith M. Humphrey, *Joseph and Aseneth*, GAP (Sheffield: Sheffield Academic, 2000), 28–37. This guide also provides a window into the long history of the novel's transmission in four text types, of which the long text *b* is the superior type, in my opinion. This too is debated. The translations below, and chapter and verse numbering, come from C. Burchard, "Joseph and Aseneth: A New Translation and Introduction," in *Old Testament Pseudepigrapha*, ed. James H. Charlesworth (Garden City, NY: Doubleday, 1985), 2:177–247.

Joseph and Aseneth

"THE SONS OF THE LIVING GOD WILL DWELL IN YOUR CITY OF REFUGE"

Joseph and Aseneth is a Hellenistic Jewish novel amplifying Genesis 41:45–50 and 46:20, which mention Joseph's wife, Aseneth (Hebrew, Asenath). The novel tells how Joseph, vice-regent to Pharaoh, meets Aseneth, daughter of the Gentile priest at Heliopolis, and how she converts to Judaism. Genesis 41:46–49, where Joseph gathers corn for the seven years of famine, provides the novel's departure point: Joseph calls at Aseneth's home while on this quest. The heroine has heard rumors about Joseph with Potiphar's wife, and is herself a virgin who keeps aloof from men, rejecting even Pharaoh's son. Surprisingly, on first sight of Joseph, Aseneth is smitten! However, Joseph keeps aloof from the idolatrous Aseneth; though he blesses her, he will not embrace her. She withdraws to her tower-chamber, repudiates her idols, and prays for forgiveness. On the eighth day, a heavenly visitor ("The Man") visits her and incorporates her into God's family. Returning to find her transformed, Joseph marries her, and they go on to have Ephraim and Manasseh, plus some adventures.

Aseneth's Apocalyptic Encounters. This romance is replete with symbolism, especially in its central chapters (chs. 14–17), which unfold like an "apocalypse," with a visual and auditory revelation, a mediating angel, a description of heavenly things, a symbolic historical narrative, and a transformation of the seer, Aseneth. Larger than life, the heroine is connected with the angel "Metanoia" (or Repentance) and is declared to be "A City of Refuge" for all Gentile penitents (15:7–8; 16:16). Details provide a marked contrast with Babylon. Aseneth is "left alone" with seven virgins, weeps, fasts, and stays awake during a time of repentance. Her tower room is cloistered from the outer world by a curtain, she grows weak in her limbs, she dresses in black, takes off her finery, and throws it (along with idols) out of the window. She loosens her hair in mourning and sprinkles ashes on her face, sitting in humiliation for seven days. On the eighth morning, when she attempts to pray, facing toward the east, she can at first only speak to herself, crying out that she is a virgin, an orphan, and desolate, hated by everyone, having neither father nor mother, and defiled by the worship of idols. In a second soliloquy, she tries to call upon the Lord's name, but falls silent. The third time, she finally "pours out her supplication," confessing her arrogance, and asking God to receive her as a father. Her language mirrors the lament psalms—particularly Psalm 22.

At this point the shining Man, like a more splendid Joseph, enters her room, calls her by name twice, and instructs her to wash and dress in her antechamber. When she returns, she is told to remove her veil, for she is accepted by God, her name is written in a heavenly book, she will be renewed, and she will "eat blessed bread of life . . . drink a blessed cup of immortality, and anoint [herself] with blessed ointment of incorruptibility" (15:4). God has always intended her as Joseph's bride and renames her "City of Refuge." We readers, like Aseneth, want to know the name of this heavenly stranger, but he only divulges that he is "chief of the house of the Most High" (15:12).

Things become strange: Aseneth is told to retrieve a honeycomb from her storeroom (which miraculously appears there), and the Man performs a ritual, feeding her with it, while he speaks of bread, a cup, and ointment, and drawing out from it two sets of bees. The good bees make a honeycomb on Aseneth's lips, but the evil ones die, only to be raised and find shelter in Aseneth's garden. Then the angel burns up the honeycomb, gives a final blessing, and disappears. The aftermath of this "apocalypse" is dramatic! Joseph arrives (in chapters 18–19) to find his beloved shining like the sun or the morning star, with cheeks red like a son of man, teeth like fighting men, hair like a vine, and breasts like the Lord's mountains. Joseph comments: "the Lord God founded your walls in the highest [as] walls of life, because the sons of the living God will dwell in your City of Refuge, and the Lord God will reign as king over them forever" (19:5). They embrace, physically and spiritually, and prepare to wed.

Here is the tale of a proud woman brought to repentance, visited by heaven, transformed, and given a revelation concerning fellow converts and enemies. She is incorporated in God's people and joined to Joseph, receiving from him a "spirit of life, of wisdom and of truth" (19:11). In the sequel, Aseneth is ambushed by Joseph's brothers, trying to abduct her for Pharaoh's son, but is rescued when she calls out to God, and has mercy on her abductors. The end of the story is upbeat.

Incorporation and Transformation. What is the point of this novel, besides being a good yarn? Its main question is the one begged in Genesis—what is a good Jewish boy like Joseph doing marrying the daughter of a pagan priest? The answer is that the marriage is God's will, because gentiles can be incorporated into Israel. The author is aware of the potential for social conflict in this transference of allegiance, for he registers this in Aseneth's cry to God, the episode of the violent bees, and the escapade with Pharaoh's son. But the author is not only interested in reflecting the (sometimes strained) Jewish-gentile relations of first-century Egypt. He also offers mystical details: the honeycomb, the bread-cup-ointment, Aseneth's transformation, the mystery of the heavenly Man, and the parallels of Joseph with "the Man" and Aseneth with heavenly Repentance. More is going on than a story of conversion and intrigue. Here is a tale of separation, transformation and inclusion, *and* the mysterious correlation between heaven and earth.

Revelation 17:1–18

"BABYLON THE GREAT THE MOTHER OF PROSTITUTES"

Though, like Aseneth, the symbolic woman Babylon sits in the heights, the two are polar opposites. Unlike Aseneth, who retires to a tower, encircled by seven other virginal women, Babylon rides on a scarlet beast, on (or by) the waters. Aseneth repudiates her idols, but Babylon's beast sports blasphemous names and aspires to the name of God (Rev 17:3–4). The naturally beautiful Aseneth strips off her decorations and clothes herself in penitence, but the "great prostitute" is dressed artificially, as she consorts with all the inhabitants of the world. She herself has a mysterious name, "Mother of Prostitutes" (17:5), rather than "Mother of Penitents." Aseneth, who has fasted, is given a miraculous meal by the heavenly Man; Babylon continually helps herself to a cup full of "abominable things and the filth of her adulteries" (17:4) and "the blood of God's holy people" (17:6). While Babylon pretends to be a great city, she actually is found in "the wilderness" (17:3); in contrast, the self-isolated Aseneth is surrounded by a garden of delight, a storehouse containing wonders, and heaven itself. The angel tells John the seer not to marvel over Babylon (17:7), but Joseph rightly marvels over his bride-to-be when he sees her transformation.

Judged by the Company They Keep. The Prostitute is associated with the "beast" who is doomed, along with those "whose names have not been written in the book of life from the creation of the world" (17:8). In contrast, Aseneth is associated with heavenly Repentance: *her* name has been written in the book from the beginning. Aseneth is worried that her people will reject her because she has turned to the living God, but the story does not in fact bear this out—God protects her from harm, and her marriage to Joseph is a joy to Egypt, with the promise of many others who will follow her example, in repentance. But Babylon's days are numbered, for "God has put it into their hearts [the hearts of those whom she oppresses]" (17:17) to destroy her. In contrast, God has put it into the heart of Joseph to bless this gentile woman (Aseneth 9:8); his blessing is fulfilled and celebrated even by those who would harm her. She becomes the mother of many; Babylon is devoured by her consorts!

As the vision continues into Revelation 18, we see why Babylon's fate must differ from that of Aseneth. Here, instead of repenting, she speaks in rebellion, calling attention to her own wealth, connections, and evil "children"—"I sit enthroned as queen. I am not a widow; I will never mourn" (18:7b). Her boasting is empty! Whereas the heavenly man blessed Aseneth in the honeycomb vision, a mighty angel in Revelation 18:21 casts a huge stone into the sea, and declares the casting down of Babylon. Her trading, light, and weddings are over, leaving three announcements of "Woe! Woe!" (18:10, 16; 19). In contrast, Aseneth is blessed—a blessing extended beyond her to her seven virgins, and beyond that to the land of Egypt, with its converts (Aseneth 17:6). Whereas the evil city loses her network, so violently and deceptively forged, the penitent Aseneth willingly gives up her natural connections, is incorporated into the heavenly community, and astonishingly brings blessing to those whose idolatry she repudiates. Revelation offers us a story of arrogance, rebellion, judgment, and isolation; the novel tells a story of repentance, confession, transformation, and incorporation. Our last glimpse of Babylon is that of an extinguished lamp and the cessation of festive weddings; but Aseneth shines on in our imagination, a partner in her own fruitful marriage.

Humility and Arrogance. Following her conversion (in Burchard's longer version), we read a psalm that summarizes Aseneth's experience. We may set its final stanza (21:21) alongside rearranged verses from Revelation 18 (see Table 15.1). Note the humbling versus the arrogance, the threefold blessing versus threefold doom, God's sovereign action versus Babylon's self-assertion, and Aseneth's incorporation against Babylon's solitude and judgment.

In parallel, these two figures show us the dynamic shared by solemn biblical texts and ancient writings composed for entertainment—God lifts up the humble and casts down the arrogant. There are, to be sure, substantive differences between the texts in genre, tone, and purpose. Aseneth beguiles the audience while Babylon is a cautionary tale: "'Come out of her, my people,' . . . so that you will not receive any of her plagues" (18:4).

Most scholars do not think that the original author of Aseneth knew the gospel of Jesus the Messiah—Aseneth breathes the air of Second Temple Judaism. Like Judith, Susanna, and Esther, it entertains while it instructs, calling the reader to be wise. In Revelation, the figure of Christ (and not a heroine) dominates, as does the urgent call to respond to God, since Christ "is coming soon" with blessing or judgment. Aseneth intimates the possibility of God's blessing for a productive life; the Apocalypse envisions eternal intimacy with the One who is Alpha and Omega. Feminine figures, then, can be used both in a novel that urges wisdom, and in a revelatory piece about the new heaven and new earth. In Aseneth, we can see a figure to emulate. By Babylon, we are driven to the One who is the Light.

Table 15.1: Psalms about the Women

Aseneth 21:21	Revelation 18
I have sinned, Lord, I have sinned; Before you I have sinned much, Until Joseph the Powerful One of God came. He pulled me down from my dominating position and made me humble after my arrogance, and by his beauty he caught me, and by his wisdom he grasped me . . . and by his spirit, as bait of life, he ensnared me. And by his power he confirmed me, and brought me to the God of the ages and to the chief of the house of the Most High, and gave me to eat bread of life, and to drink a cup of wisdom, and I became his bride for ever and ever.	"I sit enthroned as queen. I am not a widow; I will never mourn." (18:7b) A mighty angel picked up a boulder . . . and threw it into the sea, and said: . . . "The great city of Babylon will be thrown down." (18:21) "She has become a dwelling for demons and a haunt for every impure spirit, a haunt for every unclean bird, a haunt for every unclean and detestable animal." (18:2) "Give her as much torment and grief as the glory and luxury she gave herself." (18:7) In one day her plagues will overtake her: death, mourning and famine. She will be consumed by fire, for mighty is the Lord God who judges her. (18:8)

FOR FURTHER READING

Additional Ancient Texts

The following texts incorporate feminine symbolic figures, illustrating how biblical and para-biblical traditions picture Wisdom, the faithful people of God, and nations that rebel against God in this manner: Judges 19:24; Proverbs 8–9; Isaiah 47:1; 49:18; 61–62; Galatians 4:22–31; 2 Corinthians 11:2; Revelation 12, 21–22; Baruch 3:9–4:4; 4 Ezra/2 Esdras 9:26–10:59; 1 Enoch 42; Sirach 24; Wisdom of Solomon 6–10 (esp. 7:24–8:1). See also the early Christian work Shepherd of Hermas (esp. Visions 1–4).

English Translations and Critical Editions

Burchard, C. "Joseph and Aseneth." Pages 177–247 in vol. 2 of *The Old Testament Pseudepigrapha*. Edited by James H. Charlesworth. Garden City, NY: Doubleday, 1985.[2]

Cook, D. "Joseph and Aseneth." Pages 465–503 in *The Apocryphal Old Testament*. Edited by H. F. D. Sparks. Oxford: Clarendon, 1984.[3]

Denis, A.-M. *Concordance grecque des pseudépigraphes d'Ancien Testament: Concordance, Corpus des textes, indices*. Avec la collaboration d'Yvonne Janssens et le concours du CETEDOC. Louvain-La-Newuve: Université Catholique de Louvain, 1987.

Secondary Literature

Chesnutt, Randall. *From Death to Life: Conversion in Joseph and Aseneth*. JSPSupp 16. Sheffield: Sheffield Academic, 1995.

Goodacre, Marc. *The Aseneth Home Page*. www.markgoodacre.org/aseneth/.

Humphrey, Edith M. *Joseph and Aseneth*. GAP. Sheffield: Sheffield Academic, 2000.

———. "A Tale of Two Cities and (At Least) Three Women: Transformation, Continuity and Contrast in the Apocalypse." Pages 81–96 in *Reading the Book of Revelation: A Resource for Students*. Edited by David L. Barr. Atlanta: SBL, 2003.

———. *The Ladies and the Cities: Transformation and Apocalyptic Identity in Joseph and Aseneth, 4 Ezra, the Apocalypse and the Shepherd of Hermas*. SJPSSup 17. Sheffield: Sheffield Academic. Reprint Second Temple Series. London: T&T Clark, 2018.

Kraemer, Ross Shepard. *When Aseneth Met Joseph: A Late Antique Tale of the Biblical Patriarch and his Egyptian Wife, Reconsidered*. New York: Oxford University Press, 1998.

---

2. Burchard gives us an English translation of his eclectic texts, based on the longer family "b." In my view, this is the superior text.

3. An English text based on the shorter family "d" (inferior to "b," in my view), championed by Marc Philonenko and Ross Kraemer.

Rossing, Barbara. *The Choice Between Two Cities: Whore, Bride, and Empire in the Apocalypse.* Harvard Theological Studies 48. Harrisburg, PA: Trinity Press International, 1999.

Yarbro-Collins, Adele. "Feminine Symbolism in the Book of Revelation." *Biblical Interpretation* 1 (1973): 20–23.

CHAPTER 16

The Epistle of Enoch and Revelation 18:1–24: Economic Critique of Rome

CYNTHIA LONG WESTFALL

In Revelation 14:8, John describes an angel dramatically announcing that "Babylon the Great" has fallen because it made all nations drink the wine of her lustful immorality. This is an enigmatic announcement for two reasons: Babylon was not by any means a great city in the first century, and nothing more is said about Babylon for two chapters. But then the seven bowls of wrath (16:1–21) culminate in an earthquake that splits Babylon the Great into three parts, and God makes the city drain the cup of his wrath (16:19). Babylon is then personified in 17:1–18 as a "whore" with traits both of high-class and low-class prostitution.[1] She rides a demonic beast and her clients are the kings of the earth. John's description of her devastation draws on the language of Old Testament judgments of not only Babylon (Ps 137:1; Isa 13–14; 21; 47; Jer 50–51; Dan 4:30) but also Nineveh (Zeph 2:13–14), Tyre (Isa 23:1–16; Nah 3:1–7), Edom (Isa 34:11–15), and Jerusalem (Jer 9:9–10). However, the composite caricature drawn from past empires is seated on seven mountains, which would be taken by the first-century readers as a transparent reference to Imperial Rome (Rev 17:9). The intended identity of Rome as Babylon the Great is confirmed by the description of the patron-client relationship of the city with the kings of the earth, and Rome's function as the economic center and the beneficiary of the wealth of the imperial system that is vividly described in 18:1–24.

In the preceding context, Rome's domination, lethal violence, and promotion of idolatry result in the city's judgment and devastation, but

---

1. See Craig Koester, *Revelation: A New Translation with Introduction and Commentary*, AYB 38A (New Haven, CT: Yale University Press, 2014), 671–72. The offensive term "whore" conveys disgust suitable for the satire that is the tenor of John's description.

Revelation 18:1–24 primarily indicts Rome for its economic exploitation, extravagant self-indulgence, and arrogance in which the kings of the earth, the merchants, and the seafarers are all complicit. The whore's "lustful immorality" is represented primarily as gross materialism in which imperial wealth is directly linked with oppression, violence, and idolatry. Similar links between wealth and oppression, violence and idolatry are found in 1 Enoch 94:6–100:6, which form part of a major section of an apocalyptic text that was very popular in Second Temple Judaism.

The Epistle of Enoch

"IN THE DAYS OF YOUR AFFLUENCE, YOU COMMITTED OPPRESSION"

First Enoch is more technically known as the Ethiopic Book of Enoch, and is one of three pseudepigrapha (Ethiopic, Aramaic, and Latin) that are attributed to Enoch. First Enoch is the oldest and the only fully preserved version, but it is a composite work that represents a number of different periods and authors.[2] Stuckenbruck analyzes "The Epistle of Enoch" (1 En. 91:1–105:2) in the Ethiopic Book, but also takes evidence from the Greek and Aramaic texts into account in his analysis.[3] He suggests that 1 Enoch 94:6–100:6 is Discourse One of the epistle and contends that the material is consistent with conditions just before the Maccabean revolt in the second century BC.[4] Immediately before Discourse One, the ways of righteousness and the ways of wickedness are contrasted, and Enoch exhorts his children not to walk in the evil path, but to keep themselves at a distance (94:1–4), even though it will literally be located in every place (94:5).

Discourse One contains six woe oracles against the wicked (94:6–95:2; 95:4–7; 96:4–8; 97:7–10; 98:9–99:2; 99:11–16), which are often paired in the text with the consolation or blessing of the righteous. The righteous are characterized as experiencing social and economic oppression, while the wicked exercise social prestige and obtain wealth at the expense of the righteous. The first part of each oracle characterizes the traits of the wicked, which can apply to other

---

2. E. Isaac, "1 (Ethiopic Apocalypse of) Enoch (Second Century B.C.–First Century A.D.): A New Translation and Introduction," *The Old Testament Pseudepigrapha*, ed. James Charlesworth, vol. 1 (Garden City, NY: Doubleday, 1985), 5–89, see 5–6. All English translations of 1 Enoch are from here.

3. For more information about 1 Enoch, see chapter 1 by Benjamin E. Reynolds ("The Parables of Enoch and Revelation 1:1–20: Daniel's Son of Man") and chapter 2 by Mark D. Mathews ("The Epistle of Enoch and Revelation 2:1–3:22: Poverty and Riches in the Present Age") in this volume.

4. Loren Stuckenbruck, *1 Enoch 91–108*, CEJL (Berlin: de Gruyter, 2007), 189–90, 215.

nations and the disobedient of Israel (often collaborators), and the second part portrays their judgment, which consists of eschatological reversals and judgment.

Critiques of Power. The first woe oracle (94:6–95:2) critiques the power that wealth brings on a number of fronts. Building houses "with sin," acquiring gold and silver, and trusting in one's wealth are linked with oppression, deceit, injustice, and blasphemy:

> [7] Woe unto those who build their houses with sin!
> For they shall all be demolished from their foundations;
> and they shall fall by the sword.
> Those who amass gold and silver,
> They shall quickly be destroyed.
> [8] Woe unto you, O rich people!
> For you have put your trust in your wealth. (94:7–8)

The wealth of the wicked gives them the social power to oppress the righteous depicted in the second woe oracle (95:4–7): to curse, to "reward" neighbors with evil, to be witnesses of falsehood. The author of James writes similarly: "Is it not the rich who are exploiting you? Are they not the ones who are dragging you into court?" (Jas 2:6). In addition, trust in wealth is equivalent to idolatry because it is a failure to recognize that all good comes from the Lord (1 En. 94:8; 98:11).

Extravagance and Oppression. The third woe oracle (96:4–8) is particularly relevant because it indicts behaviors associated with extravagance, luxury, and consumerism as forms of oppression:

> [5] Woe unto you who eat the best bread!
> And drink wine in large bowls,
> Trampling upon the weak people with your might.
> [6] Woe unto you who have water available to you all the time,
> For soon you shall be consumed and wither away,
> for you have forsaken the fountain of life.
> [7] Woe unto you who carry out oppression, deceit, and blasphemy!
> There shall be a record of evil against you.
> [8] Woe unto you, O powerful people!
> You who coerce the righteous with your power. (96:5–8)

Extravagant self-indulgence, such as the consumption of the finest flour and large amounts of wine, is equated to economic exploitation (extravagant self-indulgence with jewelry and clothing is similarly condemned in 98:2–3). The critique of the wasteful use of water may be understood in Palestine and many other areas where drought is always a threat and restricted access to water is always an issue. One can assume that first-century readers would consider Roman aqueducts to be part of the oppressive imperial power of Rome as well. This passage particularly highlights the text's association of the indulgence of wealth with oppression and coercion. The text also confronts how money is linked to hypocrisy: it can deceptively be used to make one appear to be righteous (96:4), which is another form of social power. Prosperity can be falsely linked to righteousness as a sign of God's blessing.

Wealth and Injustice. The final three woes highlight the connection of wealth with specific acts of injustice. The fourth woe oracle (97:7–10) focuses on how injustice is used to gain wealth (97:8) and how the wicked gain immunity from criminal charges because the rich can "do whatever we like; for we have gathered silver" (97:9). The rich are indicted for having many "laborers" in their house (97:9b), which would certainly include slaves (slavery is specifically denounced in 98:4). The fifth woe oracle (98:9–99:2) critiques the love, priority, and pursuit of "good things" and the goal of satisfaction (or satiation), which characterize consumerism, one of the primary objectives of imperialism in all ages. The sixth woe oracle (99:11–16) concludes the indictments against the wicked by targeting the gain of wealth through oppressive means, such as sinful and deceitful measures (99:12), and building one's house through exploitation: "the hard toil of others" (99:13).

Consequences for the Wicked. Discourse One (94:6–104:8) is riddled with specific consequences for the wicked for their use and abuse of wealth that are parallel to John's letter to the seven churches. Of course, the negative consequences are part and parcel of the proclamations of "Woe." Retribution is certain because it is linked to a failure to understand one's primary relationship to God and to recognize his lordship:

> You shall ooze out of your riches,
> For you do not remember the Most High.
> In the days of your affluence, you committed oppression.
> You have become ready for death,
> and for the day of darkness and the day of great judgment. (94:8–9)

Three consequences for the wicked are marked throughout Discourse One: repercussions that are consistent with the offense (94:7, 10; 95:5, 7; 96:6; 98:11), a reversal of position with the poor and oppressed righteous

(95:7; 96:1–3, 8), and the suddenness of judgment (94:1, 6, 7; 95:6; 96:1, 6; 97:10). However, it is apparent in the opening of the epistle and the close of Discourse One (92:1–3; 100:1–6; c.f. 94:9; 97:1–7) that the consequences for both the righteous and the wicked are primarily eschatological and will occur on the day of judgment. The righteous will be given an active role in the judgment: they will be a reproach to the wicked (94:11), they will be given power to kill their oppressors (95:3; 96:1; 98:12; cf. 90:19; 91:12), and they will be given authority over sinners (96:1). They are meant to join God and the angels and rejoice at the destruction of the wicked (94:11; 97:2).

Revelation 18:1–24

"SHE GLORIFIED HERSELF AND LIVED LUXURIOUSLY"

Imperial Indictment. The Epistle of Enoch is arguably one of the most relevant texts for the interpretation of Revelation 18, together with the Old Testament texts previously mentioned. It is possible that John even joined these texts together intentionally in a complex way that combines the Old Testament indictments of the sins of ancient major cities and empires with a focused economic critique similar to that found in the woe oracles. In Revelation 18, the way of the wicked that was in "all places" in 1 Enoch is localized in one city (Babylon/Rome), but the imperial system of Rome was extended to virtually "all places" from the standpoint of the designated readers (the seven churches). Those who are condemned as "bedfellows with sinners" in 1 Enoch 97:4 correspond to the collaborating nations and client kings across the Roman Empire who are depicted as committing fornication with Rome (Rev 18:3). The introduction of the merchants of the earth in 18:3 characterizes them as the wicked in the light of 1 Enoch, because they "have grown rich from the power of [Rome's] luxury," which is a succinct pejorative collocation of wealth, oppressive power, and luxury. In 18:23, merchants are called the magnates, or aristocrats, of the earth because they are given the place of honor and importance in a culture that is given over to materialism.

Call to Separate. After the announcement of the fall of Babylon the Great (18:2), the call for the people to "Come out of her, my people" (18:4) could qualify as a translation of Jer 51:45 MT, but the warning against taking part in Rome's sins and sharing her plagues also closely paraphrases the separation depicted in 1 Enoch 94:3–4. John is urging people to keep a distance from the ways of Rome (the way of the wicked) rather than to physically flee a city.[5] Separation from Rome would consist of rejecting involvement in the imperial system. It is a call to resist imperial power, systemic injustice, economic collaboration, compromise with the lifestyle of luxury, and the underlying idolatry that are specified as the way of the wicked for Asia Minor.[6]

Consequences and Lament. Both the indictments of Rome and the consequences correspond in content to the Epistle of Enoch. John emphatically calls for repercussions consistent with Rome's offenses and even a double repayment of them (Rev 18:6). He specifically charges both Rome and the kings of the earth with living luxuriously (18:7, 9). He shows that Rome exhibits the arrogance that comes from trusting in wealth and power (18:7). John emphasizes the suddenness of judgment as the Epistle of Enoch does. Judgment will come in a single day (18:8), even in one hour (18:10, 17, 19).

In an ironic and artistic lament, the prophetic warnings that are characteristic of the Woe Oracles and the OT prophets are paraphrased as the mourning of the wicked, in which a series of woes are repeated. Rome's collaborators (the kings of the earth, the merchants of the earth, and all the shipmasters, sailors, and all whose trade is on the sea) are depicted as mourning, weeping, and wailing the loss of Rome because of their own loss of wealth and power (18:9, 15, 19). The detailed descriptions of Rome's gross consumerism (18:11–14, 16) reflects the same condemnations of the epistle, including amassing gold, silver, jewels, expensive building materials, choice flour, wine, luxurious clothing, and slaves, which is the crowning atrocity. However, John extends the list, which consists mostly of luxury items, including items that were supplied to Rome by the seven cities in which the designated readers lived.[7]

In contrast to the mourning of the collaborating kings, merchants, and seafarers, the saints, apostles, and prophets are expected to join God and the author in calling for judgment against Rome (18:6–7; cf. 6:9–11) and in rejoicing when it happens (18:20a). Adopting this attitude would have been quite a challenge to believers in Asia Minor, because like the collaborators indicted by John, their cities benefit from the association with Rome (cf. 3:17–18), and they must choose whether they place their trust and hope in the material benefits of the imperial system (the way of the wicked) or in God and his righteousness. All the saints are called to serve as a reproach to Rome, either as martyrs calling for vindication or as fellow claimants in a

---

5. Koester, *Revelation*, 699.
6. Therefore, the separation is not one of physical separation as in the Rule of Community in 1QS.
7. Warren Carter, *The Roman Empire and the New Testament: The Essential Guide* (Nashville: Abingdon, 2006), 108–9.

heavenly court case against Rome's violence and oppression. In a dramatic reversal of fortune, God gives judgment in favor of the righteous saints against Rome (18:20b), and all Rome's culture, industry, and social life are demolished (18:21–23). One of the primary contrasts between Revelation 18 and the Epistle of Enoch is that the author does not explicitly give the readers authority over Rome and its collaborators, nor the power to slay them at the time of its fall (but see Rev 2:26–28). However, the author concludes in 18:23–24 by stressing the same associations of Rome's wealth and luxurious self-indulgence with oppression, idolatry (sorcery), and violence.

FOR FURTHER READING

Additional Ancient Texts

For similar critiques, see Amos, Sirach, and the Rule of the Community (1QS), which opts for physical separation from the wicked.

English Translations and Critical Editions

Isaac, E. "1 (Ethiopic Apocalypse of) Enoch (Second Century B.C.–First Century A.D.): A New Translation and Introduction," Pages 5–89 in vol. 1 of *The Old Testament Pseudepigrapha*. Edited by James Charlesworth. Garden City, NY: Doubleday, 1985.

Nickelsburg, George W. E. *1 Enoch 1: A Commentary on the Book of Enoch, Chapters 1–36; 81–108*. Hermeneia. Minneapolis: Fortress, 2001.

Stuckenbruck, Loren. *1 Enoch 91–108*. CEJL. Berlin: de Gruyter, 2007.

Secondary Literature

Carter, Warren. *The Roman Empire and the New Testament: An Essential Guide*. Nashville: Abingdon, 2006.

Collins, Adela Yarbro. *Crisis and Catharsis: The Power of the Apocalypse*. Philadelphia: Westminster, 1984.

Hengel, Martin. *Property and Riches in the Early Church: Aspects of a Social History of Early Christianity*. London: SCM, 1974.

Howard-Brook, Wes, and Anthony Gwyther. *Unveiling Empire: Reading Revelation Then and Now*. Maryknoll, NY: Orbis, 1999.

Mathews, Mark D. *Riches, Poverty, and the Faithful: Perspectives on Wealth in the Second Temple Period and the Apocalypse of John*. SNTSMS 154. Cambridge: Cambridge University Press, 2013.

CHAPTER 17

Psalms of Solomon and Revelation 19:1–21: Messianic Conquest of God's Enemies

MICHAEL J. GORMAN

O f the many texts in Revelation that both disturb some readers and delight others, chapter 19 stands out because of its graphic character and celebratory tone. The chapter begins (19:1–10) with a fourfold chorus of "Hallelujahs" celebrating the demise of the prostitute of Babylon (Rome; see ch. 18) and the reign of "our Lord God." The chorus anticipates the coming "wedding supper of the Lamb." The second half of the chapter recounts three graphic visions of judgment: a royal warrior on a white horse, the "KING OF KINGS AND LORD OF LORDS" (19:11–16); an angel inviting birds to gather for "the great supper of God," where they will eat the defeated enemies (19:17–18); and the rider's defeat of those enemies, leading to the birds' feasting (19:19–21).

What are we to make of this imagery? Three things are helpful to keep in mind. First, Revelation is full of such word-pictures, like a series of political cartoons. They are not meant to be taken literally, but to stimulate the imagination and persuade the listener or reader to adopt John's perspective. Second, such imagery must be understood in light of the central image of Jesus as the slaughtered but standing Lamb (ch. 5). Third, John did not invent the image of a divine or messianic warrior; it appears in Israel's Scriptures and other Jewish writings. One such writing is Psalms of Solomon, which contains what is arguably the most important messianic text in Second Temple literature.

Psalms of Solomon

"HE SHALL STRIKE THE EARTH WITH THE WORD OF HIS MOUTH FOREVER"

Psalms of Solomon is a collection of eighteen hymns to God, compiled in the first century BC, that became part of the Greek Bible, or **Septuagint**. The messianic Psalm 17, at forty-six verses in modern versions, is the longest. The theological influences on the psalms are varied, including the canonical psalter, wisdom literature, the Deuteronomic tradition, and the prophets.

The historical context for these psalms, and particularly Psalm 17, is probably the aftermath of the capture of Jerusalem in 63 BC by the Roman general Pompey. The Psalms of Solomon also seem to be critical of the Jewish rulers the Romans essentially overthrew, the priestly family of Hasmoneans.[1] Although the Hasmoneans had given the Jews eight decades of independence, they were not descendants of David, and they had merged their priesthood with kingship. The composers of these psalms apparently believed Israel needed deliverance both from foreign oppression and from an illegitimate (if weakened) priestly kingship.

The Messiah. In Psalm 17,[2] we learn that this deliverance will come through a Davidic king, "the anointed of the Lord," or messiah (Greek *christos*; 17:32; also 18:5).[3] It can be divided into four parts:

1. Prologue: the Lord is king (17:1–3);
2. Narrative: the events that created the present crisis (17:4–20);
3. Prediction: the coming Davidic messiah, who will conquer enemies, purify God's people, and reign with justice (17:21–43);
4. Epilogue: hope because the Lord is king (17:44–46).

The description of the coming messiah in verses 21–43 is full and complex. Verses 21–25 are a prayer to the Lord to "raise up for them their king, the son of David" (17:21a), to rule Israel (17:21b), "shatter in pieces unrighteous rulers" (17:22a), purify Jerusalem from "nations that trample her down in destruction" (17:22b), "drive out sinners," and "smash the arrogance of the sinner like a potter's vessel" (17:23), "shatter all their substance

---

1. The Hasmoneans remained as client kings of Rome until the time of Herod the Great in 37 BC.

2. All quotations of Psalms of Solomon are taken from NETS.

3. There is scholarly debate about whether the original text said "the anointed of the Lord" or "the anointed, the Lord."

with an iron rod" (17:24a), "destroy the lawless nations by the word of his mouth" (17:24b), and more. Verses 26–29 emphasize the messiah's leading and judging in righteousness. Verses 30–43 tell us that he will be filled with God's Spirit (17:37) and be sinless (17:36). He will "shepherd" the people (17:40) in an era of peace, prosperity, and justice. The "peoples of the nations" will be "under his yoke" (17:30a) and "he shall strike the earth with the word of his mouth forever" (17:35a). Yet, paradoxically, he will have "pity on all the nations" (17:34b), and "he shall not put his hope in horse and rider and bow" or prepare for war (17:33).

Interpreting the Messiah. On the one hand, Psalm 17:22–24a, drawing especially on (canonical) Psalms 2 and 110 (which were often interpreted messianically), seems to portray a violent, militant warrior-messiah who will literally defeat all enemies, both domestic and (especially) foreign. On the other hand, verses 24b and 33–35a, drawing on other parts of Scripture, such as Isaiah 11 (which were also often interpreted messianically), suggest a nonviolent messiah who relies only on his words and on the Lord for victory (see Psalms 20, 33):

As this table illustrates, both literal and metaphorical battles—victory by war and by word—can be found in Israel's Scriptures. Scholars are divided when it comes to Psalms of Solomon 17. Many find it to depict a violent warrior-messiah, as in several Dead Seas Scrolls, but others disagree, stressing the psalm's focus on words. This tension and debate bring us to Revelation 19.

Table 17.1 Messianic Intertextuality in Psalms of Solomon 17

	Old Testament Texts	Psalm 17
Warfare	"You [the Lord's son, the anointed one = the king] will break them [the kings of the earth; the nations] with a rod of iron; you will dash them to pieces like pottery." (Ps. 2:9) "The Lord is at your right hand; he will crush [or "shatter"] kings on the day of his wrath." (Ps. 110:5)	"²²And gird him [the coming king, the son of David] with strength to shatter in pieces unrighteous rulers, to purify Ierousalem from nations that trample her down in destruction, ²³in wisdom of righteousness, to drive out sinners from the inheritance, to smash the arrogance of the sinner like a potter's vessel, ²⁴to shatter all their substance with an iron rod." (Pss. Sol. 17:22–24a)

Table 17.1 Messianic Intertextuality in Psalms of Solomon 17

Words	"But with righteousness he will judge the needy, with justice he will give decisions for the poor of the earth. He will strike the earth with the rod of his mouth; with the breath of his lips he will slay the wicked." (Isa. 11:4) "¹⁶No king is saved by the size of his army; no warrior escapes by his great strength. A horse is a vain hope for deliverance; despite all its great strength it cannot save." (Ps. 33:16–17; cf. Ps. 20:6–7)	"To destroy the lawless nations by the word of his mouth." (Pss. Sol. 17:24b) "³³For he shall not put his hope in horse and rider and bow, nor shall he multiply for himself gold and silver for war, nor shall he gather hopes from a multitude of people for the day of war. ³⁴The Lord himself is his king, the hope of him who is strong through hope in God, and he shall have pity on all the nations before him in fear. ³⁵For he shall strike the earth with the word of his mouth forever." (Pss. Sol. 17:33–35a)

Revelation 19:1–21

"HE IS DRESSED IN A ROBE DIPPED IN BLOOD, AND HIS NAME IS THE WORD OF GOD"

As noted above, Revelation 19 has two parts: an account of a heavenly chorus plus an angelic message (19:1–10), followed by three visions of messianic judgment (19:11–21). Some interpreters understand 19:11–21 to be the start of the last major section of Revelation, a series of visions of Christ's second coming, or **parousia**, and associated events.

The Heavenly Chorus and Angelic Message. Most of Revelation 19:1–10 is set in the heavenly throne room (19:4; cf. chs. 4–5; 7:9–17). The fourfold Hallelujah (19:1, 3, 4, 6) comes first from a great heavenly multitude (19:1, 3; cf. 7:9–10). They are joined by the twenty-four elders and four living creatures (19:4; cf. 4:4–11; 5:6–14). Next, a voice—probably angelic—invites all God's servants to join the chorus (19:5–8). This additional great multitude is made up of the "holy people" (19:8), the faithful on earth. As in chapters 4, 5, and 7, the breadth of participation in this "Hallelujah chorus" signifies that God is praised by all the faithful, whether on earth or in heaven, and by all creation.

The reason for this ascription of salvation (victory), glory, power, and praise (19:1, 5, 7) is that God has judged and defeated the great prostitute, demonstrating the Lord's justice and rightful sovereignty (19:6) and preparing for the Lamb's wedding supper (19:7, 9). The "bride" at this wedding (cf. 21:2, 9; 22:17) is comprised of the Lamb's faithful followers, clothed in the bright, pure garments of their righteous acts (19:8). The chorus of praise is followed by an exchange between the seer and the angel (who refuses to be worshiped) concerning the blessing of being invited to the supper as a part of the faithful, prophetic witness to Jesus (19:8–10).

As in Psalms of Solomon 17, the fundamental theological affirmation of Revelation 19:1–10 is the sovereignty of the Lord God over against all political and religious powers. In both texts, the people of God are enabled to participate in the peaceful and righteous fruits of that sovereignty, though the blissful existence is depicted in different images.

Visions of Messianic Judgment. At first glance, Revelation 19:11–21 looks more violent than Psalms of Solomon 17; its images are certainly more graphic. The first vision (19:11–16) is clearly a depiction of Jesus the Messiah (the "Root of David," 5:5), as echoes from the opening vision in 1:12–18 and other parts of Revelation indicate. This vision is best understood as an example of *ekphrasis*, a rhetorical device that invites the hearer/reader to encounter the person or object described. The second vision (19:17–18), of birds invited to God's great supper, offers a graphic preliminary image of the judgment and punishment that messianic (and thus divine) victory will entail. The third vision (19:19–21) briefly depicts the messiah's enemies gathered to make war. But they are defeated immediately, with the beast and his false prophet (from chapter 13, representing imperial power and worship) thrown into the fiery lake, and the rest consumed by the birds (see Ezek. 39:17–20).

The rendering of messiah Jesus and his judgment in 19:11–21 contains echoes of scriptural texts employed by Psalms of Solomon 17, including Psalm 2:9 (esp. 19:15). But Revelation's use of Isaiah 63 (see 19:13, 15), which graphically highlights wrath and blood, calls for special attention.

Whose Blood? There is a longstanding debate among interpreters of Revelation: In 19:13, is Jesus's robe dipped in the blood of his enemies or in his own blood? The echo of Isaiah 63:1–6, depicting the divine day of vengeance and the spilling of enemy blood, is clear:

Why are your garments red, like those of one treading the winepress? "I [the LORD] have trodden the winepress alone; from the nations no one was with me. I trampled them in my anger and trod them down in my wrath; their blood spattered my garments, and I stained all my clothing." (Isa 63:2–3; see Rev 19:13, 15)

Certain **Targums** interpret this text, in connection with Genesis 49:11, as a reference to enemy blood shed by the messiah.[4] What about Revelation?

If we take a narrative approach to Revelation and trace the character of Jesus, we find that "blood" is one of his defining character traits, telling us who he is and how he has achieved victory (see 3:21; 5:5): not by shedding others' blood, but by shedding his own blood (cf. 1:5; 5:9; 7:14). Jesus is not the slaughtering Lamb, but the slaughtered—and standing (resurrected)—Lamb (5:6, 9, 12; 13:8). Jesus's disciples both benefit from and share in Jesus's death/blood (6:10; 7:14; 16:6; 17:6; 18:24) by "conquering" as he did: remaining faithful in the face of death (3:21). If faithfulness to the one called "Faithful and True" (19:11) means willingness to have one's own blood shed (12:11), together with refusal to shed blood (13:10), then it would be unfaithful of John to turn Jesus into a slaughtering savior. This means that John reads Scripture christologically—in light of Jesus. Because Jesus established his messianic kingdom by dying rather than killing, John interprets scriptural images of divine and messianic violence, including Isaiah 63, nonviolently.

To be sure, Revelation can use blood as a symbol of divine judgment (6:12; 8:7–9; 11:6; 14:20; 16:3–6), but the blood associated specifically with Jesus, as the book progresses and culminates in chapter 19, is his own blood.

What Kind of Sword? What Kind of War? If blood in 19:13 is that of Jesus, then we should also conclude that his sword (19:15, 21) is not literal but metaphorical, symbolizing what is sometimes called a performative utterance: speech that actually makes something happen. It represents Jesus's own word, and indeed himself, since his name is "the Word of God" (19:13; cf. John 1). His word—his person—is the means of both divine judgment and divine salvation (see Wis. 18:14–16), no doubt associated with the "eternal gospel" that is going out to all (14:6). Together, Jesus's sword and his blood represent that divine promise of judgment and salvation.

John's warrior imagery, beginning in 19:11, including his use of Psalm 2, Psalm 110, and other scriptural texts,[5] should be understood metaphorically and christologically rather than literally and violently.

Two Kinds of Messiahs? How shall we read Psalms of Solomon 17 and Revelation 19 side by side? The two messianic portraits are constructed in

---

4. E.g., Tg. Neof. Gen 49:11.
5. See, for example, Deut 20:13; Ps 68:17; Isa 49:2.

light of similar political fears and hopes, and they draw on similar scriptural texts—texts that are sometimes in tension with one another. Together they raise the question of how those texts were read in such political situations. Will the messiah conquer by war or by word? Do we have depictions of (a) two violent messiahs, (b) two nonviolent messiahs, or (c) one of each? If the answer is (c), then which messiah is violent?

The view of Revelation offered here is that John's interpretive stance toward Scripture, politics, and Jesus in Revelation 19 is shaped by the larger narrative in which this portion of his messianic portrait appears. The jury is still out, however, on Psalms of Solomon 17. It may be another example of preferring a powerful word to a literal war, or it may highlight the distinctive messiah of Revelation.

FOR FURTHER READING

Additional Ancient Texts

Other texts about messianic/eschatological warfare include the Dead Sea Scrolls 1QM 10–12, 15–19; 1QSb 5; 4QpIsa[a]; 4Q174; 4Q285; 2 Baruch 36–40, 72; 4 Ezra 13; Sibylline Oracles 3:657–701; 1 Corinthians 15:24–28; 2 Thessalonians 1:5–2:12. For a banquet (sometimes messianic) as an image of salvation, see, for example, Isaiah 25:6–10a; 55:1–5; 1 Enoch 62:12–16; 2 Baruch 29; Matthew 22:1–14; Luke 14:7–24; as an image of judgment, see Ezekiel 39:17–20; 2 Baruch 29:4.

English Translations and Critical Editions

NETS

Wright, R. B. *"Psalms of Solomon*: A New Translation and Introduction." Pages 639–70 in vol. 2 of *The Old Testament Pseudepigrapha*. Edited by James H. Charlesworth. Garden City, NY: Doubleday, 1985.

———. *Psalms of Solomon: A Critical Edition of the Greek Text*. London: T&T Clark, 2007.

Secondary Literature

Atkinson, Kenneth. *I Cried to the Lord: A Study of the Psalms of Solomon's Historical Background and Social Setting*. Boston: Brill, 2004.

Barr, David L. "The Lamb Who Looks Like a Dragon? Characterizing Jesus in John's Apocalypse." Pages 205–20 in *The Reality of Apocalypse: Rhetoric and Politics in the Book of Revelation*. Edited by David L. Barr. Atlanta: SBL, 2006.

Barnhill, Gregory M. "Seeing Christ through Hearing the Apocalypse: An Exploration of John's Use of Ekphrasis in Revelation 1 and 19." *JSNT* 39 (2017): 235–57.

Trafton, Joseph L. "What Would David Do? Messianic Expectation and Surprise in Ps. Sol. 17." Pages 155–74 in *The Psalms of Solomon: Language, History, Theology*. Edited by Eberhard Bons and Patrick Pouchelle. Atlanta: SBL, 2015.

Zacharias, Danny. "The Son of David in Psalms of Solomon 17." Pages 73–87 in *"Non-canonical" Religious Texts in Early Judaism and Early Christianity*. Edited by Lee Martin McDonald and James H. Charlesworth. London: T&T Clark, 2012.

CHAPTER 18

The Book of the Watchers and Revelation 20:1–15: Redemptive Judgment on Fallen Angels

ELIZABETH E. SHIVELY

Revelation 20:1–15 tells the story of how God finally ousts and judges Satan. The story goes like this: on the authority of Christ, an angel binds Satan and imprisons him for a thousand years to prevent him from deceiving the nations (presumably, to make war against the saints). During that time, the saints reign with Christ. After that time, Satan is released to deceive the nations again into making war against the saints, but he is defeated and thrown into the lake of fire forever, to be joined by Death, Hades, and those whose names are not in the book of life.

This short story shares a structure, language, and ideas with other ancient Jewish texts that tell a similar story about the overthrow and destruction of Satan and his cohorts. Currents of a story about God's destruction of evil appear in Isaiah, who describes the fall of ambitious kings in cosmic terms (Isa 14:12–14; 24:21–22). Apocalyptic texts in the Second Temple period expand on Isaiah's story line to tell of how God overthrows fallen angels and human counterparts in order to make a new world for God's people (1 En. 10:4–6, 11–13; 13:1–2; 18:12–16; 19:1–2; 2 En. 7:1–2; Jub. 5:6–14; Jude 6; 2 Pet 2:4; Rev 12:7–17). Revelation 20:1–15 moves in the stream of this exegetical tradition.

Rather than identifying discrete parallels between certain texts and Revelation 20:1–15, I will look at how John employs this stream of exegetical tradition, particularly as it is reflected in 1 Enoch 10:4–8, 11–15, to tell the story of how God removes Satan to restore his rule and judge in favor of the saints.

The Book of the Watchers

"Go, Raphael, and bind Asael. . . . Go, Michael, bind Shemihazah"

Redemptive Judgment. First Enoch consists of five separate books composed over a range of five centuries.[1] First Enoch 10 belongs to the first book, the Book of the Watchers (1 En. 1–36). The centerpiece of the book is the story of how the watchers—fallen angels—leave their proper place in heaven and, as a result, bring evil to the earth (chs. 6–11; cf. Gen 6:1–13). This leads to the judgment at the flood, which represents the judgment at the end.[2] The judgment is set in motion when God's people cry out for justice against the rebel angels and their offspring. Four holy archangels intercede on behalf of humanity, and God responds by commissioning them to execute judgment (10:1–3).

I focus on God's instructions to two of the archangels, Raphael and Michael, to bind and imprison two of the watchers, Asael and Shemihazah, respectively:

> [4] To Raphael he said, "Go, Raphael, and bind Asael hand and foot, and cast him into the darkness; And make an opening in the wilderness that is in Doudael. [5] Throw him there, and lay beneath him sharp and jagged stones. And cover him with darkness, and let him dwell there for an exceedingly long time. Cover up his face, and let him not see the light. [6] And on the day of the great judgment, he will be led away to the burning conflagration. [7] And heal the earth, which the watchers have desolated; And announce the healing of the earth, that the plague may be healed, And all the sons of men may not perish because of the mystery that the watchers told and taught their sons. [8] And all the earth was made desolate by the deeds of the teaching of Asael, And over him write all the sins." (1 En. 10:4–8)[3]

> [11] And to Michael he said, "Go, Michael, bind Shemihazah and the others with him, who have mated with the daughters of men, so that

---

1. For more information about 1 Enoch, see chapter 1 in this volume by Benjamin E. Reynolds ("The Parables of Enoch and Revelation 1:1–20: Daniel's Son of Man").

2. Nickelsburg, *1 Enoch*, 7.

3. The translation is from George W. E. Nickelsburg and James C. VanderKam, *1 Enoch. The Hermeneia Translation* (Minneapolis: Fortress, 2012).

they were defiled by them in their uncleanness. [12] And when their sons perish and they see the destruction of their beloved ones, bind them for seventy generations in the valleys of the earth, until the day of their judgment and consummation, until the everlasting judgment is consummated. [13] Then they will be led away to the fiery abyss, and to the torture, and to the prison where they will be confined forever. [14] And everyone who is condemned and destroyed henceforth will be bound together with them until the consummation of their generation. And at the time of the judgment which I shall judge, they will perish for all generations. [15] Destroy all the spirits of the half-breeds and the sons of the watchers, because they have wronged men. (1 En. 10:11–15)

Binding Fallen Angels. Verse 4a gives an overview of God's instruction that Raphael bind Asael and cast him into darkness; then verses 4b–5 explain the details and time frame of that instruction ("make an opening . . . throw him there . . . lay beneath him . . . cover him . . . let him dwell there"). The instruction to "bind Asael hand and foot" conjures the image of a criminal that is arrested, chained, and thrown into a prison (cf. Acts 12:6; 21:11, 33; 22:5). The prison, Doudael, is the equivalent of Sheol, in this case a holding cell until the time of punishment by fire at the final judgment (1 En. 10:6). Bound, Asael's power and influence over human beings is removed so that Raphael may heal the earth that the watchers have ravaged (10:7).

The instruction to Michael follows a similar pattern to those given to Raphael. Verse 11b gives an overview of God's instruction to Michael to bind Shemihazah and all the other watchers who impregnated women; verse 12 explains the details and time frame of the instruction. Then verse 13 describes the fiery punishment at the final judgment after seventy generations. This is portrayed as an abyss, an eternal place of torture and a prison for demons (see 1 En. 21:7–10; cf. Luke 8:31). Yet it is also a place for which wicked humanity is bound, or restricted, together with the watchers and their offspring for eternal punishment (1 En. 10:14–15). God then instructs Michael to obliterate evil from the earth in order to prepare a renewed place for the righteous to live, using fertile earth imagery evocative of God's blessings and a new creation (10:16–11:2).[4]

In this story, the binding and imprisonment of Asael and of Shemihazah marks a watershed moment in the removal of their reign over humanity and

---

4. Nickelsburg, *1 Enoch*, 227.

the earth. It signals a regime change wherein the evil powers that deceive humanity, victimize God's people, and ravage the earth are ousted and God is restored as the rightful ruler over humankind, the world, and the cosmos.

Revelation 20:1–15

"HE SEIZED THE DRAGON, THAT
ANCIENT SERPENT"

Need for Redemptive Judgment. In Revelation, the cry of human beings rises up to God, and he responds by executing judgment against evildoers and their supernatural instigators, not unlike the basic story line in the Book of the Watchers. Specifically, the martyred saints cry out to God to avenge their blood on the inhabitants of the earth (Rev 6:10; cf. 8:3–4; 19:24). The rest of Revelation essentially unfolds God's response in a series of judgments (compare, e.g., 6:10 with, e.g., 16:1–9).

Revelation 12 reveals that the dragon/Satan is at the heart of this persecution (anticipated in 2:9–10, 13, 24). According to John, Satan is "the deceiver of the whole world" (12:9 ESV). Michael leads the angels in a war against Satan and throws him out of heaven, after which Satan's chief aim is to make war on the community of faith (the woman's children), who keep God's commandments and maintain a faithful witness to Jesus (12:17; cf. 1:2). Chapter 13 then describes how Satan wages this war: he gives authority to the beast/state so that "it was given power to wage war against God's holy people and to conquer them. And it was given authority over every tribe, people, language and nation. All inhabitants of the earth will worship the beast—all whose names have not been written in the Lamb's book of life" (13:7–8; see also 13:11–18; cf. 18:23; 19:20). In short, Satan wages war against the saints by deceiving the whole world in order to establish a pseudo-kingdom.

Climactically, Revelation 17–20 unfolds the final judgment against the nations, institutions, human beings, and, ultimately, the cosmic forces that have joined to perpetrate violence against those who refuse to acknowledge Satan's pseudo-kingdom. In Revelation 20:1, Jesus has presumably commissioned and authorized the heavenly angel by giving him the key to the bottomless pit in order to bind Satan and lock him away (compare Rev 1:18; 3:7; 9:1).

Below, I show how the story line of Revelation 20:1–15 maps onto that in 1 Enoch 10:4–8, 11–15, thus reflecting a common stream of tradition:

Figure 18.1: Revelation 20 and the Book of the Watchers

Revelation 20:1–15	1 Enoch 10:4–6	1 Enoch 10:8–11
An angel authorized by Christ	Raphael authorized by God to bind Asael,	Michael authorized by God to bind Shemihazah and others.
binds the dragon/ancient serpent/devil/Satan,	casts him into the darkness,	
throws him into the pit, and locks and seals the pit over him,	covers him with darkness,	binds them in the valleys of the earth
	and heals the earth	and heals the earth
so that he will deceive the nations no more for a thousand years.	that the watchers desolated for an exceedingly long time.	for seventy generations.
Afterwards he is released from his prison . . . [war against the saints] and Satan is thrown into the lake of fire for everlasting torture.	On the great day of judgment, he will be released to the burning conflagration.	On the day of judgment, they will be released to the fiery abyss.

Reversing the Power Dynamic. Similar to 1 Enoch, in Revelation 20 Satan is bound for a *duration* and a *purpose*. The heavenly angel throws Satan into the pit, locks and seals it for one thousand years—or a very long time—*in order that* (Gk. *hina*) he may not deceive the nations.[5] In light of the larger context of Revelation and the stream of interpretative tradition, it is most likely that the restraint of Satan's deception has to do with reestablishing God's rightful reign and reversing the state of affairs for the saints.[6] This is further supported by the fact that when Satan is released from prison, he deceives the nations so that they join him once again to make war on the saints (20:7–8; cf. ch. 13).

John has depicted Satan as "the deceiver of the whole world" (12:9 ESV) who wages war against the saints by authorizing the beast/state to establish a pseudo-kingdom and deceive the inhabitants of the earth into false worship

---

5. The degree of Satan's restraint can only be inferred from context. See Beale and Osborne for arguments that Satan is only partially restricted. G. K. Beale, *The Book of Revelation*, NIGTC (Grand Rapids: Eerdmans, 1999), 989–91; Grant R. Osborne, *Revelation*, BECNT (Grand Rapids: Baker Academic, 2002), 690–94.

6. I take those seated on the thrones and the martyrs in 20:4 as one group: the martyrs represent all the saints who have stood as faithful witnesses to Christ.

on punishment of death. Because of Satan's deception, the faithful are marginalized, subjugated, victimized, and many face martyrdom for failure to worship the beast (13:7–9, 15). The saints do not resemble the kingdom of priests who conquer and reign with Christ (1:6; cf. 2:26–27; 3:21); rather, their true status has been hidden. But now the heavenly angel reverses the state of affairs by removing Satan's power and influence to deceive the nations so that it is not possible for Satan to create an alternative world or kingdom to God's. The saints under the altar had cried out to God for judgment against their oppressors (6:10); now God finally judges in their favor ("judgment was given for them," 20:4, my translation) and they openly reign with Christ without fear, their true status on display (20:4–6).

Final Rebellion and Judgment. In the story of the watchers, the fallen angels are released from their prison immediately to their fiery judgment. In Revelation 20, however, Satan is released from his prison for a penultimate act. He deceives the nations again to muster an army for war against the saints and holy city. John further adapts the stream of exegetical tradition by fusing it with Ezekiel 38–39—the account in which Gog and Magog attack God's people—to describe Satan's final assault. It may be that John seeks to demonstrate Satan and unbelieving humanity's unrelenting hostility toward God and his people, such that their intensified rebellion demonstrates "the extent of human depravity."[7] In that case, this final act of war functions to justify God's final judgment in which Satan, Death, Hades, and unrepentant humanity are thrown into the lake of fire (20:10, 14–15).

Yet John's ultimate point is about reversing the state of affairs: Out of the obliteration of Satan's pseudo-reign emerges the new heaven and earth, and the new Jerusalem, where God and the Lamb reign with his people forever (21:1–4).

FOR FURTHER READING

Additional Ancient Texts

Second Temple apocalyptic texts depict God's overthrow of fallen angels or Satan (or the equivalent) and human counterparts, signaling a cosmic regime change that results in blessings for God's people: 1 Enoch 10:4–6, 11–13; 13:1–2; 18:12–16; 19:1–2; 2 Enoch 7:1–2; Jubilees 5:6–14; 23:23–31; 50:5; Testament of Moses 10:1; 1QM 1:5, 8–9, 12; 12:9–18; 17:6–7; 18:6–8, 10–11; 19:4–8; 11Q13. See also related NT texts: Jude 6; 2 Pet 2:4; Rev 12:7–17.

---

7. Osborne, *Revelation*, 702.

English Translations and Critical Editions

Bertalotto, Pierpaolo, Ken M. Penner, and Ian W. Scott, eds. "1 Enoch."
    In *The Online Critical Pseudepigrapha*. Edited by Ian W. Scott, Ken
    M. Penner, and David M. Miller. 1.5 ed. Atlanta: Society of Biblical
    Literature, 2006. www.purl.org/net/ocp/1En.

Isaac, E. "1 (Ethiopic Apocalypse of) Enoch: A New Translation and Intro-
    duction." Pages 13–89 in vol. 1 of *The Old Testament Pseudepigrapha*.
    Edited by James H. Charlesworth. Garden City, NY: Doubleday, 1983.

Knibb, Michael A. "1 Enoch." Pages 184–319 in *The Apocryphal Old Testament*.
    Edited by H. F. D. Sparks. Oxford: Clarendon, 1984.

———. *The Ethiopic Book of Enoch*. 2 vols. Oxford: Clarendon, 1978.

Nickelsburg, George W. E., and James C. VanderKam. *1 Enoch. The Hermeneia
    Translation*. Minneapolis: Fortress Press, 2012.

Olson, Daniel C. *Enoch: A New Translation*. North Richmond Hills, TX:
    BIBAL, 2004.

Secondary Literature

Evans, Craig A. "Inaugurating the Kingdom of God and Defeating the
    Kingdom of Satan." *BBR* 15 (2005): 49–75.

Nickelsburg, George W. E. *1 Enoch 1: A Commentary of the Book of 1 Enoch,
    Chapters 1–36; 81–108*. Hermeneia. Minneapolis: Fortress, 2001.

Parker, Harold M. "The Scriptures of the Author of the Revelation of John."
    Iliff Review 37 (1980): 35–51.

Stuckenbruck, Loren T. *The Myth of Rebellious Angels: Studies in Second
    Temple Judaism and New Testament Texts*. Grand Rapids: Eerdmans,
    2017.

CHAPTER 19

4 Ezra and Revelation 21:1–22:5: Paradise City

JONATHAN A. MOO

"Then I saw 'a new heaven and a new earth'" (Rev 21:1). This is the moment toward which all of Revelation is oriented, a vision of the new creation foreshadowed in the promises given to the seven churches in chapters 2–3 and glimpses of which have sometimes pierced through the gloom of the book's scenes of destruction, suffering, and woe. Here readers find the fruition of the victory won by the Lamb, the making of all things new (21:5), the coming to earth of the New Jerusalem (21:2, 9–27), and a restored Edenic paradise (22:1–5). It is a world taken beyond threat—no more death, mourning, sorrow, or pain (21:4). Above all, it is a vision centered on and defined by the presence of God with his people (21:3).

John's vision concerns the future, but it is a future that has broken into the present through the victory of the Lamb. It is intended to transform the life of John's readers now. If they are to flee Babylon (18:4), they need an alternative vision of the city of God to fire their imagination, a New Jerusalem to which they can belong.

Like all of Revelation, John's vision in 21:1–22:5 is suffused with imagery drawn from the Old Testament. And although no other text matches John's vision in its imaginative sweep and density of imagery, many themes that occur here are also found in other early Jewish texts. In this chapter we focus on 4 Ezra, a Jewish apocalypse roughly contemporaneous with Revelation and with which it shares not only its genre, but a number of motifs and ideas. It is unlikely that either author knew of the other's book, and it would be misleading to suggest that every point of connection or contrast is significant. But an analysis of how each text has made its own use of common traditions illuminates much that is distinctive about their respective visions.

4 Ezra

"IT IS FOR YOU THAT PARADISE IS OPENED"

Gerhard von Rad claimed that 4 Ezra is "one of the finest things ever written" in Israel.[1] Composed perhaps thirty years after the Romans had destroyed the Jerusalem temple in 70 AD (3:1), 4 Ezra contains the most daring questions found in any early Jewish or Christian text about God's justice and mercy in the face of pain and loss.[2] Like the biblical Job, the author wrestles with how a good, powerful, and loving God can allow his people to suffer. The author uses the name of the biblical Ezra, finding his situation analogous to Ezra's after the fall of the first temple. The author mourns "the desolation of Zion" (3:2), unable to find any adequate explanation for why God should have "destroyed your people" (3:30). Even if Israel's disobedience led to God's judgment, why then does God allow "Babylon" and other nations who do not keep God's commandments to prosper? This apparent injustice in God's dealing with Israel leads Ezra, in his dialogue with the angel Uriel, to ask wider questions about God's dealings with his creation: How can God allow so many of those whom he creates to perish? Why are so few saved in the end?

Ezra does not receive very assuring answers. He is directed instead to remember the limitations of his understanding and to shift his focus from the fate of the many who will be lost to the age to come and the hope of those (few) like him who will be saved. In the fourth of the book's seven episodes, Ezra, after spending seven days in a field of flowers, begins to accept the justice of God's ways, however inexplicable they might remain (7:29–37). Then Ezra encounters a mourning woman who, as he comforts her, is transformed before his eyes into a glorious city, a new "Zion" (9:38–10:59). He is rewarded with visions of God's judgment of Rome and the nations, brought about by the Messiah, and he sees the salvation of the remnant of God's people in the land—as well as the gathering of the lost tribes of Israel, a "peaceable multitude" (13:12, 39–47). This vision perhaps comforts Ezra that the number to be saved is much larger than he has realized, and that God's justice will finally be done in the end.

As this summary indicates, eschatological material is woven through all the sections of 4 Ezra, occurring not only in the visions near the end but also in the speeches of Ezra and especially in those of the angel Uriel. The table below identifies key features of 4 Ezra's eschatological vision:

---

1. Gerhard von Rad, *Wisdom in Israel*, trans. J. D. Martin (Harrisburg, PA: Trinity Press International, 1972), 41.
2. For more information about 4 Ezra, see chapter 4 in this volume by Dana M. Harris ("4 Ezra and Revelation 5:1–14: Creaturely Images of the Messiah").

Table 19.1: Key Features of the Eschatological Vision of 4 Ezra

Theme	Examples
Messiah	When the Messiah is revealed, "those who remain shall rejoice four hundred years. After those years my son[1] the Messiah shall die, and all who draw human breath." (7:28–29)[2]
	"This is the Messiah whom the Most High has kept until the end of days. . . . In mercy he will set free the remnant of my people, those who have been saved throughout my borders, and he will make them joyful until the end comes, the day of judgment." (12:32–34)
	"This is he whom the Most High has been keeping for many ages, who will himself deliver his creation." (13:26)
	"He shall stand on the top of Mount Zion. And Zion shall come and be made manifest to all people, prepared and built, as you saw the mountain carved out without hands." (13:35–36)
	"And as for your seeing him gather to himself another multitude that was peaceable, these are the nine tribes." (13:39–40)
City	"The city that now is not seen shall appear." (7:26)
	"A city is built." (8:52)
	"When I looked up, the woman was no longer visible to me, but a city was being[3] built, and a place of huge foundations showed itself." (10:27)
	"The woman whom you saw is Zion, which you now behold as a city being built." (10:44; cf. 13:35–36, above)
Land	"The land that now is hidden shall be disclosed." (7:26)
	"My salvation in my land and within my borders, which I have sanctified for myself from the beginning." (9:8; cf. 13:48–49)
Paradise	"A paradise shall be revealed, whose fruit remains unspoiled and in which are abundance and healing." (7:123)
	"It is for you that paradise is opened, the tree of life is planted, the age to come is prepared, plenty is provided, a city is built, rest is appointed, goodness is established and wisdom perfected beforehand. The root of evil is sealed up from you, illness is banished from you, and death is hidden; Hades has fled and corruption has been forgotten; sorrows have passed away, and in the end the treasure of immortality is made manifest." (8:52–54)

[1] Although the NRSV, based on the Latin and most manuscripts of 4 Ezra, identifies the Messiah as God's "son" (cf. Ps 2:7), the Ethiopic version has "servant," which may more likely reflect the original (see Jonathan A. Moo, *Creation, Nature and Hope in Fourth Ezra*, FRLANT 237 [Göttingen: Vandenhoeck & Ruprecht, 2011], 126n75). Fourth Ezra has a complicated textual history, being originally written in Hebrew (now lost) and subsequently translated into Greek (now lost); it was the Greek that formed the basis for subsequent translations into the extant Latin, Syriac, Ethiopic, Armenian, Georgian, and Arabic versions.

[2] Translations are from the NRSV.

[3] Here and at 10:42, 44, the non-Latin versions describe the city as *already* built or established, as is clear in 13:36.

A Messianic Kingdom and an Age to Come. These motifs can be divided into two complexes: one focuses on the Messiah, the land of Israel, and Zion; the other includes resurrection, paradise, and the future immortal age.[3] Although in places it is difficult to determine which complex of events is in view, in 7:26–44 they are described as two chronological stages: first, the revelation of the Messiah, land, and city yields a 400-year period of joy, followed by the Messiah's death and the return of the world to its primeval silence (7:29); then comes resurrection, final judgment, and—though it is described only in prospect here—a vision of the two options that await, the "pit of torment" or "paradise of delight" (7:36).

City and Paradise. One of the things that may be surprising about 4 Ezra's eschatology is the lack of explicit mention of a temple, but this is because the city of Zion is conflated with the temple. Thus, although in 3:24 David is said to be commanded to build the city (of Jerusalem), in 10:46 it is Solomon who built the city. Solomon, of course, built the *temple*; but, for 4 Ezra, the city of Zion and temple are considered as one. In this light, it is interesting that 4 Ezra sometimes includes elements from both complexes of events together, and, significantly, "paradise" and the "built city" are connected (8:52). This connection between city-temple and paradise is hinted at in 3:6, where the garden of Eden is said to have been planted before the creation of the earth. As Hindy Najman points out, this echoes a motif found in Jubilees 3:8–14 and 4Q265 7 II, 14, wherein the garden of Eden is pictured as the Holy of Holies, the place of God's presence.[4] Although the theme of God dwelling in the new Zion and future paradise is not developed at length in 4 Ezra, in 7:98 the greatest blessing for the righteous souls awaiting final judgment is the anticipation that they will "see the face of him whom they served in life and from whom they are to receive their reward when glorified" (7:98).

Obedience, Faith, and Nonviolence. In the meantime, God's people are called to faith and works of obedience (e.g., 9:7; 13:23; 14:34) in anticipation of receiving mercy and life after death (14:34–45). Yet no work of theirs can contribute to the city that will one day be revealed, for it is already "prepared and built" (13:36): "no work of human construction could endure in a place where the city of the Most High was to be revealed" (10:54). Fourth Ezra rejects political revolt and violence. God alone will bring in the age to come. Precluding any would-be claimants to the role of Messiah, Ezra learns

---

3. Michael E. Stone, *Features of the Eschatology of IV Ezra*, HSS 35 (Atlanta: Scholars Press, 1989), 222–25; Moo, *Creation, Nature and Hope*, 105–59.

4. Hindy Najman, *Losing the Temple and Recovering the Future: An Analysis of 4 Ezra* (Cambridge: Cambridge University Press, 2014), 108–16.

that "no one on earth can see my Son [or "servant"] or those who are with him, except in the time of his day" (13:52). The multitude that gathers to the Messiah is therefore "peaceable" (13:12, 39), faithfully keeping the law (13:42)—just as 4 Ezra expects of his readers.

Revelation 21:1–22:5

"GOD'S DWELLING PLACE IS NOW AMONG THE PEOPLE"

The New Heaven and New Earth Is the Messianic Kingdom. In 4 Ezra's vision, the focus shifts between the messianic age and immortal age to come. Although the associated motifs are sometimes blurred together, each complex of events retains different emphases and answers somewhat different questions. Strikingly, John's vision in Revelation attests to a similar timeline as 4 Ezra: there is a temporary, interim period of the rule of the Messiah and the martyrs (albeit 1,000 years rather than 400 years; Rev. 20:4–6), followed by the general resurrection and final judgment (20:11–15), and then "a new heaven and a new earth" (21:1). But the focus of John's vision of the end is almost entirely on the "new heaven and new earth." The motifs that 4 Ezra associates with the messianic age turn up in Revelation not in the millennium of chapter 20 but in the vision of the new heaven and new earth of 21:1–22:5. Ezra saw a Zion of huge foundations, a city already prepared and built; John sees a holy city, the New Jerusalem, with twelve foundations (21:14), already "prepared" (21:2) and coming down from God. Whatever John intends to convey with his brief description of the millennium, for him the fulfillment of Old Testament promises of land and temple, the place of the eternal earthly reign of God and Christ and his people (22:3, 5), and the appropriate focus of his readers' hopes belong to the new heaven and new earth, the New Jerusalem of 21:1–22:5.

City, Paradise, and God's Presence. John's description of the New Jerusalem represents a fuller development of a theme that is hinted at in 4 Ezra, the association of the city-temple with the Holy of Holies and the paradise of God. For John, there is no temple in the New Jerusalem, because God and the Lamb dwell there (21:22). It is a place defined by the presence of God with his people (21:3), where they see his face (22:4), so there is no need of a separate temple for God's presence. The entire city is described as a Holy of Holies, as indicated by the otherwise inexplicable description of the city's massive cubic shape (21:16). In this paradise-city is the tree of life, its fruit for the healing of the nations (22:2).

A Universal Hope. The presence of the nations (21:24, 26; 22:2), as well as the kings of the earth (21:24), reveals two points of contrast with the vision of 4 Ezra. Whereas 4 Ezra does not describe a future for the "nations" and kings other than judgment, in Revelation they turn up in the New Jerusalem—surprisingly, since their role in the narrative thus far has been as the enemies of God and his people. But John has emphasized throughout his book the universality of the victory won by the Lamb, who with his blood "purchased for God persons from every tribe and language and people and nation" (5:9).

Faithful Resistance and Active Witness. The second point of contrast with 4 Ezra is that not only do the kings and nations enter through the ever-open gates of the New Jerusalem, but they bring along with them their "splendor" and "glory" (21:24, 26). This is an example of a stronger element of continuity between the present age and the new creation to come in John's vision. Though the new creation is given as a gift of God and could never be brought in through mere human effort (and certainly not through violence, which characterizes Babylon rather than the followers of the slain Lamb), John nonetheless envisions a role for God's people that contributes to the adornment of the bride of the Lamb (19:8) and the splendor of the New Jerusalem. By their faithful witness to Christ, their righteous acts, their resistance to Babylon, and even cultural activity that reflects their role as a priestly kingdom (1:6; 5:10; 20:6; 22:5), there is the potential for the work of God's people to be included in the "all things" that will be made new (21:5).

Revelation and 4 Ezra inherit many of the same traditions, have some of the same hopes and expectations for the future, and share a concern to call their readers to faithfulness, nonviolence, and trust in God. Yet it is John's vision of the victorious slain Lamb at the center of God's throne (Rev. 5:1–14) that distinctively shapes his conception of life now and in the age to come. It is with this vision that he intends to transform his readers too.

FOR FURTHER READING

Additional Ancient Texts

Among many texts that describe the new creation, restored paradise, and/or a new temple or city, readers might consult Baruch 4:30–5:9; Tobit 13:16–17; 1 Enoch 24:3–25:7; 45; 90:28–29; 91:16; Jubilees 1:29; 4:26; 2 Baruch 32:6; 44:12; 49:3; LAB 3:10; 32:17; Testament of Dan 5:12; Testament of Levi 18:6–11; 1QS 4:25; 4Q174 I.1–13. Elsewhere in the New Testament, see Matt 19:28; Rom 8:18–25; Heb 11:10; 12:22; 2 Pet 3:13.

English Translations and Critical Editions

NRSV (2 Esdras)

Metzger, Bruce M. "Fourth Ezra." Pages 517–59 in vol. 1 of *The Old Testament Pseudepigrapha*. Edited by J. H. Charlesworth. New York: Doubleday, 1983.

Stone, Michael E. *Fourth Ezra*. Hermeneia. Minneapolis: Fortress, 1990.

Wong, Andy, with Ken M. Penner and David M. Miller, eds. "4 Ezra." In *The Online Critical Pseudepigrapha*. Edited by Ken M. Penner and Ian W. Scott. Atlanta: Society of Biblical Literature, 2010. www.purl.org/net/ocp/4Ezra.

Secondary Literature

Bauckham, Richard. *The Climax of Prophecy: Studies on the Book of Revelation*. Edinburgh: T&T Clark, 1993.

Henze, Matthias, and Gabriele Boccaccini, eds. *Fourth Ezra and Second Baruch: Reconstruction after the Fall*. SJSJ 164. Leiden: Brill, 2013.

Lee, Pilchan. *The New Jerusalem in the Book of Revelation*. WUNT 2/129. Tübingen: Mohr Siebeck, 2001.

Moo, Jonathan. *Creation, Nature and Hope in 4 Ezra*. FRLANT 237. Göttingen: Vandenhoeck & Ruprecht, 2011.

Najman, Hindy. *Losing the Temple and Recovering the Future: An Analysis of 4 Ezra*. Cambridge: Cambridge University Press, 2014.

CHAPTER 20

The Apocalypse of Zephaniah and Revelation 22:6–21: Angel Worship and Monotheistic Devotion

SARAH UNDERWOOD DIXON

The beginning of the epilogue to the book of Revelation (22:6–21) begins with a confident reassurance from John's guiding angel regarding the vision that he has been given: "These words are trustworthy and true" (22:6). Upon hearing this declaration, John surprises the reader by falling down in worship before the angel. It is a shocking scene, especially given that John is obviously a devoted follower of Christ. And given that John's audience would have been devoted monotheists, one can imagine that reporting such an action could have potentially discredited John and his apocalypse. Therefore, one must ask: What is the point of this scene? Why has John included it in his epilogue?

Interestingly, Revelation is not the only text to include scenes where the recipient of a vision attempts to worship an angel and is then rebuked and exhorted to worship God. The Apocalypse of Zephaniah, another apocalyptic text from sometime in the first century BC or first century AD, includes a similar scene. Indeed, the similarities between the texts make them ripe for comparison. As we shall see, comparing the two texts will reveal not only their similarities but will also highlight the theological significance of the scene in Revelation.

The Apocalypse of Zephaniah

"DON'T WORSHIP ME. I AM NOT THE LORD ALMIGHTY"

The Apocalypse of Zephaniah is a fragmentary apocalyptic text dating from sometime between 100 BC and AD 70.[1] There are three preserved texts: a short Greek quotation in Clement of Alexandria; two pages of a Sahidic manuscript; and a longer eighteen-page Akhimic text (though with a large lacuna).[2] Although it is estimated that well over half of the text is missing, the extant portions provide valuable insight into the world of Jewish apocalypses.

A Heavenly Journey and Angelic Encounters. In the surviving text, the seer, Zephaniah,[3] is led on a cosmic journey by an angel of the Lord. After a brief fragment commenting on the burial of the dead, the Akhimic text begins with Zephaniah being taken to a heavenly city located above Jerusalem.[4] There he sees both the righteous as well as the souls of those in eternal punishment. The angel then leads him to Mount Seir, where Zephaniah sees angels who record all the righteous deeds of the people, as well as those angels who record the unrighteous deeds of the people in order to pass them along to "the accuser." This juxtaposition of "angels of the righteous" with "angels of the unrighteous" continues again outside the heavenly city (ch. 4) and also in Hades (ch. 6). It is here that Zephaniah meets the accuser, who has a book recording people's sins and shortcomings. But Zephaniah also here encounters Eremiel, who holds a record of Zephaniah's good deeds.

Worship Only the Lord Almighty. Zephaniah describes meeting this majestic heavenly being:

> Then I arose and stood, and I saw a great angel standing before me with his face shining like the rays of the sun in its glory since his face is like that which is perfected in its glory. And he was girded as if a golden girdle were upon his breast. His feet were like bronze which

---

1. The following translations and comments draw from O. S. Wintermute, "Apocalypse of Zephaniah (First Century BC–First Century AD): A New Translation and Introduction," in vol. 1 of *The Old Testament Pseudepigrapha*, ed. James H. Charlesworth (Garden City, NY: Doubleday, 1983), 497–501.

2. Sahidic and Akhimic are both Coptic (Egyptian) dialects.

3. Though the text claims to be written by the biblical prophet Zephaniah, like many apocalypses it is pseudonymous. The name is probably due to the fact that the author saw himself as writing in the "spirit" of Zephaniah, or because he wanted to ascribe authority to his writing by claiming it was written by a biblical prophet (Wintermute, "Apocalypse of Zephaniah," 501).

4. Wintermute, "Apocalypse of Zephaniah," 498.

is melted in a fire. And when I saw him, I rejoiced, for I thought that the Lord Almighty had come to visit me. I fell upon my face, and I worshiped him. He said to me, "Take heed. Don't worship me. I am not the Lord Almighty, but I am the great angel, Eremiel, who is over the abyss and Hades, the one in which all of the souls are imprisoned from the end of the Flood, which came upon the earth, until this day." (Apoc. Zeph. 6.11–15)

It seems that the figure of Eremiel is so magnificent that Zephaniah believes it must be God himself. And with the description of Eremiel that is given, one can certainly see how Zephaniah might make this mistake, as God is described in similar language elsewhere. In 1 Enoch 14:20, "the Great Glory" is said to have a raiment "brighter than the sun," and in Ezekiel 1:27–28 "the appearance of the likeness of the glory of the LORD" is likened to "glowing metal, as if full of fire."[5] Zephaniah's attempted worship is actually rather straightforward: Zephaniah makes a mistake, and the author is able to use this "blunder" to reinforce monotheism.

Revelation 22:6–21
"DO NOT DO THAT! . . . WORSHIP GOD!"

Turning now to John's apocalypse, we see a similar scene unfold between the seer (the recipient of the vision) and his guiding angel:

I, John, am the one who heard and saw these things. And when I had heard and seen them, I fell down to worship at the feet of the angel who had showed them to me. But he said to me, "Do not do that! I am a fellow servant of yours and of your brothers and sisters the prophets and of those who keep the words of this book. Worship God!" (Rev. 22:8–9, my translation).

Worship God Alone. The similarities between the two texts are obvious. In both texts the seer falls down in worship before an angelic intermediary. This attempted worship is immediately refused by the angel, and the seer is urged to worship God alone. Indeed, this is the primary way in which

---

5. See also the description of the heavenly man in Dan 10:6, who is described as having a "face like lightning" and legs "like the gleam of burnished bronze."

ancient texts would use the angelic refusal tradition—to reinforce the idea that not even the most majestic heavenly creatures should be worshiped alongside God.[6] God alone is worthy of worship.

While the basic point of the angel's response in both texts is to reinforce monotheistic devotion, when we compare further details of the responses, we can easily see that the author of Revelation is doing something else as well. In between the angel's prohibition of worship ("Do not do that!") and his exhortation ("Worship God!"), he explains to John that his instructions are due to himself being "a fellow servant of yours and of your brothers and sisters the prophets and of those who keep the words of this book" (22:9, my translation). He does not simply say that he is a fellow worshiper of God, but makes a specific point of mentioning "this book." By making specific reference to the message of the Apocalypse itself, the angel is reiterating that he is not the author or originator of the vision that he has been showing John. This statement serves not only to subordinate the angel to God but also to elevate the status of his message and to lend legitimacy to John's book by reinforcing its divine authority.[7]

Take the Vision Seriously. This is confirmed when we notice what prompts the worship in the first place. Unlike the scene in the Apocalypse of Zephaniah, John's attempt to worship the angel does not seem to be prompted by the angel's magnificent appearance.[8] In fact, Revelation gives very little detail regarding this angel's appearance. What's more, this is the angel who has been with John throughout the vision, so it is not as though his sudden appearance has caused John to fall to his knees in worship. In Revelation it comes as a response to the vision itself—"when I had heard and seen [these things]," with "these things" referring to the entire preceding vision.

The importance of taking seriously the message of the vision is a major theme in Revelation's epilogue. Before the angelic refusal scene, the angel who has shown the vision to John has declared the vision to be "trustworthy and true" (22:6), and in 22:7 Christ himself says, "Blessed is the one who keeps the words of the prophecy of this book." Revelation 22:18–19 gives a warning against tampering with John's words. The reason for taking seriously this message is also clear. Christ promises in 22:20, "Yes, I am coming soon." For this reason the prophecy must not be sealed (unlike the sealed

---

6. See discussion in Loren T. Stuckenbruck, *Angel Veneration and Christology: A Study in Early Judaism and in the Christology of the Apocalypse of John*, WUNT 2/70 (Tübingen: Mohr Siebeck, 1995) and Richard Bauckham, *The Climax of Prophecy: Studies on the Book of Revelation* (Edinburgh: T&T Clark, 1992), 118–49.

7. Stuckenbruck, *Angel*, 255–56.

8. Stuckenbruck, *Angel*, 246.

prophecy in Daniel 12); its message is one of great urgency for John's audience as the day of Christ's return draws near.

The Testimony of Jesus. John's use of the angelic refusal tradition to reiterate the divine origin of his message is confirmed by a similar scene earlier in Revelation. After the description of the marriage supper of the Lamb in 19:7–9, the guiding angel says to John, "These are the true words of God" (19:9). This declaration prompts John to fall down at his feet in worship. But just as in 22:9, the angel responds, "Don't do that! I am a fellow servant with you and with your brothers and sisters who hold to the testimony of Jesus. Worship God!" (19:10).

When we compare the two angelic refusal scenes, we can see that in each instance the angel's response is nearly identical. The angel tells John not to worship him and explains that he is simply a servant of God, not God himself. The key difference between the two refusals is in how the angel describes his fellow servants. In 22:9 the angel describes himself as a fellow servant with John's "brothers and sisters the prophets and *of all those who keep the words of this book*" (my translation), whereas in 19:10 he describes himself as a fellow servant with John's "brothers and sisters *who hold to the testimony of Jesus.*"

The nearly identical wording and setting (angelic refusal scene) in the two passages is certainly no coincidence. By using nearly identical wording and then changing the way the angel's "fellow servants" are described, John is creating a parallel between "the words of this book" and "the testimony of Jesus." As one scholar notes, "Revelation relies heavily on verbal repetition to suggest meaning by creating webs of association. . . . It may be significant, then, that the most extensive and exact verbal repetition within Revelation occurs between 19:10 and 22:8b–9. 'Holding on to the witness of Jesus' has become, in the second iteration, 'keeping the words of this book.' The second may be heard as a clarification and specification of the first."[9]

This means that the vision given to the churches, which John has recorded in this book, is the testimony of Jesus himself. It is not simply John's thoughts for the churches, nor is it the angel's own message. Both John and the angel are simply servants of Christ, and their specific task is to deliver *his* message to the saints.

The point of this is not simply to elevate the text or John as an author. Revelation makes clear from the beginning that the vision John is receiving is in fact a message to the churches from Christ himself. In 1:1 the book is

---

9. David A. deSilva, *Seeing Things John's Way* (Louisville: Westminster John Knox, 2009), 135.

introduced as "the revelation from Jesus Christ"—that is, the revelation that Jesus Christ gave. In 1:2 the message of the book is labeled the "testimony of Jesus," a moniker used for the book's message throughout.[10] It is Christ himself who commands John to write down what he sees (1:11; 2:1, 8, 12, 18; 3:1, 7, 14). And finally, in the epilogue, Jesus once again acts as a guarantor of the message: "I, Jesus, have sent my angel to give you this testimony for the churches" (22:16).

So when John uses the angelic refusal scene to elevate the status of his message, he is not elevating his own status as the author, but elevating Christ himself. This is one of the many ways John puts Christ *on par* with God. In other ancient Jewish apocalyptic texts, such as the Apocalypse of Zephaniah, it is God alone who is the giver of the vision. But Revelation is making a claim that is both in congruence with and yet strikingly different from that of the other Jewish apocalypses. Like other apocalypses, Revelation claims that its message is from God himself, and that he alone deserves to be worshiped. Yet *unlike* many of these same apocalypses, Revelation makes clear that this worship of the giver of the revelation is to include worship of the crucified, risen, and exalted Christ. By using the tradition of an angel refusing worship, John is able to reinforce Christ's role as the giver of the revelation, thus elevating him to the same divine status as God the Father. The angel asserts that John must worship God alone, and the context makes clear that the worship of the exalted Christ is an appropriate and indeed required expression of his monotheistic devotion.

FOR FURTHER READING

Additional Ancient Texts

There are other early Jewish texts that include scenes of attempted angel worship. In Ascension of Isaiah 7.21–22, Isaiah attempts to worship a heavenly being but is rebuked by his angelic guide (see also the angel's correction when Isaiah calls him "my Lord" in 8.5). Tobit also contains a similar scene (12:16–22), although it is not clear whether Tobit and Tobias fall down in worship or in fear. This same ambiguity is found in a similar scene in the Apocalypse of Paul.[11]

---

10. See Sarah S. U. Dixon, *The Testimony of the Exalted Jesus in the Book of Revelation*, LNTS 570 (London: Bloomsbury, T&T Clark, 2017).

11. Although the Apocalypse of Paul is an explicitly Christian text, I've included it here as it draws directly from Jewish apocalyptic texts.

English Translations and Critical Editions

Wintermute, O. S. "Apocalypse of Zephaniah (First Century BC–First Century AD): A New Translation and Introduction." Pages 497–515 in vol. 1 of *The Old Testament Pseudepigrapha*. Edited by James H. Charlesworth. Garden City, NY: Doubleday, 1983.

Secondary Literature

Bauckham, Richard. *The Climax of Prophecy: Studies on the Book of Revelation*. Edinburgh: T&T Clark, 1992.

deSilva, David A. *Seeing Things John's Way*. Louisville: Westminster John Knox, 2009.

Dixon, Sarah S. U. *The Testimony of the Exalted Jesus in the Book of Revelation*. LNTS 570. London: Bloomsbury T&T Clark, 2017.

Stuckenbruck, Loren T. *Angel Veneration and Christology: A Study in Early Judaism and in the Christology of the Apocalypse of John*. WUNT 2/70. Tübingen: Mohr Siebeck, 1995.

Glossary[1]

Ancient Near East, ANE: The phrase describes the peoples who lived in Egypt, Palestine, Syria, Mesopotamia, Persia, and Arabia from the beginning of recorded history to the conquest of Alexander the Great, though some also informally use this to refer all the way up to the first century AD.

Antiochus IV Epiphanes (c. 215–164 BC): A ruler of the Seleucid Kingdom, the Hellenistic state in Syria partitioned from Alexander the Great's vast empire. Antiochus provoked the Maccabean conflict by trying to Hellenize the Jewish people.

Anthropology, anthropological: Literally "the study of humans." This includes topics such as human composition (e.g., body, soul), human ability (e.g., free will), and human diversity (e.g., Jew, gentile).

Apocrypha, Apocryphal (also known as the **Deuterocanonical** Books): A collection of Jewish texts written after the Old Testament period and which are combined with a Greek translation of the Old Testament to form the Septuagint. These were considered authoritative by patristic Christians and accepted by Roman Catholic and Orthodox Christians as canonical but are rejected by Protestants as Scripture.[2] In nonacademic settings, "apocryphal" is often used as a description of stories that sound true but are not.

Apocalypse, Apocalyptic, Apocalyptic tradition: An apocalypse is literally a "revelation" of previously hidden things. These terms are most associated with the revelation of God and of heavenly realities through visions and dreams, and the revelation of divine actions to establish God's (future) rule among his covenant people and the whole world. Thus, there is often focus on spatial (heaven/earth) and temporal (present/future) dualisms.

Canonical: Texts are considered canonical when they are included in a collection of texts considered to be inspired and authoritative Scripture. The OT and NT are indisputably part of the Christian canon, whereas different Christian traditions dispute the inclusion of the Apocrypha. See *Apocrypha*.

---

1. Some definitions are adapted from Mark L. Strauss, *Four Portraits, One Jesus: A Survey of Jesus and the Gospels* (Grand Rapids: Zondervan, 2007).

2. Strauss, *Four Portraits*, 526 (*modified*).

Christology, Christological: This term generally refers to the person and work of Jesus. More specifically, the term relates to Jesus's role as the Christ. "Christ" (*christos*) is Greek for "anointed one," and it often served as the direct translation of the Hebrew term "messiah." See *Messiah*.

Covenant, covenantal: An agreement between two parties that places obligations on each party. Important covenants in the Bible include the Abrahamic covenant (Gen 15, 17), the Mosaic covenant (Exodus; Leviticus; Deuteronomy), the Davidic covenant (2 Sam 7), and the New covenant (Jer 31; Ezek 34–37).

Covenant community: Jewish groups who believed they were faithful to God's covenants with Israel considered themselves to be a "covenant community." This conceptuality is sometimes used by groups (like those at Qumran) to distinguish themselves from other Jews who are not considered faithful to the covenants. See *Dead Sea Scrolls*.

Dead Sea Scrolls: An ancient library discovered in caves near the Dead Sea in 1947 and likely associated with the first-century Jewish community at Qumran.[3] The scrolls include copies of biblical and other Jewish literature as well as sectarian texts arising from the Qumran community. See *Sectarian*.

Deuterocanonical: See *Apocrypha*.

Deuteronomic theology (or pattern): A theological view, expressed most fully in Deuteronomy, whereby God issues to his people material blessing and protection for covenant obedience, and cursing and suffering for disobedience.

Eschatology, eschatological: Literally "the study of the end times." The term indicates any event or idea that is associated with the final days. In Jewish and Pauline studies, though, the term "eschatology" does not refer simply or only to the end times, but to God's action to restore his rule through key agents or events.

Eschaton: The final state after God brings resolution to history. See *Eschatology*.

Hasmoneans, Hasmonean Period (167–63 BC): The Jewish family who ruled a semi-autonomous and later fully autonomous kingdom as the Jews secured independence from the Seleucids. As a result of infighting among the family, the Jews lost their independence to the Romans in 63 BC. See *Maccabean Revolt; Seleucids*.

Hellenism, Hellenistic, Hellenization: The spread and influence of Greek language and culture in the ancient world, particularly after the military conquest of Alexander the Great (c. 333 BC).

---

3. Strauss, *Four Portraits*, 528.

Josephus (AD 37–ca. 100): Once a Jewish Pharisee and military leader, Josephus was taken captive during the Jerusalem War against Rome and eventually made a Roman citizen and dependent of Emperor Vespasian. His four extant works are very important for our understanding of the history and culture of Second Temple Judaism: a history of the Jewish people (*Antiquities of the Jews*), an account of the Jerusalem War (*Jewish War*), a work in defense of Judaism and the Jewish way of life (*Against Apion*), and an autobiography (*Life*).

LXX: The abbreviation for the Septuagint. See *Septuagint*.

Maccabean Revolt (or crisis/conflict): The Jewish rebellion against Seleucid rule in 175–164 BC. The conflict is titled after "the Maccabees" (Hebrew for "hammer"), which was a name given to Judas and his brothers who led Israel during this period.

Messiah, messianic: A transliteration of a Hebrew word meaning "anointed one" and which is translated into Greek as "Christ." There was no single Jewish view about the Messiah, though all views envision this person as God's agent who will deliver his people.

Nero (ca. AD 38–68): Nero was a Roman emperor (AD 54–68) from the Julio-Claudian dynasty. Ancient Roman sources are critical of his reign, and he is known to have persecuted Christians as scapegoats for the Great Fire of Rome.

Pharisees: One of the Jewish sects mentioned by Josephus and throughout the gospels. They were widely known for their skill in interpreting the law.

Philo (ca. 20 BC–AD 50): A diaspora Jew influenced by Platonism from Alexandria, Egypt. He authored numerous philosophical treatises and exegetical studies on the Pentateuch. See *Platonism*.

Platonism: Plato is a famous Greek philosopher who lived in Athens (c. 428–347 BC). He wrote a number of philosophical treatises on ethics, physics, creation, logic, and rhetoric, among other things. There are various forms of Platonism that draw in differing ways from Plato's thought, but a primary aspect was a dualism based on a distinction between the realm of conceptual realities (immaterial and unchangeable) and the realm of concrete realities (material and changeable).

Pseudepigrapha, Pseudepigraphic: Literally "falsely ascribed writings." A pseudepigraphic text is a text written under the name of another, often centuries earlier, person. The Pseudepigrapha specifically refers to Jewish pseudepigraphic texts not included in the Apocrypha, but since this was a common practice for Second Temple Jews, the term pseudepigrapha has generally become a catch-all for all Jewish texts not included in another specific category, such as the Apocrypha or Dead Sea Scrolls, or authored by specific writers, like Josephus and Philo.

Qumran: A site located near the Dead Sea and close to the caves in which the Dead Sea Scrolls were found. The common view is that the community who lived there during the Second Temple Period where Essenes and responsible for producing the Dead Sea Scrolls.

Second Temple Period, Second Temple Judaism, Second Temple Jewish: The period in Jewish history roughly from the return from exile (about 516 BC) until the destruction of the Temple by the Romans in AD 70. Other phrases used for all or part of this time period are Early Judaism, Middle Judaism, and the Intertestamental Period.

Sectarian: That which pertains to a particular religious group, notably the texts composed by and for the Dead Sea Scroll community. See *Dead Sea Scrolls.*

Seleucids, Seleucid Kingdom (312–115 BC): A kingdom in the region of Syria that was formed after Alexander the Great's kingdom was subdivided after his death. Judea was eventually ruled by the Seleucids who attempted to force the Jews to assimilate to Hellenism. See *Hellenism; Maccabean Revolt.*

Septuagint (LXX): A collection of authoritative Jewish texts in Greek that includes the Greek translation of the Hebrew Bible as well as other Jewish writings. The abbreviation LXX is the Roman numeral for 70 and is based on the tradition that 70 (or 72) men translated the Hebrew Pentateuch into Greek.

Testament: A "testament" is a literary genre in which an author records a person's last words of advice and instruction to his children. This genre was popular in the Second Temple period, the most well-known being the Testament of the Twelve Patriarchs.

Two-ways paradigm: A theological view in which humans are presented with the options of good or evil and can determine for themselves which path to follow. This perspective is rooted in Deuteronomic theology. See *Deuteronomic theology.*

Theodicy: A defense or explanation of how God is just, even though evil exists, especially with regard to the righteous who suffer unjustly at the hands of the wicked.

Zealots, zeal: Jews during the Second Temple period who sought freedom through military means to free Judea from foreign domination. They were not only looking for political independence but also Torah purity, not attainable with a pagan presence in the land.

Contributors

Garrick V. Allen (PhD, University of St. Andrews) is lecturer in New Testament at Dublin City University.

Ben C. Blackwell (PhD, University of Durham) is associate professor of Early Christianity at Houston Baptist University.

Ian Boxall (DPhil, University of Oxford) is associate professor of New Testament at the Catholic University of America.

Jamie Davies (PhD, University of St. Andrews) is tutor in New Testament at Trinity College Bristol.

David A. deSilva (PhD, Emory University) is Trustees' Distinguished Professor of New Testament and Greek at Ashland Theological Seminary.

Sarah Underwood Dixon (PhD, University of Cambridge) is an affiliated lecturer in New Testament at the University of Cambridge.

John K. Goodrich (PhD, University of Durham) is associate professor of Bible at Moody Bible Institute.

Michael J. Gorman (PhD, Princeton Theological Seminary) is Raymond E. Brown Chair in Biblical Studies and Theology at St. Mary's Seminary and University.

Dana M. Harris (PhD, Trinity Evangelical Divinity School) is associate professor of New Testament at Trinity Evangelical Divinity School.

Ronald Herms (PhD, University of Durham) is dean of the School of Humanities, Religion, and Social Sciences at Fresno Pacific University.

Edith M. Humphrey (PhD, McGill University) is William F. Orr Professor of New Testament at Pittsburgh Theological Seminary.

Jason Maston (PhD, University of Durham) is assistant professor of Theology at Houston Baptist University.

Mark D. Mathews (PhD, University of Durham) is senior pastor of Bethany Presbyterian Church, Oxford, Pennsylvania.

Jonathan A. Moo (PhD, University of Cambridge) is associate professor of biblical studies at Whitworth University.

Ian Paul (PhD, Nottingham Trent University) is an independent researcher and managing editor of Grove Books Ltd.

Benjamin E. Reynolds (PhD, University of Aberdeen) is associate professor of New Testament at Tyndale University College.

Elizabeth E. Shively (PhD, Emory University) is senior lecturer in New Testament Studies at the University of St. Andrews.

Cynthia Long Westfall (PhD, University of Surrey Roehampton) is associate professor of New Testament at McMaster Divinity College.

Benjamin Wold (PhD, University of Durham) is assistant professor in Ancient Judaism and Christianity at Trinity College Dublin.

Archie T. Wright (PhD, University of Durham) is associate professor of Ancient Judaism and Christian Origins at Regent University.

OLD TESTAMENT APOCRYPHA

Tobit

Wisdom of Solomon

Sirach

Baruch

1 Maccabees

2 Maccabees

2 Esdras/4 Ezra

Subject Index

Author Index

Reading Romans in Context

Paul and Second Temple Judaism

Ben C. Blackwell, John K. Goodrich &
Jason Maston, Editors

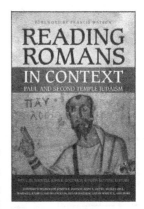

Readers of Paul today are more than ever aware
of the importance of interpreting Paul's letters
in their Jewish context. In *Reading Romans in
Context* a team of Pauline scholars go beyond
a general introduction that surveys historical events and theological
themes and explore Paul's letter to the Romans in light of Second Temple
Jewish literature.

In this nontechnical collection of short essays, beginning and intermediate students are given a chance to see firsthand what makes Paul
a distinctive thinker in relation to his Jewish contemporaries. Following
the narrative progression of Romans, each chapter pairs a major unit of
the letter with one or more sections of a thematically related Jewish
text, introduces and explores the theological nuances of the comparative text, and shows how these ideas illuminate our understanding of the
book of Romans.

ZONDERVAN
ACADEMIC

Reading Mark in Context

Jesus and Second Temple Judaism

Ben C. Blackwell, John K. Goodrich &
Jason Maston, Editors

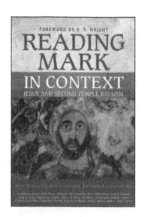

Over the last several decades, the Jewishness of
Jesus has been at the forefront of scholarship,
and students of the New Testament are more
than ever aware of the importance of under-
standing Jesus and the Gospels in their Jewish context. *Reading Mark
in Context* helps students see the contours and textures of Jesus's engagement with his Jewish environment. It brings together a series of
accessible essays that compare the viewpoints, theologies, and hermeneutical practices of Mark and his various Jewish contemporaries.

Going beyond an introduction that merely surveys historical events
and theological themes, this textbook examines individual passages in
Second Temple Jewish literature in order to illuminate the context of
Mark's theology and the nuances of his thinking. Following the narrative
progression of Mark's Gospel, each chapter in this textbook (1) pairs a
major unit of the Gospel with one or more sections of a thematically
related Jewish text, (2) introduces and explores the historical and theological nuances of the comparative text, and (3) shows how the ideas in
the comparative text illuminate those expressed in Mark.

ZONDERVAN
ACADEMIC